Dharamsala Days
Dharamsala Nights

The Unexpected World of the Refugees
from Tibet

Pauline MacDonald

To my uncle: for his endless patience, encouragement, tutoring, and editorial support. To my son: for his willingness to live an unusual life. To my Tibetan friends: for accepting me into their world and for their knowledge, help, and friendship. And to my Indian and other foreign friends: for their insight and friendship. You know who you are.

Prologue

I first became interested in Tibet in the late 1980's. My boyfriend at the time had spent several months in Tibet in the mid 80's, illegally hitchhiking overland through Kham to Lhasa, sometimes hidden by sympathetic Tibetans under sacks in the back of trucks. The Tibet that Mike spoke of was populated by people much like him: smart, funny, good with weapons and therefore handy in a fight, yet kind hearted and religious. He told me of the horrifying destruction perpetrated by the Chinese and of the ongoing oppression in the country despite reforms that had been implemented.

Once in Lhasa, a Chinese policeman had asked him where he was from. When he answered, the policeman became very excited, "Canada is very good!" the policeman exclaimed, pulling from his belt a cattle prod with a "Made in Canada" label. Mike's stories, photographs, and the books that he recommended awakened in me what became a lifelong interest in Tibet. In the years that followed, I read dozens of books on the topic, but it wasn't until 2003 that I met my first Tibetans.

In the summer of 2002, I discovered that, from what I had read on-line, one could live and volunteer in Dharamsala very cheaply. I wanted to go but I had almost no money, and I was the single mother of a nine-year-old son. Lying in bed one night, I realized that I could (but just barely) afford to get by in India for a year. At that moment, I decided that we would leave the following April. The next morning, I began telling my friends and family that we were going. I knew that some people —including my own inner voice —thought that I was crazy or irresponsible, especially because I was taking my nine-year-old child, but I decided to forge ahead regardless.

Over the next eight months, I scrimped and saved to pay off bills and packed up our lives. Very little practical information was available on the Internet or in books at that time, so I had almost no idea of what I was getting myself into. Fortunately, I was able to connect with an expert on Tibet who had visited Dharamsala countless times. She gave me much valuable advice on what to expect in McLeod Ganj, as she had lived there and visited regularly since the 80's. She reassured me that everything would be fine, but I didn't know if she was made of far stronger stuff than I. I had never even seen a photo of the town other than pictures of monasteries and locals in traditional dress. That didn't tell me much. India I had seen only in movies and documentaries. It looked like a depressing, poverty-stricken place. I read *A Fine Balance* by Rohinton Mistry, which only exacerbated my foreboding. I told friends that if we hated it, we would return home in a few weeks.

In the spring of 2003, my son and I flew to India via Hong Kong on an almost empty flight. There were twenty three passengers on an airplane that could hold more than two hundred and seventy. SARS was at its peak, and almost no one was travelling to Asia. I had considered cancelling our trip, but my friend Daphne, who lived in Hong Kong and with whom we were to be staying, had informed me that the outbreak was concentrated only in certain neighborhoods. My sensible sister also surprised me by encouraging me not to abandon my plans, although as we waited in the almost deserted Vancouver airport, I felt some trepidation. In Hong Kong, we appeared to be almost the only tourists. My small son was overjoyed to visit a virtually abandoned amusement park and go on ride after ride without having to line up. We flew on to India with four bags of possessions, mostly his toys, and what seemed an ample budget of 11,000 rupees, $330 a month for the two of us.

Back then, McLeod Ganj—the Tibetan enclave in Upper Dharamsala—was far more primitive than it is now. Only a handful of restaurants catered to foreigners. There were no cappuccinos and but three tiny shops on Bhagsu Road that stocked a handful of imported goods such as Ovaltine, Cornflakes, and outrageously priced tinned ham. The sewers were not covered, and the potholed streets and the hillsides were repositories for rubbish. But traffic was not a major problem and the foreign visitors were mostly a hardy lot.

Within two months of arriving, I was sharing two rooms in an apartment building entirely populated by newcomer Tibetans from Amdo, with my son, a Tibetan boyfriend, and his two destitute friends.

We shared a single toilet and a cold water tap—which more often than not produced no water —with up to thirty neighbors. My boyfriend had an income of 1,500 rupees each month (at that time worth about $40 Canadian), but our other roommates had no incomes whatsoever and other penniless friends often dropped by to eat.

Although we later moved to an apartment where we shared a toilet with only one other family, we lived in the same conditions for a year. I bathed from a bucket in the malodorous and filthy toilet, which was visited by enormous spiders and home to strange insects, which appeared to subsist entirely on a diet of urine and feces. I washed dishes and did laundry outside in glacial tap water sometimes in winter rain and snow. When it was very cold, my hands would turn red and burn like fire and then go numb. We were the wealthiest among our friends; our small, grubby, damp, and moldy two room apartment, with a tiny kitchen that had no sink, contained four beds, a T.V., a cassette player, and a simple wooden chair, and was considered upscale by our impoverished Tibetan friends. Years later, many laughed when remembering how fancy it seemed at the time. "I remember how impressed I was because you guys had a chair," Rabgey recalled.

Introduction

Much has been written about Tibet and the suffering of its people. In these pages, I have attempted to tell a mostly untold story—that of the people who have escaped from Tibet in the past fifteen years or so and the small world that most of them inhabited—Dharamsala. My aim is not to provide an exhaustive historical and political overview, but rather, based on my experience and research, to describe the world of the newcomers and the difficulties they have faced. As we shall see, some problems are shared by most if not all Tibetan refugees, in Dharamsala and elsewhere.

It should be noted that Tibetans who fled to India around the same time as the Dalai Lama, who escaped into exile in 1959, and those Tibetans who were born and raised in India are usually referred to as "settlement Tibetans." As the term seemed too cumbersome, I have adopted the term "settler." "Newcomers" are those Tibetans who have fled Tibet since the 1970's. Most of the newcomers that I write about escaped to India in the 1990's and 2000's and are continuing to do so as I write. The distinction between the two groups is important because newcomers are effectively ruled by the settlers, who make up the majority of exile Tibetans and hold most positions of power in the exile government and Tibet-related human rights organizations.

When I set out to write this account, I anticipated that some of what I would say might be disturbing, but nothing prepared me for what I was to discover: the problems with the ways that escaping refugees have been managed are far worse than I ever imagined. It seemed everyone's interests were being served: the settlers', India's, and China's; the only interests not being considered were those of the recent refugees from Tibet.

Although many Tibetans knew that I was writing a book, they were entirely unaware of what exactly I was saying. Many of my findings were so disturbing to me that I couldn't bear to discuss them with my friends. I did not want to add to their trauma or incite impotent anger when none existed. It seemed best not to share information until the book was completed. Anyone who is offended by my findings and opinions should be aware that I came to them on my own. All that anyone, Tibetan or Westerner, friend or interview subject, knew was that I was attempting to write the story of the newcomers. I sat alone at my computer for a year and a half, chasing information through cyberspace, reading tens of thousands of pages, and writing about what I had learned and experienced.

At the risk of appearing uncomprehending or negligent in my research, I have left out some sensitive material, as will be obvious to some. If the drawbacks of sharing information outweighed perceived benefits, I left it out. Almost all who are mentioned, unless they are public figures or representatives of organizations who participated in formal interviews or spoke publically, are protected by one or more pseudonyms, and some small details have been changed to further protect identities. People shared intimate details of their lives with me, including shocking or potentially embarrassing things that they had done. They were also frank and forthcoming with their opinions. I didn't want their honesty to ever hurt them.

I anticipate that once they start reading this account, the first thing that many people will want to know is what the Dalai Lama's role is in all of this. My answer is that the Dalai Lama is entirely dependent on his advisors for accurate information. The problems were and are very complex, and it appears that no one in an advisory capacity has really understood them. The solutions that were devised have never been questioned. The United Nations High Commission for Refugees has said nothing. Most of the issues that I address have never been analyzed by researchers. Some were, but it appears that no one in the related departments of the exile government either read the reports or followed the recommendations. Journalists have never exposed flaws within the existing system. Human rights organizations have been silent; in some cases, perhaps because they are so out of touch with newcomers that they have no idea what has occurred. Furthermore, the Dalai Lama's own track record is exemplary; he employs newcomers in his offices and has provided financial support to countless numbers of them both through individual sponsorship and donations to organizations that benefit and employ them. I am unaware of any attempts to draw his attention to the issues that I will discuss. "He has enough to deal with already," I was told when I asked why newcomers had not taken their troubles to him. Given these facts, it seems preposterous to hold the Dalai Lama accountable.

I am not an academic, and I have no post-secondary education. I never even set out to write a book. I went to Dharamsala because human rights were important to me, and I found myself in a position where human rights violations were going on around me, but I was doing nothing about it. The situation was so complicated that I didn't know what to do. I spent a total of three years in Dharamsala between 2003 and 2012, but little was changing for the better; in some ways conditions got worse. Explaining some of the problems of newcomers met with the same reception as if I had stated that Elvis lived downstairs from me or I had an alien life form stored in my freezer. Those who were aware usually had a "blame the victim" mentality that could not be changed through discussion. I realized that if anything were to change, I needed to carefully examine and write about everything that I knew. I thought of writing a short academic paper, but I wanted to reach as wide an audience as possible because, as we shall see, many people in positions of power and influence know the worst of what transpires, but harsh judgments and uninformed justifications predominate. Because I could see no other way to make an impact, I have tried to write an at least somewhat entertaining book that addresses serious issues.

Throughout the process, I had very mixed emotions. Writing about newcomers involved criticizing and exposing some of the unpleasant realities of life in Dharamsala and beyond. Exile Tibetans (both settlers and newcomers) have done a remarkable job of adapting to a new country while maintaining their unique society. Despite some serious flaws, they are arguably the most successful and stable refugee group in the world. India is a developing nation that faces enormous obstacles in providing for its citizens. Exile Tibetans have in so many ways succeeded against incredible odds in providing employment, education, and health care for many of their people. For example, as

India struggles to provide education to its population, the literacy rate among Tibetan youth in India is around 98%,[1] virtually matching that of the West.[2]

Unfortunately, within days of first arriving in Dharamsala, I found something that was all too familiar to me. I grew up in a small town in Canada where racism against First Nations (Native American) people was endemic. That some of them had serious problems is well documented, but when I was a child, the causes were not well understood. First Nations were all stereotyped as unemployed and drunk even when there was ample evidence that such was not the case. Our society marginalized them and tried to train the "Indian" out of them, with tragic consequences. The injustices perpetrated are now being addressed somewhat and the problems are well understood, although far more remains to be done. As a white Canadian, I have to live with the legacy of my ancestors.

What I observed in the Tibetan community in India is, in some ways, different and should prove far easier to repair. Indeed, some may be enraged by my comparison. But I believe that anyone who studies such things will see some obvious parallels when they read what I have written and examine the policies, actions, and attitudes of the society. Although I use much anecdotal evidence, I also provide ample source documents that are available to the general public. It is my greatest hope that the issues that I bring up will be further explored and addressed. The information contained within could prove useful to anyone who works with refugees and minority sub-groups.

Many feel that criticizing exile Tibetans and their society is unfair and that discussing negative aspects of the exile experience is in some way disloyal. Some Tibetans whom I spoke to became angered by anything that they perceived as criticism. Writers, including Tibetans, who dare to mention flaws or bring up obvious problems are often accused of being on the side of the Chinese or of attempting to tear apart Tibetan society; accusations of Chinese influence are often used by Tibetans to silence or belittle those with differing opinions and to enforce social conformity. Despite my concerns that some of what I had to say could be used as propaganda by the Chinese regime, I continued writing because my commitment was to human rights and equality and to those Tibetans who suffer from the lack of both, foremost within Tibet but, as we shall see, also in exile.

Initially, I planned to write only about the Salai gyals (more or less pronounced *Sally jas*), as many Tibetans called them. These were the young Tibetan men, many new arrivals from Tibet but also some settler Tibetans, who dated foreign women and often ended up going to the West. I felt that the Salai gyals were a small but important and misunderstood part of Tibetan exile history that should be written about. As I began researching in earnest, I realized that I couldn't write about Salai gyals without discussing the broader situation of newcomers and the problems that they faced. The men with foreign women were really a small symptom of far larger problems.

As the newcomers came to know that I was writing about them, people came to me to share their stories. Those who didn't know me would hear what I was up to and track me down in order to suspiciously grill me on my intentions and then often shared their insights once they came to understand that I was planning to create an honest yet sympathetic portrait. A few were obviously not willing to take chances and would barely speak in my presence. Friends whom I had known for years were the most open and the most reliable source of information and inspiration in that I already knew many of their stories.

"Tell the story of the unimportant people or they will be forgotten. Write the truth," Karma Phunsok, one of the few newcomer university students urged. When I was filled with despair, a Tibetan writer friend told me, "Just keep writing. Don't worry what people will think." I suspected that he would be very surprised, possibly furious, when he read some of what I was saying. Although a newcomer himself, he often played the devil's advocate when he talked with me and provided a lot of useful information about problems that some of the newcomers had created and the extreme challenges faced by many settlers. "Go to the settlements in the south. Go to Arunachal Pradesh. Then you will really see. Newcomers think that they are the only ones with problems. Ha ha ha! Settlement Tibetans have a lot of problems too."

I couldn't go. My son was keeping up with school by correspondence, and his work was always behind schedule. I was a student with classes to attend, and I also didn't have much money. Not travelling had its benefits. In many ways, I knew only the India of a typical newcomer: Dharamsala and a few months in Delhi comprised my exile world. This limitation perhaps made it easier for me to understand their frustrations and empathize, although I learned as much as I could about the current conditions in the settlements and the early struggles of the refugees.

There was no point in even attempting to hide the focus of my writing from the newcomers. I had been a well known part of their community for almost a decade and many were good friends, but when most other people around town asked me what I was doing, I told them that I was "writing a book about this place." It may surprise some that most people were not interested in hearing about it and with good reason.

Dharamsala is full of often mentally unhinged and unemployable foreigners who spend months every year hanging around the town. Many have inherited money or received divorce settlement packages from former spouses, allowing them to stay in India to try to "find themselves," often through Buddhism. Others claim to be working on behalf of the Tibetans, even fundraising in that regard, but appear to produce little or nothing of substance. My friend Lucy attempted to make conversation with one of these creatures: "What do you do?" she asked, curious to learn what sort of career would allow a foreigner, far below retirement age, to spend the better part of each year in Dharamsala. "I'm a Buddhist," was the dramatic reply that ended the conversation. Some, I suspected, were modern versions of the centuries old tradition of remittance men, dysfunctional black sheep of the family who were given money by their families to stay far away from home.

India is very cheap compared to the West, and in recent years Dharamsala has become so modern that even the fussiest—and these people are often very fussy—can find a cappuccino or pizza that at least partially meets with their satisfaction. They grumble endlessly about the traffic, the weather, and the food. Their neighbors are always defective, and the barking of the street dogs keeps them awake at night. They are endlessly disappointed with the locals, who seldom live up to their expectations. But they keep going back.

Many of these people claimed to be writing books, so my statement that I was writing one was a wonderful yet entirely honest way to be written off as a person of no importance. I was more than willing to answer any questions that anyone wanted to ask about my project, but most locals had met pseudo writers too many times to take me seriously. Some would react with fear, apparently expecting me to begin ranting on about strange theories of Buddhism or Tibetan culture like an escaped lunatic. As a result, people continued to be unguarded with their words and opinions.

Before I move on to the narrative, I should clarify a couple of points. In order to avoid confusion, it needs to be clear that when I speak of Tibet, I am not referring to the Tibetan Autonomous Region, as the Chinese call it. I am referring to ethnic Tibet, the Tibetan Plateau, which has been inhabited almost solely by Tibetans for millennia. The northern extremities belong to Muslim neighbors, and Tibet contained pockets populated by or shared with Mongolians. Small numbers of Muslims, Chinese, and other ethnic groups were peppered throughout the plateau, particularly along its eastern border. Tibet draws attention to itself on a topographical map due to its high altitude, which may explain why the Chinese don't use many topographical maps on their websites. The Tibetan regions— Kham, Amdo, and U-Tsang—were incorporated into the Chinese provinces of Gansu, Qinghai, Sichuan, Yunnan, and, not surprisingly, the Tibetan Autonomous Region.

Other clarifications are of importance, as well. The exile government, as I call it, is officially known as the Central Tibetan Administration or C.T.A. for short. That name, too, I discarded. Tibetans are, technically speaking, foreigners in India; however, when I use the term "foreigners," I am speaking of non-refugees, usually tourists and other visitors from outside India and the Himalayan region. When I speak of Tibetans soliciting funds from or dating foreigners, I am not just speaking of foreigners from the West; the same occurs with Asians from Korea, Japan, Taiwan, etc. In Dharamsala, the term "Westerner" is sometimes used to describe anyone from abroad even if he or she is not actually from the West. I almost always use common spellings of Tibetan words in English rather than the Wylie transliteration system, which, although of great use to those accustomed to it, is very confusing to those who have not learned to read it. For example, the name commonly spelled "Tashi" is rendered in Wylie as "Bkra shis." As imperfect as many common spellings are—regional differences in pronunciation are sometimes vast —I have used them.

My sincere hope is that rather than creating anger and retribution, this book will inspire dialogue and productive changes. So much beauty and sincerity exists in the world that the exiles have created and there is so much to admire about their relationships with India, the Indian people, and the world.

Pauline MacDonald
July 25, 2012

Chapter 1

"It's natural for small differences to crop up and the reason why more of this is happening now is that the old Tibetans who came in the 1960s were the true Tibetans, reared and imbued with genuine Tibetan cultural and social ethos. But the new arrivals, who began coming after 1988, are products of a harsh Chinese regime. They have known only violence and life under the red flag and are intolerant."[1]

Samdhong Rinpoche, Prime Minister of the Tibetan Government in Exile from 2001 to 2011

I noticed them on my first day in Dharamsala in 2003, young, often stylish Tibetan men, many with long hair, loitering in the square, watching the streets from rooftops, and sometimes sauntering around town in the company of foreign girls and women. People told me that the young men, most of whom had recently escaped from Tibet, were bad boys who loved to fight and callously chased foreign tourist women for money and marriages that would get them visas to the West, but as I came to know them and their situations, I discovered that things were not so simple. The vast majority were good and gentle people.

Before I went to Dharamsala, the home of the exiled Tibetan spiritual leader, the Dalai Lama, I knew that each year thousands of Tibetan refugees were escaping the oppressive regime in China by making a dangerous, often month-long trek through the frozen Himalayas to apparent safety in India. Some died on the way as a result of freezing to death or falling into crevasses. Others were shot by Chinese border police. Women were raped. I had read about their plight in countless books, news reports, and documents provided by human rights groups. Much to my shock, I came to learn that "newcomers" were not welcome to stay in India. Almost all were expected to make the perilous journey back to Tibet. Those refugees considered too old to be educated were allowed to stay for just a short "pilgrimage," while almost all of the rest received permission to remain only until their studies were completed.[2] (At the time of writing, this abhorrent policy has not changed.[3]) Many did not want to return, but in India they had very few options.

Since the 1980's, tens of thousands of refugees have escaped to India, although since 2008, the exodus has slowed dramatically. When thousands were arriving each year, the established Tibetan exiles had little means to support or provide newcomers with opportunities to lead productive lives in exile. Some say that they barely tried. Most of the newcomers who stayed had to find their own ways to make lives for themselves, usually without family support or other guidance and in many cases without access to documentation allowing them to stay and work legally in India. Many toiled in low-paying service industry jobs. Some became successful, but unemployment was extremely high, and, for those who were employed, the wages were usually very low. Even the very bright often roamed the streets, sometimes hungry, looking for a way out.

For more than a decade, from the 90's to the late 2000's, young men that I learned were referred to as "Salai gyals" hung around downtown McLeod Ganj every afternoon and evening. Although at any given time there were never more than a hundred or so of them, they came to represent, both to the public and the media, the newcomer presence in Dharamsala. Many were penniless and on the hunt for foreign women. As human beings in difficult circumstances, they craved affection, and as men of marriageable age, they desired sex, but what some of them did bordered on prostitution, for many would sleep with seemingly any woman, for any period of time, as long as she provided meals and often alcohol, clothing, or, hopefully, gifts of cash. Western friends often referred to McLeod Ganj as "Thailand in reverse" because seemingly any foreign woman, regardless of her personality, flaws, or age could hook-up with a young Tibetan "hottie" almost instantly if she wanted to and even marry him. It wasn't unusual for women to tell me that they had been proposed to within days or weeks of meeting their Tibetan boyfriends.

Some of what went on really was outrageous. "Do you remember the twenty-one-year-old Tibetan boy who married the fifty-two-year-old European woman?" Lucy asked me. Her tone was disapproving, but her eyes sparkled with humor and her lips curved into a subtle smile. We were having tea and discussing the sometimes strange world of love in Dharamsala. When I replied in the negative, she went on, "This was back around 2002. He said he was twenty-one, but he looked about twelve. He didn't really speak any English. The woman's daughter showed up for the wedding, and she looked so embarrassed to be seen with them. I don't know what those women were thinking. There were so many relationships like that. Back then there seemed to be a wedding every week." She wasn't exaggerating. Although I could not find all-encompassing data, I later learned that between January and November of 2004, forty Tibetan men had married Western women at the Dharamsala district court house.[4] Six months later, the average had apparently climbed to two a week.[5]

When they had money or women who would pay, many of the Salai gyals partied all night and slept all day. As warm and kind as they were to foreigners, they were often rude or unfriendly toward the India-born Tibetans and Indians. A few of them would try to pick fights for almost any reason. Based on their behavior, there was a perception in the community that all newcomers tended to be immoral and ill-mannered. I was repeatedly told by settler Tibetans that the behavior of the young men was due to the degradation of Tibetan culture inside Tibet as a consequence of Chinese rule.

From almost the beginning, it was apparent to me that many other factors were at play. The more Salai gyals and other newcomers whom I talked to and the more time that passed, the more certain that I became of my deep-seated suspicions. The newcomers themselves were often very aware of some of the sources of their problems, but no influential people were interested in what they had to say. The situation was, at least publically, almost entirely ignored by the Tibetan exile government: it was an obvious source of embarrassment.

I returned to Dharamsala in 2010 to study at the Library of Tibetan Works and Archives and immediately noticed that something had changed dramatically. There were no Salai gyals hopefully lurking in the streets, and Tibetan men in the company of foreign women were relatively few and far between. I saw some players and gigolos, but those in relationships were often seriously committed and usually in no rush to go to the West. There was one foreign woman in town who had a parade of Tibetan boyfriends. She seemed to have a new one every week. Her success in obtaining them was only tempered by the speed with which they dumped her; it seemed that she had deep-seated psychological problems, and Tibetans were no longer willing to put up with such shenanigans—her failures were one of the striking hallmarks of change. The newcomer youths were more confident and dignified and less angry and frustrated. During my year and a half stay, among my large circle of friends and acquaintances, only four marriages to foreigners occurred. Two of those were to Tibetans who had gone abroad long ago. It is with this knowledge that we begin our journey back and forth in time through the world of the newcomers and the Salai gyals and the society that rejected them.

Before exploring the newcomer world and the more bizarre aspects of Dharamsala, it seems fitting to immediately talk a little more about Salai gyals. Within weeks of arriving in McLeod Ganj, I first heard the term used, often negatively, to describe Tibetan men who are romantically involved with foreigners. Over the years, I have been party to much debate over the definition of the term. Many people could not even agree on its spelling and hence etymology.[6] Most use the term broadly to refer to any Tibetan man who dates or marries a foreigner; no term exists for the few Tibetan women who date and marry foreign men. Some, such as my friend Karma Phunsok, consider Tsongtsan Gampo, the great 7th century Tibetan king, a Salai gyal due to his marriages to two foreign princesses. These marriages, like other strategic marriages of alliance throughout history, were not love marriages: in fact, the women came with gifts, including valuable and sacred statuary. Others use the term "Salai gyal" sparingly to refer to Tibetan men in India who date foreign women as a vocation and specifically to procure visas to the West through marriage.

Most of the Salai gyals whom I have known were "Amdo Boys," young men from the Amdo region of Tibet, but many Salai gyals were not Amdowas. "Before the Amdo Boys there were the Lhasa Apsos," a

Western friend, who has spent several decades visiting Dharamsala and who is an expert on human rights issues in Tibet, informed me. My own observations told me that huge numbers of Khampas were also Salai gyals as were a lesser number of settlers. A highly cultured newcomer friend advised, "You must write about the Salai gyals of the 1990's. They were really something, educated and sophisticated, not like the ones that came later;" I was unable to verify his statement, but it made sense given that intellectuals tend to be trail-blazers: open-minded, bold, and adventurous. A very knowledgeable friend concurred, elaborating on what constituted a Salai gyal, "You need to write about the now high ranking officials who married Westerners. Write about the lamas who married foreign women and had foreign lovers. Write about the geshes, the monks, the ex-monks, the newcomers, the Tibetans who grew up in India, the women, and the gays. You can't ignore the ones who were straight but had to sleep with foreign homosexuals. They are all so important."

Even having long hair was enough for individuals to be labeled Salai gyals, for a lot of them did have long hair. I was sitting in McLlo bar, in the heart of McLeod Ganj, one night with one of my young Salai gyal friends who, like many Sali gyals in recent years, had short hair. A Tibetan man around forty years old with shoulder-length hair walked in. It was obvious from his dress that he was visiting from abroad. He waved at me as he passed by our table. My young friend snickered rudely, "Who is he? Some old Salai gyal?" "No," I replied icily. "He is a scholar that I met at a conference."

Although there was a tendency to look down on anyone who might be a Salai gyal, one of the most revered Tibetan intellectuals of the 20th century was certainly one. His lifestyle made most modern Salai gyals seem like saints, so it is doubtful that he would have been better accepted by today's society. His story is important given the level of respect that he now receives from a society that still imposes harsh judgments on those who fail to conform. Undoubtedly, he qualifies as a Salai gyal, for in 1938, he published an extraordinary sex manual, based on his experiences with Indian women, that combined his own ideas with those of the *Kama Sutra*.

Gendun Chophel is considered by the majority of historians to be the most important Tibetan literary and artistic figure of the 20th century. In his tragically short life, he produced an astonishing diversity of work and excelled at a startling array of disciplines. Based on his own writings, it is thought that he was born in 1902, although the date is open to debate.[7] What is certain is that he was born around the turn of the 20th century in a staunchly conservative society in which art and literature were almost exclusively reserved for religious expression.

As a young monk, in Amdo and later in Lhasa, Gendun Chophel excelled at debate and poetry, scandalizing his contemporaries with his provocative views on Buddhist philosophy.[8] In his youth, in order to support himself, he began painting portraits of photographic quality as well as beautiful and unique religious works known as thankas, a practice that he continued throughout his life. In the mid 1930's, Choephel travelled to India and ceased to be a monk. He began producing works hither-to unknown to Tibetan literature, which were ground breaking, highly literate, and sometimes beautifully self-illustrated. He also drank copiously and slept with numerous Indian women.

Choephel completely scandalized Tibetan society with the publication of his book *The Arts of Love*. Basing his writing on the *Kama Sutra*, Choephel reworked the material, infusing it with ideas from his own obviously copious experiences. Friends who travelled with him in India remember him as being a frequenter of prostitutes. In the book, he makes several references to widows as suitable sex partners, and he mentions completing his writing in the home of an Indian lady friend.

Choephel seldom had a reliable source of income. Some Tibetan intellectuals whom I spoke to thought that he just slept with cheap prostitutes; others believe that he was supported, at times, by his Indian sex partners. Choephel's concern for and obvious experience with giving women pleasure —the major reoccurring theme of the book—would certainly have made him a desirable house guest for lonely ladies. As a travelling Tibetan and a penniless scholar and artist, his presence in widows' homes would not necessarily have been terribly remarkable. The *Arts of Love* closes with a passage which appears to support the theory that he had at least one Indian woman sponsor who was also his lover.[9]

It is uncertain as to whether or not Gendun Choephel ever slept with Western women. Given the time of the publication of *The Arts of Love*, it seems very unlikely. His brief descriptions of the sexual performances of Western women appear to be based on his experiences with hard-core pornography, some of which involved bestiality, rather than personal encounters.

Following the book's publication, Choephel remained in India for a further seven years. He wrote and illustrated a travel guide to India and Sri Lanka in Tibetan, complete with maps and guides to rail routes. Most people in Tibet were entirely unaware of current events, history, science, and technology. Choephel informed and sometimes outraged them with articles–often self-illustrated–that he wrote for magazines distributed in Tibet. He became proficient in English, painted and drew prolifically, and assisted George Roerich in translating the *Blue Annals*, while staying with this renowned Russian family of artists and intellectuals at their Institute of Himalayan Studies in Kullu. His sexual exploits during that time remain so far unknown.

Toward the end of his time in India, he became involved with a communist group dedicated to the modernization of Tibet. The extent of Choephel's participation in the organization and his political beliefs are not so far entirely known. Shortly after his return to Lhasa, he was arrested on charges of counterfeiting and/or treason by the Tibetan government—the reasoning and details remain foggy. He was flogged repeatedly, and his writings and drawings were confiscated. Most were never returned and their fate remains unknown. Gendun Choephel's health, both physical and mental, was ruined during his time in prison, and he died, a broken man, in 1951.

Although there were obviously historical Salai gyals, the term itself seemed to have modern origins. Most Amdo Tibetans whom I spoke to thought that the term originated from a popular comedy series

Ru sde thra mo (Small Village),[10] created by the legendary Amdo performer and writer Menla Kyab in Tibet in the mid 1990's. The program aired on radio in Tibet and was also widely distributed on cassette, including among the Amdo diaspora. In the series, Menla Kyab used comedy to encourage people to examine a broad range of social issues. "Salai Gyal" was the name of a character who outraged his family and fellow villagers by having a romantic relationship with a female Western researcher.

An acquaintance, Jamyang, contacted Menla Kyap in Tibet and asked him what he thought of the term's use in India. Menla Kyab said that he was very busy and didn't have time to discuss the issue; I wondered whether he wanted nothing to do with someone writing about Dharamsala. He was kind enough to tell Jamyang that he thought that the exile term was not related to the character in his program and was very different in meaning. He thought that it had evolved independently in India and pre-dated his radio play. I was unable to find out whether this was true.

Menla Kyab's Salai Gyal program remains famous in the Amdo community in Dharamsala. Dozens or maybe even hundreds of people referred to it over the years. Back in 2003, I heard it many times and sat in dumb silence as my friends roared with laughter; unfortunately, I didn't understand Tibetan. Later, as I was writing this book, many people spoke with great authority and at length in regards to exactly what Menla Kyab had intended the character to represent. Unfortunately, almost every analysis was quite different, and they all admitted that they had never spoken to Menla Kyab directly. Even the plot summaries that I was provided with were different. Sometimes, Salai Gyal married the girl. Other times she was a peripheral character. Most frustrating of all, no one whom I spoke to had a copy of the program. The situation was comedic and fascinating. The inconsistencies that were delivered with such authority became more interesting to me than the facts, although I much later learned that Salai Gyal eventually received permission to marry the girl, but she went back to America and never returned, an ending familiar to Salai gyals in India.

Typically, the term "Salai gyal" was used to describe almost any Tibetan man who dated or married a foreigner. Usually, it didn't seem to matter how serious the relationship was, especially to people who didn't know the couple. A man with a career who had a single long-term relationship with a foreign woman with whom he was deeply in love was as likely to be called a Salai gyal as a guy who slept with a different woman almost every night for fun or financial assistance. Tibetans who dated Western women were seen by many as opportunists, man-whores, and/or traitors to their race. In many circles, the Tibetan community emphasized keeping blood lines pure, something not easily understood by Westerners from multi-cultural countries. Many Tibetans worried that their race would die out. Others felt that it was very important to have children who were purely ethnic Tibetan and, most importantly, to raise them in a Tibetan environment so that the culture would not be lost. But for many Tibetans, whom they loved was not to be decided solely by their race.

Despite or perhaps to thumb their noses at prejudices, some embraced the term. Amdo Tibetan intellectuals of all ages practically lined up to discuss the topic. "Do you want to hear my Salai gyal stories?" many offered with a grin when I politely suggested that I would appreciate their analysis of the phenomena. They would go on to tell me stories, often of innocent encounters and romances in their distant pasts. Others would begin by launching in with sharp criticisms of the Salai gyals. After they had completed their rants, they would suddenly switch to light heartedly telling their favorite Salai gyal stories: "He had sex with a foreign woman nine times in one night. He was so exhausted that he literally collapsed in front of the Snow Lion Hotel the next morning," a highly regarded Amdo intellectual who was often harshly critical of Salai gyals told me gleefully.

One intellectual's opinion changed with the passage of time: "When I first came here and saw what they were doing, I thought that they were stupid. But after I was here [in India] one or two years, I wasn't so sure anymore. I became more like them." He shared a number of his own Salai gyal stories with me, enough so that when I suggested aloud that I should talk to more Salai gyals, he questioned why I needed to: "You should have enough stories. I've told you all of mine!" One was particularly funny, if not sad. He had experimented with on-line dating. When the woman arrived from abroad, she did not resemble her photographs at all— she was obese and balding. "I saw her waiting, but I didn't go meet her. I was so angry with her for lying to me. But later I started feeling sorry for her, so I took her for lunch."

Critics missed the most obvious of facts. Because of fear for their personal safety, very few women escape from Tibet, and thus there are far more single men in exile than women. A striking example of the skewed demographics occurred at a Losar party in 2010. Everyone in attendance was young and single and from the same region of Amdo, but there was just one girl in attendance. The guys were quick to point this out: "There are more than twenty unmarried guys here [in Dharamsala] from our part of Amdo and only one single girl," She was dating an Amdo guy who worked for the U.N. "People criticize us for dating foreigners," Rabgey told me bitterly, "but there are not enough women here, so who are we supposed to marry?"

A glance at statistics immediately paints a startling picture. The 2009 Tibetan Demographics Survey reported a sex ratio of 131 males to every 100 females among Tibetan refugees in India,[11] a figure which would leap to the attention of any demographer who came across it. China and India, both of which are experiencing serious social consequences as a result of abnormal sex ratios, pale in comparison, reporting figures of 113/100 and 112/100, respectively.[12] The skewed demographics among Tibetans in exile are not a consequence of selective abortion because the sex ratios among children are within digits of standard norms. The ratios become highly abnormal among those above the age of ten, clearly pointing to a different cause.[13] The Demographics Survey mentions that the disturbing data are a result of high numbers of male refugees coming from Tibet.[14] A mention is also made of the high numbers of monks, but as we will later learn, many do not remain monks forever; indeed, at least half of my Tibetan friends are ex-monks.

According to the 1998 Tibetan Demographic Survey, only 14.4% of Tibetans who had come from Amdo in the previous four years were female; the ratios were badly skewed for the two other regions as well.[15] After monks were factored out of the equation, there were 1532 more lay men than women in India,[16] and given the fear of authorities and essentially homeless status of many newcomers, I suspected that many were not counted. Although the exile government was unwilling to provide me with current figures regarding young adult newcomer lay people[17], I obtained useful information from a study conducted at the Tibetan Transit School, where they are sent for education. The researchers reported the student body as 28% female.[18] Two other studies showed similar figures.[19] Obviously, serious social and psychological consequences would be expected to result from the extreme shortage of women. The problem wouldn't be as big as it is if Tibetan men intermarried with Indian women and settler Tibetans, but, as we will see later, with a few rare exceptions, they don't.

Despite intensive searching, I couldn't find any research that had touched on this problem in the past twenty years. I read every paper that I could find that looked at social problems, mental health, and substance-abuse issues in the Tibetan exile community. Problems associated with skewed demographics were never mentioned, nor in most cases the other extreme challenges, such as denial of documentation, bigotry, chronic unemployment, and the lack of access to proper education faced by adult and youth new arrivals as they tried to adapt to life in exile. Most newcomers whom I knew in 2003 were also consumed with guilt because they were unable to provide financial support to their impoverished families back in Tibet.

In one study, Ministry of Health officials from the Tibetan Government in Exile and Buddhist leaders informed the researchers that newcomers had difficulty coping with exile life and suffered more from mental health disorders because they lacked sufficient education in Buddhism and did not access appropriate spiritual guidance; I can't imagine the reaction if Canadian Ministry of Health officials suggested that mental health problems in Canada were related to church attendance and bible study. Some to whom researchers spoke did acknowledge that newcomers lacked family support in exile, although no mention was made of the shortage of newcomer women.[20] The

Tibetan exile government appears to have never acknowledged the problem, although it leaps to the eye from its published data.

Most papers focused on torture victims and/or the coping mechanisms of settler Tibetans. I had a number of friends who were torture victims or who had escaped for political reasons. They did suffer greatly from what had happened to them in Tibet, but what kept most of them awake at night and caused tremendous stress was their difficulties finding gainful employment and, for the men, finding a wife. Other newcomers had the unappealing but possible option of returning to Tibet. The ex-politicals, as political activists who escaped Tibet without being arrested are referred to by Tibetans, and the ex-political prisoners don't have the option of returning to their homeland. Their futures weighed very heavily on their minds.

Men who had escaped from Tibet were demonized and mocked for their dating habits and social problems, but one clear cause had been ignored. The problem was in everyone's view, particularly in the early to mid-2000's. Young men were roaming all around town with barely a girl to be seen. "I thought that they were just shy and stayed home," a foreign resident later told me. The bars were full of single guys often getting drunk night after night and even sometimes fighting over the few available women. Although everyone wasn't drinking, most of the young men whom I spoke to were miserable because they couldn't find wives or girlfriends. Many, including those who were financially self-sufficient or even successful, dove into unsuitable relationships with the first foreign or Tibetan women who came along because they didn't want to lose a chance at getting married.

Unemployment and the lack of access to higher education and other opportunities drove some of the brightest newcomers to the brink of madness. Others cultivated carefree and sometimes arrogant public images, but in private they would occasionally admit to feelings of despair and humiliation. Binge drinking and alcoholism were widespread. Counselling was unavailable, but I was told that the exile government gladly paid for bus tickets back to Tibet.

The Tibetan Government in Exile did not have the financial resources to provide newcomers with the education or other opportunities that they needed to thrive, but it also did nothing to encourage other countries to take them or even publically address their predicaments. The Government of India made further changes to prevent new arrivals from going abroad, which were neither publically discussed nor objected to by human rights organizations.[21] Aid money to feed the hungry and house the homeless was apparently not requested. Although I did not uncover many instances in which exile government officials lied directly about how new arrivals were managed, it seemed that they left out crucial information when speaking with those who might not agree with their actions. In a U.S. government cable released by Wikileaks, no mention is made of the situation of newcomers with the exception of one comment that implies puzzlement: "Interestingly, according to statistics obtained from the Dharamsala Refugee Reception Center, of the 87,096 refugees that were taken in by Center from 1980 to November 2009, over half –46,620 people –returned to Tibet after a short pilgrimage in India and audience with the Dalai Lama."[22] One third of those who escaped Tibet are reported to be children, who are entitled to remain in India at least for the duration of their educations,[23] as are young adults. Not surprisingly, many newcomers were filled with anger and resentment towards the Tibetan government in exile and the "Indian Tibetans," as they often called the settlers.

The few older and successful newcomers tried to act as role models and mentors, but often with little success. Most of the mature adults had been forced to go back to Tibet, so there were few of them, and, in any event, most of the young refugees were followers, not leaders or entrepreneurs. They saw successful newcomers as god-like creatures to whom they could not relate. Although they stayed awake late into the night discussing their dreams and plans for the future, very few newcomers had the disposition required to create something out of nothing. It was impossible for them to figure out a way to become business people or gain their desired education as they sat penniless in their tiny dingy rooms. The older and more successful newcomers would encourage or chastise them when they had the chance, but the young men, who were often mired in well-concealed depression, couldn't find a path through their internal darkness.

In any event, there were just too many refugees for everyone to make a living. While exile-born Tibetans their own age and often with lesser intellect headed off to university or at least had a high-school diploma and spoke Hindi to give them an advantage, newcomers mostly faced severe competition for low-paying jobs in the service industry. Even those with qualifications could not apply for jobs with the Tibetan exile government unless they had documents allowing them to work in India. Most newcomers were not entitled to obtain them legally.

The 1998 Tibetan Demographic Survey reported that in Dharamsala, 77% of twenty to twenty-four-year-olds were not employed, as were 53% of twenty-five to twenty-nine-year-olds.[24]. It is unclear how monks and nuns were recorded, but if included, the unemployment rates would still be enormous. The figures were almost as bad for Tibetans throughout India, so migrating to other parts of the country, an option that some critics around the time suggested, would not solve their problems. To gain skills, most attended free English classes in McLeod Ganj— the demographics survey reported many students—but the teachers were often unqualified volunteers who were unable to effectively teach those ready for advanced study. When not attending classes, many of the young men could be found in the streets, dressed in their most stylish clothes, hoping against hope to meet foreign women who could save them by taking them to a new life abroad, or at the very least buy them dinner.

A profound sense of hopelessness pervaded. What truly amazed me was that no one whom I knew ever committed suicide, although several admitted that they had contemplated it, and some appeared hell bent on drinking themselves to death. Although many were not exactly what one would think of as religious, their faith seemed to give them an ingrained resilience, and even in the toughest of times, people would roar with laughter at almost anything, including misfortune and poverty, especially their own. Foreigners were often shocked at the darkness of the humor and the resilience of Tibetans. Strangely, as the fortunes of newcomers have improved, the laughter has died away.

Chapter 2

The location of Dharamsala in some ways exonerates the settlers and others from damning condemnation for their ineptitude when dealing with the newcomers. Dharamsala is not a small city as one might imagine, but rather a town, and not a large one at that, located in what was until recently a very remote backwater of India. One friend explained the necessity, in the 1980's, of going to an office in Lower Dharamsala in order to use a telephone, the call put through by a switchboard operator. Another friend described e-mails in the early 1990's being sent and received only through a computer operator at an exile-government office. That conservative, simplistic views have predominated is not surprising given its isolated locale and, it should be mentioned, a lack of job-specific education among many in decision-making positions. That the Tibetans have achieved as much as they have is little short of miraculous.

"Dharamsala!" For most, the name of the town evokes images of the Dalai Lama, maroon-robed monks, deeply religious Tibetan refugees, and peaceful political activism. That Dharamsala does exist, but some visitors and indeed many locals are disappointed that the town doesn't always resemble the stereotypes. Perhaps, now it will be helpful to journey overland to the town circa 2011 and peek at the place itself, its foreign visitors, and some of their odd expectations.

To reach Dharamsala one must fly, take a train to the nearest station, which is hours away, or, as most do, travel for twelve hours by bus or occasionally car, usually through a dusty night, first across the seemingly endless northern Indian plains, then finally through the foothills of the Himalayas. As the sun begins to rise, the bus winds its way through the Shivalik Hills, a 2,400km long mountain chain parallel to the great Himalayas, slowly growing over the millennia via often catastrophic earthquakes, as the earth's crust buckles and folds, pushing the ranges to greater heights. The bus passes through the small towns and villages of Himachal Pradesh. Most residents are still asleep, and the metal shutters of shops are closed, many bearing the imprint of advertising for what appears to be Himachal's most popular consumer purchase—cement. The air is cool and fresh. The road, which has been created by blasting with unknown tons of dynamite, twists and turns along steep hillsides. Rivers tumble among massive boulders through the narrow valleys far below. The landscape is strikingly lush. You have a sense that you are going somewhere very remote and not long ago virtually inaccessible. The massive Dhauladhar range, of the outer Himalaya, comes into view. As the bus makes its way up through Lower Dharamsala and then follows the long route up through the nearby army base, most passengers stir from fitful sleep. Shortly thereafter, they disembark bleary eyed into an enthusiastic crowd of taxi drivers and porters at the McLeod Ganj bus station.

Dharamsala is not one town, as many who have never been there might imagine, but rather a collection of towns and villages spread over several kilometers. Lower Dharamsala, where most of the Indian community resides, is a relatively large, thriving Indian market town. For those who live in the surrounding villages, Dharamsala is the place to go if you want to purchase clothing, electronics, kitchen supplies, bedding, and other goods. It is a friendly town that does not appeal to the tourist crowd and is therefore, I found, a delight to visit. Residents are used to visitors from abroad, but their income does not depend much on them directly, so they pay no special attention to foreign faces and the shops mostly have fixed prices, with discounts offered rather than fought for. Sometimes, on a whim, I would wander through the back streets. There I did attract some stares, but only because white faces are so rare that residents gave me a quizzical look as if to say, "What on earth are you doing here? Are you lost?" There are some beautiful homes with lovely gardens, many houses dating to the time of the British and some even earlier, especially down below the Superintendent of Police offices.

The British relocated to Lower Dharamsala after McLeod Ganj, which was at that time a fairly major hill station, was essentially destroyed in a massive earthquake that rocked the Kangra valley in 1905. Few buildings survived the earthquake even in Dharamsala, which is somewhat flatter and more stable, but tucked away on a quiet street right near the heart of Kotwali Bazar is arguably the most interesting and best-preserved building in town, the Hotel Grace, a former manor house built in the early 1800's. In the market, old shops, some with their walls bulging and threatening to collapse, perhaps as a result of the long-ago earthquake, sit side by side with modern fashion emporiums and small businesses with tailors at work on old-fashioned sewing machines, delectable sweet shops, and dhabas, informal roadside restaurants, some terrifying looking, with blackened walls and peeling paint, where I could procure a delicious sweet chai or a light and heavenly parantha – an Indian stuffed pancake.

When I needed to purchase reading glasses, an optician, a kindly older man, took me into a small room which contained eye charts and perhaps the most interesting dentist's office that I have ever seen. It appeared not to have been used in a decade or more; the rusting tools lay on trays as if waiting in vain for the owner's return. There was an enormous hand-held power drill, worthy of a carpenter of the 1960's, a once state-of-the-art chair of a similar age, and a wonderful wooden cabinet that looked as though it might have been around for a century. "These are best quality," the optician told me, as I tried not to stare at his unusual office while he presented me with a pair of spectacles. Despite much abuse, they have performed perfectly ever since.

Far down the ridge, Dharamsala boasts what must be one of the most stunning cricket stadiums in the world, modern and shiny with a breathtaking view of the Himalayas. In the shadow of the cricket stadium lies a teeming slum, its plastic tents home to more than 800 people. Despite the slum's desperate appearance, hope is not lost thanks to a monk from Tibet who taught himself Hindi and set to work providing educational opportunities to the children and health care to all of the residents. In the winter, huge wild poinsettia trees bloom in the most unlikely places throughout the town, even in the slum.

By following a steep winding road up the hill, or better yet by walking up one of the paths where Morning Glories and a myriad of other flowers blanket the hillsides, one comes to Gangchen Kyishong, locally referred to as Gankyi, where the Tibetan Government in Exile operates from a collection of practical but not entirely charmless office buildings. Many Tibetan officials and other employees, as well as Indian families, inhabit nearby apartment blocks and houses, many with pretty gardens teeming with flowers.

Each day when I would go to Gankyi to attend language class, I would marvel at the rugged beauty of the Library of Tibetan Works and Archives, which was built from concrete and brick but in the traditional architectural style of the U-tsang region of Tibet. Those builders of old knew what they were doing when they built such squat imposing structures with their extremely thick walls on the seismically unstable Tibetan plateau. Due to the techniques used, seismologists discovered that the library is one of the only buildings which they surveyed in the area that will not be at high risk of collapse during the next major earthquake.[1]

Below the Library, the Nechung Monastery, home of the Tibetan state oracle, is tucked away discretely, its golden roof glistening in the sun. For some reason, nearby Men-tse-khang, the Tibetan institute of traditional medicine, reminds me of Japan, with its neatly swept lane and tidy blocks of classrooms, offices, and simple apartments. Farther up the road, Tibetan Delek Hospital might not inspire confidence with its utilitarian appearance, but untold lives have been saved there, including possibly my own, for I once came down with a virulent case of dysentery and spent almost a week in a spartan ward receiving a quick and accurate diagnosis and the kind of treatment—or better than—one would receive at a gleaming new Western hospital.

The road continues to wind more steeply up and up. The hillsides are scattered with sometimes massive pines and rhododendron trees, the latter producing spectacular red blooms in the spring. During monsoon, the jungle floor bursts with moist dripping plant life in every shade of green imaginable, and enormous yet charming golden-brown slugs roam through the almost primeval landscape. Later, in the dry seasons of fall and winter, the gnawing of domestic animals exposes the hillsides, which bear the scars of earthquakes of past centuries and the detritus of landslides produced by the life-giving monsoons.

About a kilometer farther up, the road levels somewhat for a few hundred metres as it passes through the hamlet of Jogibara. Several small motorcycle repair shops and tiny eateries line the road. Small farms, guest houses, and apartment blocks are scattered through small meadows. One can hear the roar of a small river in the valley below. On clear nights, thanks to an absence of streetlights, the sky above the darkened village is blanketed with stars.

It seems impossible, but past Jogibara, the road becomes even steeper than before. Finally, a kilometer further, one arrives at McLeod Ganj, home of the Dalai Lama and the bulk of the Tibetan population. McLeod Ganj clings precariously to a ridge that juts off the massive Dhauladhar mountain chain. The surprisingly small town literally spills off the edge of the narrow ridge, like a ragged spider web, with guesthouses and small apartment blocks clinging higgledy piggledy to the unstable slopes. After the modest nature of the towns and villages of the Kangra Valley and much of the Indian plains, the cosmopolitan atmosphere of McLeod Ganj and its embracement of tourism on a massive scale can come as a shock. Innumerable guesthouses, along with shops selling a dazzling array of handicrafts, imported foods, books, clothing, and art line the eight narrow streets. Restaurants are everywhere, offering Indian, Tibetan, Italian, Thai, Japanese, Israeli, Korean, Nepali, and even Bhutanese food. McLeod, as it is commonly referred to, may have more coffee shops per capita than anywhere on the planet. In 2010, a Tibetan friend named twelve that had cappuccino machines, and more have opened since.

Here and there in the urban jungle, one comes across Gaddi farm houses, some with a cow or more in the yard, reminding the visitor of the town's not so distant rural past. A few tiny mostly makeshift cabins made of wood, some clad with flattened tin boxes, are tenuous physical reminders of the extreme poverty and resourcefulness of the first Tibetan refugees. Many of the old homes and walls incorporate stones that appear to have been cannibalized from the ruins of British buildings destroyed in the 1905 earthquake. Like the farm houses, very few cabins remain, and those that do mostly cower in the shadows of new developments.

All this might be too much, too urban, too crowded; certainly, it can seem so during busy seasons when foreign tourists can sometimes be heard, over the blaring of car horns, shouting with impotent rage and frustration as they attempt to navigate the sidewalk-less, traffic-jammed streets. But the town is saved by its steep terrain, which allows for panoramic views of the breathtaking mountains and valleys from almost every location. The hillsides are so steep that as one sits on the usually tranquil balconies and roof tops, hawks, eagles, and kites are observed circling at eye level and below as they ride on updrafts searching for prey and sometimes frolicking and diving playfully, seemingly without a care in the world.

Occasionally, from those same tranquil patios, there are reminders that McLeod Ganj is only fifty miles from the Pakistan border. Sometimes jets can be heard far off in the distance, at times non-stop for hours on end. Although I never learned for certain what was going on, the distant roar often coincided with rises in political tensions between the two neighbors. Locals seemed mostly unaware and unconcerned. Most had never seen an airport or recognized the sound of a jet in flight. But I always felt a sense of wonder and excitement.

The trees and bushes teem with a myriad of other bird life. One friend who had conducted birding tours around India told me that she had never witnessed such diversity in such a small area. Mongooses scurry through the underbrush. Sometimes, I watched them amuse themselves by playing elaborate games of tag through torn tarpaulins and discarded cement bags. In winter, troops of often enormous and disarmingly human looking shy and gentle Langur monkeys pay a welcome visit to the town.

One morning in the depths of winter, I awoke before dawn to a frozen winter wonderland. Deep snow had fallen and the temperature in my room had dropped to almost 0 C. Icicles clung to the eaves and Jack Frost had made patterns on the windows. The trees sagged under the weight of the new-fallen snow. The electricity had been knocked out by the storm, not that it would have mattered as we, like almost everyone in town, had no heating. I struggled into layers of clothing and fumbled with freezing fingers as I made coffee on the gas stove.

Wearing two pairs of fingerless gloves, I checked my e-mail and read news on-line, thankful for the generous battery life of the tiny Samsung notebook computer that relative poverty had forced me to buy. As the winter sun peeked over the mountain, I stepped out onto the balcony where I was greeted by the most charming of sights. The forest below was peppered with dozens of enormous Languor monkeys and their tiny offspring, waiting in the highest branches of the tallest trees for the first rays of sun to brush the tree tops.

Other creatures are not so welcome. Like elsewhere in India, McLeod Ganj is home to hundreds of Rhesus monkeys. Long ago they abandoned their traditional foraging methods and now subsist mostly on garbage and other stolen food. They have sharp teeth, can be aggressive, and often thieve by intimidation. Woe is to those who leave a door open or food within reach through a barred window. They are intelligent creatures who seem to prefer their food packed for easy transportation. How often I have seen a monkey galloping along electrical lines between buildings clutching a take-away bag stolen from a restaurant, an enraged employee helplessly hurling curses and sometimes projectiles in its wake.

For some reason, the monkeys also seem to especially enjoy dried noodles —similar to fettuccini—which are used for making a type of thukpa, Tibetan noodle soup. I would often observe them tearing open packages of the noodles, stolen from god knows where, and munching contentedly. Leaving a door open is an invitation to a home invasion. Even when confronted by occupants ready to defend their properties, the scallywags bar their teeth and leap, growl, and threaten so aggressively that most allow them to help themselves to the contents of their kitchen for fear of bites from the nasty invaders.

Still, one cannot help but sometimes feel sympathy for the creatures. We had a grizzled old monkey friend who would shelter on our balcony during monsoon with his small family. When I first went to chase them off with a chair, rather than barring his teeth, he stared at me with a resigned expression and made as though to leave. We took pity on the family and allowed them to seek haven during downpours. The monkeys seemed to appreciate our kindness and allowed us to use the rest of the balcony, without protest, when they were taking refuge in their corner. Even when my son would, in an occasional fit of boredom, approach the window and make obnoxious teasing gestures, the old monkey would only glance at him disdainfully and then turn his face away.

By far, though, the most curious animals to pass through the community are human. What was and continues to be essentially a refugee camp has morphed over the decades into a major tourist destination. Locals rub shoulders—often literally in the crowded streets—with a bewildering array of visitors, including outrageously clad and sometimes dreadlock-bedecked hippies and other sometimes scantily clad foreign visitors—they often have a fondness for what my friend Dolkar named "Shit Pants," a variation of traditional Indian ladies' baggy trousers marketed to tourists, with bulky crotches that droop unflatteringly to the knees and even the ankles, creating an impression of over-sized toddlers in dangerously overloaded diapers. They are joined by middle-class domestic tourists, ranging from families munching on ice creams to ill-mannered groups of horny young men in town to party, and a plethora of foreign and Indian Buddhists. Often, the crowds on the streets of McLeod Ganj resemble an assemblage of extras in a multitude of entirely unrelated films. Some of the tourists and "expats," as many of the long-term foreign visitors refer to themselves, indulge in dope smoking and excessive drinking while others immerse themselves in Buddhism with the torturous enthusiasm of recently born-again Christians. Certainly, many visitors are perfectly ordinary, but the circus-like atmosphere is hard to miss, especially during peak tourist seasons.

Most locals manage to live ordinary lives in this strange environment, but its impact does not go unnoticed. "Western culture is ruining this town," remarked a modern young Tibetan woman shortly after I met her. I did my best to explain that what she saw represented was not Western culture but rather Western holiday culture. My new friend drank and smoked in public, radical behavior for a Tibetan woman in India, but she, like many of the Tibetans whom I have spoken to over the years, felt that many of the tourists went too far with their excessive and self-indulgent behavior. Such cross-cultural disillusionments go both ways.

"It is disgusting how they have lost their culture," grumbled a French lesbian with whom I was sharing a taxi. The object of her derision was a cluster of cheerful looking young Tibetan men who were standing in the market, dressed in black with spiky hair, leather jackets, and skinny jeans. She didn't seem to see the irony of her comment as she and her partner sat in the taxi in matching Crocs and frumpy generic travel clothes. They themselves hardly epitomized traditional French culture. I thought that she should be grateful that the Tibetans had "lost their culture," for the young men may have been the descendants of bandits from times of yore and, in an alternate reality, would have appeared on horseback clad in traditional dress as she made her way back in the dark to her guest house following dinner, robbed her, and left her for dead at the side of the road. I imagine that one of my friends would have met with her approval, given his penchant for Tibetan dress and his eloquence discussing Tibetan religious history. She would have beamed with pleasure in his company, blissfully unaware of the collection of pornographic images of him and a number of Western woman engaged in sexual acts that he had shown me on his cell phone.

"What do they need phones for anyway?" barked another disgruntled Western woman several days later. The comment was so inane that I didn't know what to say. "Maybe they want to call their Mom in Tibet or let their boss know that they can't make it to work because they are sick," I replied lamely. In India, Tibetans have embraced technology with a fervor that I have not witnessed elsewhere, and this, too, is at odds with some visitors' expectations. Tourists and even journalists are often bemused or even disappointed by the sight of Tibetans, especially monks, talking on cell phones, texting, and using the Internet. Elsewhere in India, outside of tourist areas, Internet cafes are few and far between, but in McLeod Ganj, they are everywhere, and the majority of the customers are Tibetan. (This is slowly changing as more locals have access to the Internet at work and at home). I sometimes wonder if the desire to be wired and connected stems from centuries of being essentially cut off from the outside world and the loss of statehood that self-imposed isolation may have played a part in.

Tibetans use technology to keep in touch with friends and family back in Tibet as well as those who are, increasingly, scattered around the globe. Information on the human rights situation in Tibet is generally passed on via phone and the Internet these days. Home phones are difficult to have installed, so the entire country has embraced India's extremely affordable mobile phone technology and services with a vengeance. Even though I called North America regularly and spent a lot of time talking to friends around India, my phone bill was seldom more than $8 a month. My teenage son, who spent what seemed like half the day texting, spent just $1.50 a month. Almost everyone but the Tibetans themselves seems to be surprised to see monks with cell phones. Tibetans would be much more surprised to see a monk without one.

The Internet is the isolated hill station's most important connection to the outside world. Like people almost everywhere these days, Tibetans e-mail, read newspapers, conduct research and do business, use Facebook, chat, look at rubbish, and watch videos on-line. Once, in 2009, after most Internet cafes were closed for three days over Losar, I waited for hours to access a computer terminal as dozens of Tibetan youths busied themselves playing Farmville on Facebook.

The tourists, for their part, are sometimes disappointed that the Tibetans have refused to allow their society to remain quaint and picturesque, virtually frozen in time as it was sixty years ago, ignoring the obvious folly and impracticality, not to mention dullness, of living like feudal people in the 21st century. When you see others as your equal, you generally do not expect them to conform to expectations that you yourself would reject outright. I never wish that I could confiscate my Tibetan friends' phones, computers, and fake North Face jackets and banish them to the mountainsides to herd yak or sheep, while dressed in traditional costumes. The tourists draped in Indian shawls while buying up Tibetan jewelry and music C.D.'s in the streets of McLeod Ganj and planning their next exotic meal are often the same people who complain bitterly when they see a Tibetan youth with spiky hair listening to a hip-hop track and sucking on a cappuccino. "Oh but that is different," they exclaim. Of course, it is exactly the same thing when you think about it.

Surprisingly, Facebook, currently considered by many to be one of biggest time wasters on the planet, has proven very beneficial to Tibetan language preservation. Previously, many newcomers, who, unlike most of those born in India, are usually quite literate in Tibetan, seldom had much reason to write in their language and didn't read often unless they were intellectuals. Ordinary Tibetans now use Facebook and chat in their own language. Fingers fly over the keys as people post comments, exchange gossip, or comment on news articles in Tibetan. A literacy renaissance is taking place, often under the disapproving gaze of foreigners.

Many Tibetans are amused by the unrealistic expectations placed upon them, while others feel frustrated. I spoke to the young India-born Tibetan founder of the Tibetan Art Collective, an organization that showcases the work of Tibetan artists, including writers and filmmakers, regardless of whether or not their work is Tibet related and that seeks to "discourage the perpetuated stereotypes or notions of Tibetan identity." He spoke eloquently and at length of the frustration that he and many other Tibetans feel at being expected to conform both creatively and personally within narrow parameters to fulfill expectations, both of their own people and outsiders. I couldn't help but feel fortunate, as I so often did in India. Canadians have never had to face such restrictions. Arguably, the most popular cultural icons at that moment in my country were the Trailer Park Boys, perpetually unemployed drunk and stoned white trash immortalized in a television series.

I spent a lot of time thinking about culture and its preservation, coming to the conclusion that most outsiders like to see other cultures preserved in ways that are picturesque, politically correct, and convenient for them. The tourists would whine with indignation if no one spoke English and they could find only truly traditional Tibetan home cooking in local restaurants. Great lumps of boiled meat, endless bowls of tsampa (roasted barley flour), hard malodorous dried cheese, and heavily salted tea mixed with often rancid butter would not likely meet with their approval. I often wish that I could dress the disapproving visitors in starched collars and stove-pipe hats or corsets and hoop skirts and send them down the hill back to Delhi in a covered wagon.

Chapter 3

I awoke at dawn on the morning of February 18th, 2012 and opened my Facebook account. I had returned to Canada a month earlier. Not being in Dharamsala to witness how unreported and apparently unnoticed events were unfolding was weighing on my mind. A tragedy had been playing out in Tibet for almost a year. Over the course of that time, almost two dozen Tibetans had lit themselves on fire in protest against Chinese policies. (The first self-immolation within Tibet had been an isolated event in 2009 when Tapey, a young monk of the Kirti Monastery in Amdo, had lit himself ablaze.) Those who hadn't died at the scene were whisked away by the Chinese authorities.

Demonstrations were reported to have been flaring up in various communities throughout the Tibetan plateau. Many parts of what had once been Tibet were under unofficial martial law, and the entire Tibetan Autonomous Region was scheduled to be closed to foreign visitors. Tibetans were planning to boycott their traditional New Year's celebrations, and the anniversary of the unsuccessful uprising of March 10th, 1959 was approaching. The Chinese did not want outsiders to witness potential dissent.

As usual, Tibetan friends and Tibet supporters were posting news stories on their Facebook walls. Since I had last checked Facebook the night before, another self-immolation had occurred; this time it was a forty-year-old monk who had spent several years in India during the 1990's.[1] Tsering Woser, the most prominent Tibetan blogger in China, who has long been exiled to Beijing but has somehow so-far avoided imprisonment, reported that elsewhere in Tibet, a thirty-three-year-old writer had been arrested for reasons unknown.[2] People were still posting a video that had been released by the *Guardian* a week earlier of the tremendous police and military presence in Amdo Ngawa (Also known as Ngaba by those from Central Tibet and called Aba by the Chinese) where many of the self-immolations had occurred.[3] None of this was unusual or unexpected. I had been looking at disturbing photographs and videos of self-immolations and charred corpses and reading accounts of arrests and futile demonstrations for months.

What captured my attention was something else. I noticed two posts that brought into sharp focus a question that had been weighing on my mind. The first had been made by a friend who, several months earlier, had been brutally beaten by Indian police in front of horrified onlookers who had witnessed the assault from a second-floor restaurant window. He had been planning to go back to Tibet, and the incident only deepened his resolve. I was still somewhat surprised to read his Facebook post. Apparently, he had received a phone call from home warning him not to return, but it appeared that he had, so far, not changed his mind. The second post was more unsettling. Another friend had written of a father with whom he had just spent the evening. The family was planning their return to Amdo, taking their four children with them. I had wondered if, despite the dramatically deteriorating conditions in Tibet, newcomers would continue to intentionally choose to head home.

Over the past several years and for reasons unknown, on a fairly massive scale, the Chinese had begun to issue travel documents to newcomers wishing to return to Tibet to visit or resettle there permanently. During the year and a half that I was in Dharamsala beginning in September 2010, familiar faces had disappeared at an alarming rate; most never returned. Their departures will be described in more detail later. The question that is best answered first is why so many were going back to Tibet by choice, especially those who had lived in India for a decade or more and had, before restrictions were harshly enforced, managed to obtain documentation that allowed them to remain in India. Some of the answers are obvious to those who know the community.

Although mostly relatively harmonious on the surface, the Tibetan exile community is fractured and dysfunctional. As in most societies, often a social disconnect exists between conservative (some would refer to them as traditional, while others would call them narrow-minded) inhabitants and those who have adopted modern, seemingly Western lifestyles. This divide is often attributable to the millennia old griping of older people around the world about the younger generation. But further, deeper, and more troubling divides exist between those born in India and the newcomers who were born and raised in Tibet. Even among the newcomers themselves, there are divisions based on the areas in Tibet that they are from. Certainly, friendships and marriages among the communities exist, but relations between those born in India and those from Tibet remain mostly poisoned.

Such divisions really surprised me when I first went to Dharamsala. From everything that I had read over the years, I envisioned exile Tibetans as one big happy family. I imagined the settlers welcoming those who came from their homeland and seeking out the newest arrivals for news of their ancestral hometowns. I imagined people from the various communities exchanging knowledge and information. I was told that many of the oldest settlement Tibetans who had grown up in Tibet before the Chinese invasion did seek out and befriend newcomers, but sadly, quite the opposite was true of the vast majority of the rest. Initially, I thought that the Chinese must be somehow using agents to destabilize the community, but over time, I realized that this was not the case. The problem was just too deeply entrenched and the spite too personal to be the work of outside forces.

In 1989, the Dalai Lama won the Nobel Peace prize, ushering in an unprecedented era in Tibetan history. The current Dali Lama's success at unifying his people in a so far almost entirely non-violent struggle against the Chinese and his tremendous compassion and gifts as a teacher have captivated both Tibetans and foreigners. In past centuries, Tibet had been mythologized, but most accounts produced by the few foreign visitors to the country had presented a balanced perspective. Unfortunately, nowadays there is a perception that Tibetans are an extremely advanced race spiritually, embodying the characteristics personified by the current Dalai Lama. This view, combined with the focus on the many positive aspects of Tibetan Buddhism and the remarkable success of the Tibetan refugees, has created an atmosphere in which Tibetan exile society is perceived, by most Tibetans and many foreigners, as being superior to that of other cultures. Foreign media and the gushing praise of many visitors who fail to look below the surface have reinforced this myth. Those who do notice serious problems usually want to be supportive of Tibetan refugees, so they say nothing. Meanwhile, an insidious and crippling climate of bigotry has flourished unabated within exile Tibetan communities.

I was able to locate only one article written by a Tibetan confronting the situation directly. It was published on an obscure website in 2005. Ironically, the author, a settler, expressed fear of opening a can of worms by publishing his article, but it had not even created a ripple. I could find no reference to it anywhere in cyberspace. The article echoed much that I had seen, but when I contacted the author in 2012 for clarification of a term that he had used, he wrote back insisting that I not quote it. He has lived in the United States for many years and now feels that his previous "notion of everyone in exile being prejudiced and hostile makes no sense."

In the past, problems within the newcomer community itself had been almost as destructive. I was told that they mostly stemmed from regional loyalties. To a certain extent, social divisions are also natural products of linguistic differences because some Tibetan dialects are almost mutually unintelligible. It is possible that competition for the few available jobs and women contributed to the problem, for newcomers told me that people within Tibet were nowadays generally not prejudiced against each other; to grossly simplify a complicated history, in old Tibet, there had been a lack of unity and disputes over territory. In Dharamsala in recent years, the flood of refugees arriving from Tibet has slowed dramatically, and those newcomers who remain in India have become far less judgmental, but often people were and, in some cases, still are close friends with only those from the same small region in Tibet.

My former husband, an Amdo Tibetan, was very proud of the fact that in Dharamsala in the early 2000's, he had cultivated friendships among people from all parts of Amdo and brought people together socially who had never mixed before: "Even educated people like xxxx and xxxx are like this," he told me at the time, but he couldn't explain why. In India, he had been very hostile towards "Indian Tibetans," as many newcomers called the settlers. Later in Canada, he swore that if he returned to India, he would try to befriend some of them, "A lot of them were rude to me and called me "newcomer beggar," but some of them seemed cool but I wasn't willing to give them a chance." We discussed the social divides often, "It's a really big problem, and not easy to change," he would tell me.

The social chasms often surprise and even create problems for foreign visitors and researchers. I've attended and heard torturous tales of innumerable disastrous dinner parties where foreigners invited their like-minded Tibetan friends to meet one another and have a good time. Most, especially young Tibetans, wouldn't even make the effort to make polite conversation even if only to please their hosts. Instead, they sat in stony silence or spoke comfortably only to people who had grown up in the same place as they had. The foreigners were shocked because they never expected this, or if they had been warned, they assumed that the person who told them was friends with idiots.

Foreign researchers can be in the worst position because they often work with translators. Getting people to answer questions honestly, or at all, when a translator is not from the right place can be extremely difficult. One researcher told me that he couldn't get a Tibetan exile government official to even answer his questions because his translator, a newcomer who spoke excellent English, wasn't deemed appropriate. Occasionally, I had to put off interviewing people for months as I waited for just the right translator to come along. Sometimes, I was forced to give up. I knew that if the translator and the interview subject weren't at ease in conversation, the effort would be useless.

Unexpectedly, unfortunate events led to improvements in the social environment. In 2008, demonstrations flared up throughout far-flung regions of Tibet for the first time since the Chinese invasion. The Chinese cracked down hard, arresting anyone even remotely suspected of involvement. Since then in India, I have noticed a warming of relations between newcomers from the various Tibetan provinces. Formerly, it was common to hear people from Amdo put down people from Kham or U-Tsang and vice versa. The change in attitude towards more universal appreciation and respect has been dramatic, although many don't think that things have improved enough. "Tibetan groups need to start holding parties for people from all over Tibet so that we can talk and get to know each other," Nyima told me at the bar one night after he had quizzed me on my opinions regarding relations between newcomers from different regions. "Things are getting better, but it is not good enough."

Still, in India, many Tibetans from various regions who would never have spoken a few years ago now greet each other with a smile and exchange friendly banter. Completely dysfunctional dinner parties are mostly a thing of the past, although usually only as long as the Tibetans present were all raised in Tibet. Rather than curtly describing someone as being from Kham or Lhasa, newcomers are more inclined to say that individuals are from Tibet; when they do say the name of the region, their tone almost always now implies respect. Unfortunately, I have not yet noticed much in the way of similar improvements in relations between the settlers and the newcomers.

Looking back through the years, I'd be hard pressed to count on two hands Tibetans born in India who haven't made some sort of bigoted comment about newcomers if the subject came up: "Newcomers don't work," "Newcomers think like Chinese," "Newcomers live off Western sponsors," "Newcomers are always fighting," "Newcomers are drunk," "Newcomers are dishonest," "Newcomers are rude," "Newcomers can't speak Tibetan properly," "Newcomers want to marry foreigners so that they can have an easy life in the West." Sometimes the remarks are subtle, but they are endless, coming from settlers of all ages and from all walks of life, from the most uneducated to monks and university graduates. "You are always hanging around with newcomers," or "you really like newcomers," many said to me with the knowing smirks of those talking to a fool. A young newcomer scholar told me that the problem was not as bad in some settlements as it is in Dharamsala and he hoped that people like him who studied with settlers and lived in both societies could eventually build bridges between the communities. But for now, bigotry against newcomers from Tibet is so deeply entrenched that at times I wondered if it was taught in the exile schools and monasteries as a matter of course, "Bigotry 101."

Aside from such generalizations being predominantly untrue, one of the ironies in the Tibetan exile context is that, in the Tibetan language, writers, radio and television journalists, and scholars are almost all newcomers. The depth of prejudice depressed and disturbed me. Some of my favorite people that I met in India were settler Tibetans. The ingrained and unjustified prejudices that most embraced starkly contrasted their other beliefs and actions.

As I shared a home with three newcomers in McLeod Ganj for a year in 2003, a constant stream of their impoverished countrymen, many of whom I barely knew, dropped by our room almost every day to visit or eat. There were no bank machines at the time, so once a month I went to the Western Union and collected 11,000 rupees, which I had transferred from my bank account. It was considered a small fortune at the time; a tiny room, with no kitchen or toilet, could be rented for as little as 500 rupees a month back then. The money sat on a shelf in my room, barely hidden under a stack of clothing; eventually almost everyone who visited our house knew that it was there. I found it truly remarkable that no one ever stole any. Despite the poverty that most newcomers were suffering from at the time— many were often hungry and some were essentially homeless— thieving was extremely uncommon. What few robberies did occur in McLeod Ganj seldom seemed to be solved, so the low crime rate could not be attributed to effective policing.

The dozens of young newcomers whom I knew were, almost without exception, kind and helpful to me, perhaps because I shared what I had and lived as they did. They had only each other to depend on for survival; loyalty and generosity were not optional among the new arrivals at that time. They repaid my small kindnesses with kindnesses of their own. Friends and visitors to my home would often cook and wash dishes. Some would do so even if I asked them not to. They solved disagreements between me and my Tibetan husband. Much to his chagrin, they were always on my side. They patiently explained even the subtlest details of Tibetan customs and culture. If I went out of town, someone would always be waiting early in the morning at the bus stand to carry my bags home when I returned. They listened to my boring problems and offered often valuable advice. People invited me for dinner or enraged me by paying my bill without my knowing in restaurants. They gave me and my son gifts which they could ill afford. Many of them worked very hard at often menial jobs, far beneath their capabilities, with little complaint. Like people everywhere, most were not without flaws, but the kindness and friendship of these marginalized people changed my life forever.

While the settlement Tibetans have their own prejudices, foreign visitors often have a variety of other illusions regarding people who have escaped from Tibet. For example, many are under the impression that newcomers are mostly illiterate. I had dinner one evening with a friend from Europe who had been visiting Dharamsala for years. She was intelligent, educated, and up-to date on the Tibetan political situation. I mentioned what a waste it was that so many bright young people from Tibet could find only low-paying jobs in restaurants. One of the girls who worked in the extremely successful and upscale Tibetan-owned restaurant where we were eating had previously mentioned to me that her wages—far less than the state's legal minimum wage—were so low that she could only afford to live in a building where she had no access to a toilet. "They don't have many other options," my European friend told me sadly, "They are illiterate."

It is a complex problem, for the situation in Tibet is dire and the culture is under tremendous threat. There are serious problems with illiteracy and lack of access to education in Tibet, but the majority of young adult newcomers arrive literate or quickly become so in exile. More than half of those who escape are monks and a few are nuns. They may not all have excellent Tibetan, but literate they are. Most of the younger nomads and farmers whom I have met, especially the men from Amdo, arrived in India literate to a certain degree. Some had been taught at home, while others had gone to schools where instruction was in Tibetan. Many of the latter were also literate in Chinese. Many highly educated people have also escaped.

The raw data from the 1998 Tibetan Demographic Survey clearly show that newcomers were, in most cases, more literate in Tibetan than the settlers. I visited the exile government's Department of Home in hopes of obtaining the raw data from the more recent 2009 survey, but I was told that I could not have it without permission from "the boss," who was out of town. Since I had no credentials whatsoever, I never went back. In 1998 in South India, where the majority of newcomers are monks, Tibetan language literacy among those born in Tibet between the age of twenty and thirty four was above 99%, as opposed to 88% among those born in exile. In the north, among the same demographic, 84% of those born in Tibet were literate in their own language compared to 81% of those who were exile-born. [4]

The highest number of illiterates is among the demographic that escaped with the Dalai Lama into exile. This is not unexpected because like elsewhere in much of Asia, literacy levels were extremely low in Tibet prior to the 1960's. Due to the Cultural Revolution and other Chinese policies, illiteracy remained extremely high in Tibet through the 1960's and 70's and in many regions continues to be to this day. Many of my friends were tutored in Tibetan at home by relatives because schooling was unavailable or instruction was mostly in Chinese. Many families could not afford school fees and others did not want to send their children to Chinese boarding schools. Some joined monasteries, not always because they were very religious, but because they wanted to be educated in Tibetan. I heard many stories of kindly or dictatorial relatives, usually uncles who were or had been monks, who taught children in Tibet at home.

In 2011, a young blogger who called himself "Angry Tibetan Guy" addressed this issue in his casual yet often pointed style: "One thing I still don't understand is that why people from Tibet are better in Tibetan language especially writing. You will hear this frequently in school, 'Tashi is good in Tibetan because he's from Tibet.' What makes them better? I thought Chinese govt. don't let them study Tibetan in Tibet. Or am I missing out on something?"[5] Angry Tibetan Guy made a number of other thought-provoking posts, but he suddenly backed off and then stopped blogging altogether. I noticed on a forum on the high-profile Tibetan news website Phayul that he was accused by some of being a Chinese sympathizer. I suspected that he had received hate mail. Vicious personal attacks are common on Tibetan forums and blogs.

Angry Tibetan Guy was right. In India, until very recently, Tibetan schools for children devoted most of their curricula to studies in the English language. Tibetan Transit School, which is for young adults from Tibet, focuses heavily on Tibetan language instruction. Those adults who were illiterate when they escaped to India but went on to complete their studies at Tibetan Transit School quickly become literate in Tibetan and at least somewhat literate in English.

Derogatory attitudes and bigoted views are even accepted and embraced without question by some who should know better. This lesson I learned when I read Pico Iyer's book about the Dalai Lama, *The Open Road*. Iyer is an acclaimed author and journalist who writes for magazines such as *Time* and *Harpers*. His book *Video Night in Kathmandu*, which he wrote in the 1980's, had a major impact on my life, filling me with desire to visit the faraway lands that he so eloquently described. On one of my first nights in McLeod Ganj, I saw a man who bore a striking resemblance to the idol of my youth in Khana Nirvana restaurant at one of its sometimes painfully amusing open-mike nights.

This was my first time at open-mike, but it was to become a part of my routine for many months. It was an outing that didn't involve spending money, and it was a chance for newcomers to meet girls, so a lot of them went every week. My husband was handsome, charismatic, and long haired. He was not the world's greatest singer, so he always sang the same simple song. Most foreign girls were enraptured by his jaunty rendition of the Tibetan alphabet, having no idea that he was singing a children's song. Another highlight was an Israeli girl with huge boobs who wore an unsupportive bra. For a time she was a regular. She acted out not terribly brilliant poems of her own composition. Most people who were witnesses will never forget the performance of her breasts during her poem *Running*.

On that first night at Khana Nirvana, I was sure that I must be mistaken. With more than a billion people in India, the man I saw sitting casually with other tourists in a Japanese-style seating area, curtained by a few plants suspended in somewhat grubby macramé hangers, couldn't possibly be Pico Iyer. It had to be someone who resembled him. The next day, one of the volunteers working in the restaurant told me that "some writer called Pico Iyer" had been there. I was really disappointed that I hadn't taken a chance and said, "Hello."

I was excited to read *The Open Road*, for it had received a glowing review in the *New York Times*. I expected something insightful, but I was beyond disappointed. I discussed the book with friends on Facebook: "It is a book of paradox putting H.H. the Dalai Lama in the list of men of all time, yet dehumanizing those of us who hail from Tibet," a student who had arrived from Tibet young enough to qualify for education at a Tibetan Children's Village school eloquently wrote.

Iyer spent a long time in the town over a period of decades conducting research and, by his own account, devoted a great deal of time to hanging around with the Dharamsala elite. He admits that at least some of his views come directly from them. No mention is made of the many contributions of newcomers to exile society. Iyer, who had the time and connections to do careful research, entirely ignores the Tibetan-language intellectuals and artists who have escaped from Tibet, not to mention the thousands of principled and hard-working ordinary people. The Tibetans he met who came in 1959 and those born in exile are painted as marvelous individuals, whereas newcomers without exception are portrayed as inferior, uneducated, ignorant, pathetic, backwards, and opportunistic. This is particularly sad because the newcomers who worked in the coffee shop that he frequented considered him a friend.

Iyer describes those who arrived in Dharamsala, following their arduous escape from Tibet on foot, as "wild Tibetans,"[6] as opposed to wild looking, who would, once their education was complete, go back to Tibet "as real Tibetans who know their language and their history."[7] The Tibetan language was and indeed still is in crisis in exile. Most of the children would take little home in that regard. To make matters worse, few would return able to speak the dialects of their regions. Would his "worldly exiles"[8] arrive in any better condition following such a nightmare journey? Would the exile ladies have their eyebrows waxed and their lipstick in place? His descriptions once again reminded me of Native Americans who were portrayed in the era of residential schools as savages needing to be "civilized."

I, too, had seen the newest arrivals. I had walked past the old Reception Center hundreds of times. Until 2010, the Reception Center was located in downtown McLeod Ganj on one of the most sunless and dismal stretches of Jogibara Road. This was where until recently newcomers spent their first month or more in India. To me, most new arrivals appeared traumatized, lost, and homesick. Some of the youth affected boisterous swaggers, but their eyes told a different story. They could not understand the languages spoken in India, including the exile-Tibetan dialect, which contains many unique pronunciations and includes many Hindi and English words. Their faces were burned by the sun and the wind. Some were political activists who had fled for their lives. Some had been tortured. On the walk from Tibet, many had witnessed the death of companions. Some of the women had been raped. Children often sat on the steps staring blankly into the congested, dirty street, perhaps pining for their mothers far away in Tibet. I saw them as survivors of one of the world's great tragedies.

Iyer wrote of the torture and abuse that those who returned to Tibet faced but then belittled those who wanted to leave India. Did he not notice the shortage of women or the lack of opportunities in exile? Did he think they should grow old cheerfully delivering cappuccinos to rich foreigners like him or risk their lives trudging back to Tibet through the high mountain passes to face oppression in their homeland? I am quite certain that I know one of the people whom he wrote of personally. He was a bright and adventurous young man in his early 20's who was trying to find his way in life and was respected by intellectuals from Tibet for his brains and disposition, despite his youthfulness and playful nature. He, like many Tibetans, dreamed of seeing the world and becoming a citizen of a country other than China.

The "Global Soul," as Iyer has referred to himself, had no compassion for such men who wanted to live freely and see the world for themselves.

According to Iyer, newcomers talk of their experiences or discuss the Tibetan situation with foreigners only for personal gain. In his view, they "will use Tibet whenever it suits them, even if they are not Tibetan in knowledge (how could they be? The very use of the Tibetan language in schools is fading in Tibet.) They have little motivation to hold onto the culture and history that made them, though every motivation to turn it to global advantage."[9] I thought of respectfully removing the portrait of the Dalai Lama from the cover, then tossing the book off my balcony to compost swiftly in the monsoon-drenched jungle below, but I decided to keep it, in that it was a valuable document insofar as it personified the depth of prejudice and lack of insight and compassion that were prevalent in the community.

Gossip and rumors were also major contributors to the problems. One night in the winter of 2011, I spent the evening at Black Magic, a local bar. An Amdo man, whom I know well as a quiet guy and not a trouble-maker or a fighter, was attacked outside the bar by six exile-born Tibetans from Norbulingka, a Tibetan enclave down in the Kangra valley. The fight was apparently over a foreign girl. In front of a group of foreign tourists, they beat him with motorcycle helmets and smashed beer bottles on his head. A Canadian journalist, who recounted the details to me when I arrived outside moments after the assault had ended, had tried to stop the attackers and as a result had had a beer bottle smashed over his own head. The journalist was wearing a thick hat, so fortunately he wasn't injured. Apparently intimidated by the journalist—for he was large and undaunted—the perpetrators ran off. The newcomer was rushed to the hospital where he required numerous stitches.

Several weeks later, a Western friend told me that she had heard the story from a prominent exile-born activist who had not been present that evening. As he related the version of the story that he had heard, the details were the same, except that now it was a group of newcomers who had attacked. This happened often. If I heard talk of a fight started by persons unknown, it was at first "probably newcomers" and with retelling "newcomers."

Some of the prejudice was more direct. In 2011, I took the beginner Tibetan class taught by an apparently educated nun at the Library of Tibetan Works and Archives. During class one day, she began criticizing newcomers. During a rant that lasted almost twenty minutes, she taught the class that newcomers all receive free education, are entitled to documents allowing them to remain permanently in India, receive enormous sponsorships from overseas, and are, in her words, "spoiled." She also claimed that newcomers who sell trinkets in the street earn vast sums of money. "One pair of earings—150 rupees!" she cackled.

Street vendors can do well in busy seasons, but competition is fierce. The streets of McLeod Ganj are lined with dozens of makeshift stalls. The vendors are usually elderly, barely speak English, or both. They sell similar items, mostly Tibetan-style jewelry and hand-knitted woolen goods. The peak tourist season lasts from April to early July before being put more or less to an end by Dharamsala's torrential monsoon, which lasts almost three months. During that time, those vendors who do venture out huddle under tarpaulins, often for hours, sheltering from the downpours while they wait for a break in the weather and a chance to make a sale. The Himachal Tourism website reports an average of 290 centimeters of rain in Dharamsala each year.

Things pick up again in October until mid November when the advancing chill of winter drives most of the tourists away until spring. Some of the vendors migrate south for the winter and do well selling sweaters, but many handicraft sellers stick it out, sitting stoically at the side of the road through the bone-chilling winters. If selling costume jewelry at the side of the road was really a lucrative and reliable trade, the settler Tibetans wouldn't bother opening restaurants and shops or working for the exile government or the Library of Works and Archives. They would have cornered the trinket and knitted-hat market long ago.

I once bought ten C.D.'s from a street vendor in January. The woman looked so happy that I was worried that she was going to cry.

Even though I never bought anything again for many years after, she beamed at me every time that we ran into each other and shook my hand vigorously. Her English was not good, but she explained to me that she was a single mother of eight kids. She was often ill, probably from sitting at the side of the street all day inhaling exhaust fumes, which are so bad that the jewelry that I bought from street stalls usually needed to be washed with dish soap to remove a thick grey coating of oil and dust.

When I attempted to express the reality of newcomers' lives to my Tibetan teacher, particularly regarding their legal status in India, she became enraged and belligerently accused me, in front of the class, of not knowing the truth. "They get R.C.'s," she shrieked—R.C.'s are Registration Certificates; the documents that Tibetans need to live legally in India—"There are always notices posted in Tibetan telling them to apply for R.C.'s." Students nodded in approval at her wisdom and gave me dirty looks. I overheard her making snide comments about me as I entered class several days later. I wrote to the school administration, and she must have received a talking to, for several days later, she showed up in a foul mood that didn't improve for the rest of the semester. On the up-side, the students then ceased to hang on her every word. Ironically, about a month after my teacher's rant, the street vendors were banished by Indian authorities, fortunately temporarily. Once several days had lapsed, and they paid large bribes, they were allowed to lay out their wares once again. Shortly thereafter monsoon began.

Although there is no real excuse for this sort of ignorance, most settler Tibetans have limited interactions with newcomers and lack knowledge of their situation. Exile-Tibetan news sources focus almost entirely on issues related directly to Tibet. Problems in exile are mostly ignored. A Canadian friend with deep roots in the community pointed out that there was absolutely no excuse for the opinions expressed by my teacher because she could easily learn the truth from her newcomer colleagues and others at the Library. When I related the story to an American PhD candidate, he wasn't surprised. He told me that an exile-born acquaintance, an employee of the Tibetan

Government in Exile, had told him, with absolute certainty, that if newcomers find lice in their hair, they transfer the creatures to their clothing rather than discard them on the ground or kill them.

Almost all of the foreigners whom I spoke to who have spent extended periods of time in Dharamsala were bothered by the prejudices against newcomers. So sure are many exile-born Tibetans of their bigotry that they seldom refrain from expressing these views to those who are close friends with, volunteer with, or work with newcomers. I wondered if my opinions regarding newcomers and their position in exile society were true or based on my unique yet copious experiences, a personal bias in my research, and the opinions of most of my friends. I began searching English-language writing available on-line and elsewhere for any references to newcomers in order to see what others had to say and find views and experiences which contrasted with my own. What I found surprised me. Although the newcomer experience has not been written about extensively by foreign academics and writers, I unearthed far more references to endemic prejudice and stereotyping than I did to tolerance.

Interestingly, I noticed that two of the writers had worked or done research in the field of medicine where they were in daily contact with a broad range of Tibetans from various backgrounds. In *Precious Pills: Medicine and Social Change among Tibetan Refugees in India*, Audrey Post refers to newcomers as being seen as "contaminating agents both socially and physically"[10] by settlement Tibetan society. Mona Schrempf in *Soundings in Tibetan Medicine* writes, "The tension between earlier refugees and newcomers is potent in Dharamsala. Newcomers are the object of all suspicions and the recipients of accusations for multiple social ills."[11] Besides their criticisms of newcomers' fashion sense, Paul Christiaan Kliger notes that "many exile Tibetans complain that the new arrivals have bad behavior and love to fight."[12] In *Immigrant Ambassadors*, Julia Meredith Hess observes, "On many occasions Indian-born Tibetans would express their distaste and bafflement at the direct manners of new arrivals—essentially considering them rude, too direct, and sometimes even prone to violence."[13] She had introduced the topic with the not surprising statement: "Newcomers told me that they feel like outsiders in exile society."[14] In *Echoes from Dharamsala*, Keila Diehl writes, "it is important to address the confused reception of *sar jorpa* (recent escapees born and raised under Chinese rule in Tibet) by Dharamsala Tibetans who are often embarrassed, scornful and suspicious of the 'Chinese' ways of their compatriots. Rather than being valued as fresh connections to the increasingly remote homeland as one might expect, these Tibetans more frequently caused disappointment by failing to validate the hopeful dreams of those living in exile."[15] I read for several days, but eventually I had to stop. There seemed to be no end to such quotes, and many of the books and papers that I came across outlined the ways in which newcomers were stereotyped and marginalized, although not necessarily intentionally. It was all too depressing.

I couldn't be cheered by an infrequent sunset that had burned its way through the cloud-laden sky of monsoon season, and I was contemplating an unopened bottle of tequila on my shelf. Instead, I decided to read a dissertation by Mati Bernabei, who has a long history of association with the Tibetan exile community outside of academia. I knew that she had received positive feedback regarding newcomers from settler teachers that she had interviewed, so I looked forward to reading different perspectives.

Unfortunately, not everything that I read painted a rosy picture. One of the teachers who had come from Tibet to India for schooling as a twelve-year-old told the story of the welcome that he received as a newcomer child: "I had ponytail hair, and earing, and fur coat. [Traditional Tibetan hair and attire.] They were all taken. They shaved me and then all my clothes back in Nepal. All were taken... Oh my hair – it was cut twice – once at Pathankot [a town en route to Dharamsala] at Tibetan hotel. He cut short. He said, 'There's no boy having hair like this one in Dharamsala. Not proper to go like that.' And he cut it short. Then was the second phase – shaved. It was very sad. Sad and lonely you know. I came from Tibet from Western side. Different dialect. Our own. It was Tibetan language but different dialect. It was unusual the language used here. Very fast. And everyone was new. I was changed."[16] His story couldn't help but bring to mind accounts that I had read of the experiences of Canadian First Nations students when they arrived at residential schools.[17] I imagined his mother carefully preparing his clothing and jewelry for his new life in India and his sorrow and confusion over the loss of those tangible links with home.

Still, it was heartening to read the comment of one of the teachers who works with newcomers: "It was my first time I saw new arrival Tibetans. They are totally different from Tibetans in India. Their way of talking, eating. I got to know how they talk, how they look, their nature. And I was very much impressed to see the true Tibetan. We were very much influenced by Indians,"[18] a settler Tibetan teacher told Mati.

Although this example was encouraging, my mind couldn't help but go to dark places. I recalled a conversation that I had had with someone who should have known better. "Wow you are so brave," an employee of Tibetan Woman's Association told me when I said that most of my friends were newcomers. "They are dangerous. I would be so afraid to hang around with them."

I put on lip-stick, grabbed my bottle of tequila, and headed to the bar. I polished off the better part of the bottle with assistance from the random collection of newcomer friends and acquaintances assembled. Cheered by the unexpected arrival of the hitherto unknown liquid from Mexico and delighted with the ritual of knocking back shots with lemon and salt, they thanked me by filling my beer glass enough times to obliterate any trace of the angst I felt about my research. Despite the in some cases copious amount of alcohol consumed by those present, as usual nothing untoward occurred.

Chapter 4

There were many causes for the prejudices, as I further learned when I spoke with an historian whom I will call Dorje Wanggyal. He told me that although Tibet was virtually sealed off from the 1960's through the 1970's, "in the 1970's, several Tibetans managed to escape and more followed. When the first newcomers arrived in India, they were heroes to the settlement Tibetans. Everyone wanted to meet them. Parties were thrown for them. They were given money and food, sent to study, and offered jobs. They were really important to the exile community."

Following the death of Chairman Mao, China began a series of reforms in the 1980's. For several years, Tibetans were allowed to visit India, and exiles were able to visit Tibet. Although reforms were underway, the destruction wreaked throughout Tibet since the 1950's was massive. People from Tibet who visited exile communities saw that Tibetans in exile were able to manage their own affairs under the capable leadership of the Dalai Lama, practice their religion freely, receive access to modern education, and were not subject to discrimination and humiliation for practicing and preserving their culture and religion.[1] Exiles were also able to visit Tibet, and some, no doubt homesick and encouraged by the reforms and the business opportunities created for English speakers as Tibet opened up to international tourism, decided to remain permanently.[2]

Unfortunately, the policy of openness and the period of relatively open borders were short lived. Beginning in 1986, border disputes between China and India and deterioration in Tibetan exile-Chinese relations were among the first signs of a change for the worse. Within Tibet, calls for further reform and a series of demonstrations in Lhasa beginning in 1987 led to hardliner and soon-to-be Chinese leader Hu Jintao being brought in to run the Tibetan Autonomous Region. In March of 1989, a few days before the thirtieth anniversary of the 1959 Tibetan uprising and three months prior to the Tiananmen Square

Massacre, demonstrations in Lhasa were violently suppressed and martial law was imposed.[3] The open door slammed shut.

Refugees then began fleeing Tibet in greater numbers. Restrictions on movement within China were no longer as strict as during the Cultural Revolution, so it was easier for Tibetans to gain access to border regions, particularly for those from Amdo and much of Kham. These two Tibetan regions had mostly been incorporated into Chinese provinces rather than being included in the Tibetan Autonomous Region where movement of individuals remained highly regulated. Many of those who escaped were ex-political prisoners and other good people who had suffered greatly. The exile Tibetans were at first delighted, supporting those who came by giving them money, finding them jobs, or placing them in monasteries. More and more kept coming until the trickle became a flood. By the early 1990's, an average of 2,500 Tibetans were escaping to India every year. The refugee population in India was fewer than 100,000 at that time, and the exiles lacked the facilities, resources, and finances to deal with the new arrivals.

According to Dorje Wanggyal, himself a newcomer who escaped into exile in the early 1990's, it did not take long for the settler Tibetans to discover that some of the new arrivals were not the heroes that they had imagined. In a lengthy interview, Dorje outlined the many problems. Some of the newcomers fleeced the exile Tibetans out of money. Some were so diabolically clever that they managed to scam tens and even hundreds of thousands of rupees, even from the Dalai Lama. Others were discovered to be rapists and murderers. One Lhasa Tibetan who had been given a good job raped and killed a girl at the staff canteen near the exile-government's offices. Several had been trained by the Chinese to conduct espionage and plot assassinations. Others who had been given positions where they had access to sensitive information turned it over to the Chinese either because they were willing spies or their families were under threat if they didn't co-operate. "Some guys married sweater sellers and had children with them. Then they ran off stealing the family's life savings and went to Nepal. Some of the newcomers were really tough and ruthless. People were really afraid of them," Dorje explained. By the early 90's, when he had arrived in India, the settlers' attitudes towards newcomers were already tainted.

Then in February of 1997, something unimaginable happened. One of the Dalai Lama's closest advisors, the elderly principal of the Institute of Buddhist Dialectics, as well as two younger monks, were brutally murdered. The perpetrators were identified as newcomer monks who were affiliated with the worship of Dorje Shugden, a practice that had been banned by the Dalai Lama in 1996, with much opposition and complaints of discrimination from practitioners. Dorje Wanggyal felt that this was the final straw: "You can't underestimate the impact of attempts by the Shugden worshipers to ruin the Dalai Lama's reputation and then the murders. It was unimaginable that anyone would do something like that, especially monks. The Dalai Lama was responsible for the Tibetans' survival in India. Everything that they had was because of him. The Shugden practitioners were almost all newcomers. Settlement Tibetans began to deeply, deeply hate newcomers. Maybe it's not fair that all newcomers were blamed for the behavior of a few rotten ones, but people are people. They don't always use logic. Whether it is right or wrong is another issue. That is what happened. The good things that newcomers brought, especially in regard to Tibetan language and culture, were acknowledged by educated people at the time, too."

Back then, communication between Tibet and India was nearly impossible, so the exiles had no way of verifying who was honest and trustworthy and who wasn't. Unless the newcomers had substantial proof of their activities in Tibet, the settlers became increasingly unwilling to take chances. Dorje Wanggyal told me that even some of those who had received assistance by claiming to be former political prisoners turned out to have been criminals and frauds.

Technological advances and the subsequent flow of information between Indian and Tibet now allow background checks to be performed with greater ease. Reputable newcomers in exile can establish, through their contacts in Tibet, the validity of most new arrivals' claims. Unfortunately, the climate of mistrust has not really abated. Several prominent settler Tibetans told me, in casual conversation, that they did not think it wise for any newcomers to be employed by the exile government or work with the Dalai Lama.

Through volunteer work, I came to meet Sonam, the director of the Tibetan Centre for Conflict Resolution. She is a strikingly beautiful and seemingly delicate young Tibetan woman who was raised in India, but from almost the moment that she began speaking in her soft voice, I realized that she had a mind like a steel trap. She intrigued me, for she exhibited none of the mindless intolerance that I had come to associate with settlement Tibetans.

When I initially interviewed Sonam, I learned that her centre was set up to address conflict within the Tibetan community, as well as between Indians and Tibetans. Its mandate is to teach and promote understanding and tolerance, goals which are mostly achieved through workshops. Sonam has been with the centre since its inception, and the depth of her understanding of issues within the community was immediately apparent. Months later, I e-mailed her and asked if I could interview her for my book regarding problems with newcomer/settler relations. When I arrived at her office, she ordered tea from the kitchen, we sat down, and I turned on my recorder.

"I think that the issues between those of us who are born here and those who are from Tibet are of very deep concern," she told me immediately. "There are prejudices and misconceptions on both sides, and we are working to change that. We are brothers and sisters, and we need to learn to understand each other. Whenever we [she meant people like her who were born in exile or escaped Tibet with the Dalai Lama] hear about people in Tibet doing something [meaning political], we just want to weep because they are our people being tortured and dying. We care about them so much. But when we come face-to-face with people from Tibet, the small things start to matter.

When you live side by side, you have different ways of believing things or doing things or act in different ways. So many things creep up. When we first started doing our training, we realized that this was something that we needed to deal with. When we first took this to the community, they said that there was nothing wrong with our relationship and nothing has to be done because it is perfect already. But that is not what we saw. When we hold seminars in the community, we always discuss the issues."

The background information that she provided echoed much of what Dorje Wanggyal had said, although Sonam was of a younger generation, "In the late 90's and early 2000's, there were so many Tibetans coming. Some of them were political activists who were so dedicated and came here as a last resort, but others were sent here by outside forces [meaning the Chinese] to spy or create problems. Some of them came here for education or to try to go to the West so that they could earn money to send back to their families. People in Tibet were so poor at that time. Most of the so-called development work in Tibet was happening in the cities. For so many reasons, people were coming here, and for all of them, one common thing was to see His Holiness the Dalai Lama.

Here in exile the problem was that there was a large influx. All of a sudden, all of these people who we looked at with nostalgia were right in front of us and in such large numbers. Some of them were fighting, some of them were having problems with the local Indians for small reasons, and the Indians were blaming all Tibetans even over little things. It was actually a situation that was quite difficult to handle. It was very hard for the exile community to absorb the enormous influx of people."

Sonam wasn't exaggerating or making excuses. Since 1990, when the United Nations High Commission for Refugees began recording numbers, an average of 2,500 new arrivals passed through the refugee reception centre in Nepal each year enroute to Dharamsala. Thousands of them ended up in the tiny town of McLeod Ganj. By 2001, when her centre first opened, the town was inundated.

Chapter 5

Since the mid 1990's, the policy of the Tibetan Government in Exile has been to provide young adult newcomers with free education at Tibetan Transit School. Technically, they don't have a choice, as they cannot stay legally in India unless they are going to school. Those over the age of twenty five who are neither monks nor nuns appear to be allowed to enter India only as pilgrims; I met a number of Tibetans who had lied about their age so that they could go to school. Like all newly arrived refugees, they receive an opportunity to meet the Dalai Lama, which is, without a doubt, one of the highlights of most newly escaped Tibetans' lives. They are also entitled to a short stay at the Reception Centre. After that they are expected to return to Tibet. The younger adults are sent to Tibetan Transit School (T.T.S.).

Initially, T.T.S. students received one year of education while living in very primitive conditions, but the program gradually expanded to allow students to remain for five years, and the facilities were greatly improved, although I was told that men and women are still housed separately even though many students arrive with their spouses and graduates are often thirty years old or more. Among my friends, drop-out rates among married couples were extremely high, and sometimes the husband or wife was too old to qualify. Students received no academic credentials for further education although they qualified for higher studies at non-accredited Tibetan exile schools. (In 2012, I was told that a new program offering legitimate high-school education had begun. The first batch of students was completing Grade 11.)

The training that newcomers receive is not geared towards adapting to life in India. According to Bhuntuk Shastri, the director of T.T.S., "We keep them here for five years and give them basic education. We do not teach them Hindi, because the ultimate aim is that they should go back to Tibet and educate our people there. Unfortunately, only 10 per cent of them return. The rest assimilate into various settlements or migrate to the West."[1] I'm not sure where the figure of 10% came from: elsewhere, I saw a more likely figure of 70%,[2] but I do know that most former students had not been eager to head back over the mountains into the hands of the Chinese.

A teacher-training guide produced for T.T.S. in 2004 did not anticipate graduates having many rosy prospects: "Few of them will get jobs, but some can work at cyber cafés, in small business, like street hawkers, at hotels & restaurants, in the army, as Thanka painters, tailors, musicians and singers. Some will be monks or nuns, some go to the army, some go abroad, some go 'after foreigners,' some create small ventures like cooking classes, massage centres, some will teach Tibetan to foreigners or translate. Some go for entrance exams to get employed in exile government. Some who are good at Tibetan may go to higher Tibetan studies and later work in institutes."[3]

Many former students who had completed the program were critical of the standard of education offered. Those who had arrived in India illiterate or barely literate expressed the most appreciation; some of them were very pleased and thankful. Those who were already educated when they arrived in India or were very motivated were less generous. "The school was not very good, but you could learn a lot if you used your free time for your own study," Karma told me bluntly in his almost impeccable English. Others were more dismissive. "Was T.T.S. a good school? Did you learn a lot?" I asked one friend, a recent graduate, who had managed to remain in India and now worked for a Tibetan language N.G.O. "It was good," he replied instantly. But he then immediately changed his mind. He smiled, as Tibetans often do when imparting negative or depressing information, "It was no good. I learned little bit. Not much. Before I came here, I went to university in Tibet. I have a BA."

In some respects, T.T.S. is a shining star compared with many other exile schools. Most recent graduates whom I spoke to in 2011 had solid Tibetan language skills and a good knowledge of Tibetan history as opposed to graduates of other exile Tibetan schools, many of whom could barely read or write in Tibetan and often knew as much about Tibetan history as one would learn from reading a few pamphlets. Some of the T.T.S. graduates already had good or even excellent Tibetan when they came into exile, but most told me that they knew next to nothing of Tibetan political history before arriving in India.

Their biggest gripe was the absence of real-life qualifications: "People work so hard for years and only get a useless certificate. It is good for nothing," a former student told me. The certificate certainly was useless, for it did not qualify graduates for recognized universities and colleges. If an employer googled the school, the information to be found, even on the school board's own website, was far from impressive. The Tibetan exile government did accept the T.T.S. certificate as an alternate to a Bachelor's degree in job advertisements that I came across, although I didn't find out how many T.T.S. graduates it hired. I didn't meet any. A valid R.C. is required to work for the exile government, and most newcomers were not entitled to renew theirs once they left school. It seems like false advertising.

Opinions about the school had improved dramatically since I lived in McLeod Ganj in 2003. At that time, T.T.S. had a horrible reputation. "It is like a hell," my ex-husband had told me. "The rooms are made of metal. They are either really hot or really cold. The water and the food are bad and everyone is sick all the time." He was inclined to exaggeration, but I heard very similar stories from everyone who had studied there. I didn't know many people who had lasted at T.T.S. for more than a few weeks or months in the 1990's and early 2000's. Now, opinions are quite favorable regarding the new facilities, mostly funded by the European Commission and completed in 2005.

Finding information on-line about Tibetan Transit School was very difficult. I found a lot of information in the media and from medical professionals about the seemingly endless health crises at the school, but there was little in terms of information about its facilities, curricula, and needs over the years. Much was made of the number of people fleeing Tibet, and money had been raised as a result of awareness of their escapes, but it was difficult to find out what exactly was being done to provide for them and how they could be helped.

Sambhota Tibetan Schools Society, which runs T.T.S., devotes two paragraphs to the history of the school and two sentences to its curriculum: "It facilitates them in learning of English and Tibetan language as well as vocational skills. Imparting of spiritual and cultural education is also given due importance."[4] This lack of information is in stark contrast to the abundance available on-line about other important Tibetan exile schools.

It wasn't until I was doing research for this book that I saw photographs of the old accommodations for the first time. T.T.S. is located a few kilometers from Dharamsala in a rural area, and unofficial visits are discouraged, so I had never been there. It was as appalling as I had been told. The students had been housed in low-roofed shacks constructed from bare metal sheeting. They resembled oversized and elongated makeshift garden sheds with flimsy metal shutters. "Oh my god, that is where they lived? It looks like something that animals would be kept in," was one foreigner's reaction when I showed her a picture. Tibetans who had studied there often laughed diabolically when I showed them photos and asked what was depicted. "T.T.S. ha ha ha!"

A teacher who had spent a year volunteering at the school in the late 90's outlined the same pathetic conditions that my friends had described. She was disturbed to learn that her students could not legally remain in India following their studies unless they could afford to pay bribes for documents (even that is now no longer possible) and instead would have to go back to Tibet and would "undoubtedly be tortured, or even killed." She heard the same sad plea that I had heard so many times from newcomers, "Is there no country where we can be free?"[5]

The sheds were situated in an open field. Due to the scorching hot summers and winter temperatures that dipped close to freezing in the valley, they would have been a nightmare to live in. They also provided little protection from monsoon and other violent rain storms that regularly drench the valley almost year round. They compared unfavorably, in many ways, to the tents of many of the homeless Indians in the slum in Lower Dharamsala. No wonder so many newcomers who attempted to study there at the time had been so bitter and in many cases chosen a life of poverty, hunger, and even virtual prostitution in McLeod Ganj over enduring living in such conditions. Even the most humble home in Tibet or slummy room in McLeod Ganj was a palace in comparison.

Even after the new campus was built, unsanitary conditions prevailed and no safe drinking water was available. The people arriving from Tibet were often physically weak and lacked immunity to the parasites and diseases that plagued the school water supply and were inadvertently served in meals from the kitchen. Everyone who had studied at T.T.S. in years past spoke of chronic diarrhea and vomiting. "I was so lucky. I didn't really get sick. After I first went there, I had to spend one month in hospital, but after that I didn't get sick again," a former student who had escaped to India in 2006 told me earnestly.

Former students usually had little understanding of what caused their ill health. The school didn't seem to teach students about water-borne illnesses and food poisoning. Considering how vulnerable they are, to me it seemed that this was one of the first things that new arrivals should have learned. Knowledge wouldn't have helped much however, as the students were at the mercy of exile-government officials, administrators, and staff, who were either ignorant themselves or willfully negligent.

For many years, the school used water from a creek that passed through settlements up-stream. People in Dharamsala and other communities in India urinate into watercourses, and open sewers sometimes drain into them, so it's wise to be suspicious of even the most sparkling waters. Food poisoning was common. One outbreak hospitalized fifty-eight students.[6] The school was plagued with TB, malaria, typhoid, and even cholera.[7] T.T.S. students died of preventable illnesses and diseases over the years.

I had a friend who had had a very close call as a result of residing there. Tseten had been a scrawny guy, little more than a kid, living in a small, dark, and grubby room that he shared with another friend when I met him in 2003. I knew that he had left T.T.S. shortly before because he had been sick. He barely spoke English back then, so I didn't realize the extent of his illness. By 2009, he was a robust fellow who cut a dashing figure with his stylish clothes and thick, fashionably disheveled hair. When I was visiting Dharamsala that winter, he told me what had happened, "When I was at T.T.S., I got bone TB. It was so bad that I couldn't walk. People had to carry me... I was in hospital for a really long time... When you met me, I was just starting to get better." I'd never even heard of bone TB, so I looked it up. He had been very lucky. Spinal Tuberculosis can kill or leave patients disfigured for life.

During an outbreak of gastroenteritis in 2006, which sickened 118 students and turned out to have been caused by contaminated meat and unhygienic food preparation practices, researchers explored every possible cause. Their findings exposed the sources of ongoing problems that doctors had been complaining about and reporting fruitlessly for more than a decade:

> The food handlers & their cooking conditions in the kitchen were unhygienic...Upon inspection, the water tank was smelly and muddy, suggesting poor maintenance. There was no practice of chlorination. The government source of piped water came from an ill maintained and poorly chlorinated reservoir made in the mountains. The water from the stream was used for scrubbing the kitchen utensils. The laboratory of the medical college considered water samples from these three water sources unsatisfactory.[8]

Fortunately, the depressing report did contain some unintended humor: "We could not lift any ingested food sample or their vomit from the case patients or from the spot, as there were a lot of resistances, resentments, and refusals on this account."[9] Although it really wasn't funny, I couldn't keep myself from laughing as I imagined the earnest Indian researchers trying to collect diarrhea and vomit samples from a bunch of sick and self-conscious young Tibetans.

Finally, in 2008, a reverse osmosis system was installed in the school, the result of a single fund raising event held by Los Angeles

Friends of Tibet after the organization became aware of the problem. Rebecca Novick, the producer of The Tibet Connection, had recommended the project. "I will never forget the exhausted face of a Scottish doctor as he explained to me the connection between contaminated water and TB," she explained in a report on the project. "These young Tibetans were dying in his arms simply because they didn't have clean water." Los Angeles Friends of Tibet chose to fund the project because the solution was simple, and it "wanted to fund something that wasn't getting the attention or financial support that the more 'popular' programs get." Lisa Kelly, the president of LAFOT was emphatic, "To risk your life escaping from Tibet only to die later of a preventable disease is tragic."[10] Finally, fifteen years after the school opened, the students received access to safe water.

Chapter 6

I was waiting to use the toilet at Mountview Bar one night in the fall of 2011. Standing side by side, also waiting, were a Tibetan man and a large Punjabi with a bushy black beard. Up sauntered a young North American who, in his board shorts and expensive flip flops, looked as though he had just stepped out of a frat party. As we all stood waiting, the North American made friendly conversation. "Are you from Tibet?" he asked the Punjabi.

I noticed over the years that the experiences of Western tourists who visit the town had changed: travel in India used to be reserved for the relatively tough and adventurous, but improved tourist facilities and easy forms of communication with home were enabling the most unworldly and disengaged people to travel and spend their holidays in a bubble. How, I wondered, could such people make their way from the nearest international airport to Dharamsala without noticing that Tibetans look vastly different from most other inhabitants of the country? Obviously, it had become possible. The boy didn't seem particularly stupid, but he was in the company of similarly dressed tourists who were obviously travelling together in a group.

Several activists told me that far fewer tourists had any knowledge of or interest in the Tibetan situation. I thought of the unlikely but important role that Salai gyals had played in educating visitors and piquing their interest. Most of the Salai gyals had depended on foreign tourists for their survival and the provision of a party lifestyle. The group of trendy-looking and obviously moneyed young North Americans would have instantly attracted them. Serious-minded newcomers were inclined to seek out respectable-looking tourists to practice their English with, but the results were essentially the same. Most new refugees had poor English skills, so conversation was limited. One of the first things that they seemed to learn in English class was how to tell the story of their flight from Tibet. Many of their accounts were harrowing.

A typical escape from Tibet took over a month of walking in the dead of winter through remote Himalayan passes at extremely high altitudes. Newcomers described the sadness of leaving their homes and the journey by bus to Lhasa. Many were unable to say good-bye to their families and friends due to the secretive nature of their escapes, while others, not realizing the implications, had run away on a whim. Supplies for the long journey were purchased in Lhasa: noodle soups, tsampa, butter, tea, a tarp to protect them from the cold, an extra pair of shoes, and a few items of warm clothing. Intellectuals usually carried their books and other written material. One friend told me that along with supplies for the journey, he carried out around twenty-five pounds of notebooks. Then they waited in fear, for days or even weeks, before the time came to depart. In the dead of night, their guides fetched them. They were hidden in the back of trucks and smuggled to their points of departure. Often, the trucks were stopped at check points, the escapees huddling in silent fear, praying that none of their companions would give them away by coughing or sneezing.

Eventually, the long and dangerous walk began. The only way to hope to avoid detection was by crossing passes such as the Nangpa La, which is 5,800 metres above sea level, usually in the winter. The groups often included families as well as unaccompanied children who were being sent for education in India. Strangers would help to carry the kids on top of their already painfully heavy loads. Sometimes companions became ill or injured and had to be carried. If carrying them became impossible, they had to be abandoned, lest the whole group succumb to the cold or be discovered. It could only be assumed that these unfortunate individuals perished in the frozen wasteland of the Himalayas. Others fell into crevasses and despite attempts could not be rescued. They, too, were left to their demise. Everyone's lives depended on moving on. Starvation threatened, hypothermia was a constant peril, and to compound their misery, the mountains were patrolled by Chinese border police who would arrest or shoot on sight those that they could.

Sherab, who escaped young enough to attend a T.C.V. school and is now on a scholarship at university, described his experience thus:

"We slept during the day and walked during the moonless nights; we crossed the dangers of wild animal-attack zones and faced stormy weather. Unluckily, we were caught by the merciless Chinese border soldiers after a month of arduous journey. To a homeless fourteen-year-old orphan boy, it was not easy to bear the cruel treatment and torture that I subsequently went through in Chinese jails. For instance, they used electric gadgets on my body until I was completely unconsciousness, hung me from the ceiling of a dark cell by my thumbs, and forced me to stand naked on biting ice during the freezing winter nights. I cried every night as I was so sad and felt so lonely. I was badly tortured, in four different Chinese jails, both physically and emotionally for a year, which made me feel that I was in some kind of inferno." Upon his release from prison, Sherab repeated his journey and escaped from Tibet successfully.

Hortsang Jigme wrote of his own escape and the experiences of others. The refugees were not even safe once they entered Nepal:

> During the day we slept in the forests, making sure no one saw us and journeying at night. In the forests there also roamed gangs of Nepalese thieves as well as soldiers who would not hesitate to arrest escaping Tibetans. They did this because escapees are stateless, without anyone to care for them. They were easy prey from whom the Nepalese could extract extra income by robbing them of whatever money, clothing, and belongings they had. Another reason why they preyed on the Tibetans is that after dispossessing them of everything that they had, the gangs would hand the escapees over to the Chinese, thereby getting a monetary reward.
>
> Even more horrific was that some Tibetans were killed in the most bloody and gruesome way, as if they were mere pawns in horrible games, which included raping the women. For instance when Tsayue Chagdrug and his wife were travelling together, they were caught by Nepalese soldiers. Chadrug was brutally beaten and his hands and feet were tied and bound. Right before him seven or eight soldiers raped his wife. Such instances are many. Not knowing where to go,

many refugees using an escape route through the Mount Everest region got stuck for days and nights in that icy environment and as a result lost either hands and feet or fingers and toes[1].

Even those who had relatively safe journeys were usually scarred in some way by their ordeals. My friend Gonpo Dorje escaped in 2000 at the age of sixteen. The journey took forty-three days. Towards the end, he was running out of food and completely exhausted. He became unconscious and had to be carried: "Luckily we were a group of thirty-one. There were no women or children. They took turns carrying me." His journey didn't end once he finally arrived in India. It continued in his sleep: "I had nightmares for several years after. Sometimes I was walking. Sometimes the military was after me or I was falling somewhere or I had lost my group. You keep this fear inside of you for years. Even now, [2011] it feels like it only happened yesterday. I think that there is no one on the planet who deserves to go through an experience like that."

Stories like theirs—there were tens of thousands of them—were shared with countless visitors to Dharamsala over the past decades. Reading such accounts is harrowing enough, but something is shocking and personal about hearing first-hand accounts like these from an otherwise often quite ordinary person with whom you have just struck up a casual conversation. These days, far fewer newcomers strike up conversations with tourists, and the settlers, many of whom, especially among the older generation, suffered their own difficulties escaping from Tibet or growing up in exile, are mostly jaded when it comes to foreign visitors. The voices are going silent.

Many newcomers told me that they had become embarrassed to be seen talking to foreigners. "If people here see us talking to foreigners, especially women, they think that we are trying to get something from them, so I never talk to them," one friend told me. I was tempted to laugh as he was telling me—a Western woman—this over a beer in a bar. Still, I knew that it was mostly true. I'd seen the man around for months, and he had never returned my smiles or said "Hello" until he overheard me discussing newcomer issues with another Tibetan.

"Look at her," he said gesturing towards the only other foreign woman in the bar. The rest of the customers that night were Amdo guys. I knew them all. They had been in exile for a number of years and most were single. The woman was young, attractive, and friendly looking. She was sitting alone at a table, drinking a beer and reading a book. He elaborated, "A few years ago one of them would have talked to her right away. Now they are all ignoring her on purpose. I feel sorry for her. She looks lonely."

Life had been very different for newcomers when I had first lived in McLeod Ganj eight years earlier. Back then, they had very few options. The drop-out rate at Tibetan Transit School was very high, so most quickly ended up in McLeod Ganj. They didn't usually move to other parts of India because there were very few newcomers in other Tibetan settlements, and they needed a network of friends to survive and find jobs. It was also not easy to move to a new community when they couldn't produce R.C.'s proving their legal status in India. Most didn't speak more than a few words of Hindi, and many barely spoke English. In McLeod Ganj, they felt safest, and they could find a sense of community among the other newcomers. The other big draw was the possibility of help from foreign visitors.

Linguistic and cultural differences between newcomers and settlers were perhaps the most important reasons that the newcomers were socially isolated and stuck together, mostly in McLeod Ganj. To further understand these problems, one needs to look back in time. It is impossible to accurately articulate any important aspect of Tibet's complex history in a few pages, but the following is an attempt.

The first wave of Tibetan refugees followed the Dalai Lama when he escaped into exile in India in1959. Prior to the Chinese invasion, ethnic Tibet was loosely divided into three traditional provinces: U-Tsang, Kham, and Amdo. Much of Tibet is inhospitable and mountainous, and there were virtually no roads, so travel in those days was done on horseback, usually with yak caravans. A journey across Tibet took months. As U-Tsang was closest to Tibet's borders with India and Nepal, its residents had the best opportunity to escape with the Dalai Lama. Few from Kham and Amdo got out, as their regions were farthest from the border and had been invaded and occupied by the Chinese communists since the early 1950's. Being located in the far north east, the people of Amdo had the least chance of escape.

Essentially, Tibet is home to three major dialects, along with numerous sub-dialects. Tibetans share the same written language but, the dialects are often mutually unintelligible, although because they are so closely related, with a little effort, Tibetans can learn at least the essentials. Many people in Tibet, particularly those involved in interregional trade or business, are fluent in more than one dialect, and newcomers quickly learn to communicate with settlement Tibetans. But in most cases, settlement Tibetans make no effort. Quite literally, linguistic differences are Chinese to them.

Upon arriving in exile, the Tibetan leadership—who almost all originated from Lhasa—chose the Lhasa dialect as the official language of exile institutions. In exile over time, the Lhasa dialect evolved into a distinct Indian-Tibetan sub-dialect. Obviously it is beneficial to having a mutually intelligible language for oral communication, but I could find no evidence of the exile government's encouraging the preservation of dialects in exile, discouraging discrimination against dialect speakers, or celebrating regional linguistic differences. Instead, the goal was assimilation and the homogenization of both language and culture, not easily or willingly accepted among the newcomers, who were proud of their distinct dialects and traditions.

A study conducted by students from Oxford University published in 1994 looked at the reasons and methods used to suppress regional differences in exile[2]. In the years previous to the Chinese invasion, Tibetans were united by religion, written language, a myriad of cultural similarities, and, of course, ethnicity, but the Lhasa government did not administer the entire country. Tibetans in other regions typically saw themselves as, for example, Amdowas or Khampas—or perhaps more commonly as people of a region, such as Golok—and were hostile towards the administrators and aristocrats of Lhasa. Now, in the 21st century, despite their differences, Tibetans in both Tibet and India have a strong identity as a people, but this was not the case when the first refugees arrived in India.

The researchers found that the Tibetan exile government had chosen to go about creating a strong national identity among Tibetans in exile by eliminating regional loyalties through various steps including making the Lhasa dialect the official language, intentionally mixing children from the various regions in schools, and mandating that teachers speak in a dialect similar to or the same as that of Lhasa. Measures were also taken to deregionalize associations with music and dance, although performances themselves were not suppressed. The idea was to create a strong national Tibetan identity. The result is that what most settlers now consider to be authentic and "proper" Tibetan language and culture has evolved from its Lhasa-centric base and has been infused with a big enough dose of Indian influence to make it recognizable yet unfamiliar to anyone from Tibet.

In contrast to the way that the exile government usually tries to break down regional affiliations, Tibetan exiles in India vote for representatives of their Tibetan province of origin rather than for a representative of their community of settlement. In the 1970's, the Central Tibetan Administration proposed that voting no longer be conducted along regional lines. Members of the C.T.A. from Kham and Amdo felt so strongly that this would be disastrous for their interests that they resigned until the proposal was withdrawn. The change of plan was in some ways fortunate, as it would have remained difficult for the exile government to continue to try to represent the people of the regions of Tibet if exiles were, for example, voting for representatives from Karnataka or Delhi instead of Kham or U-Tsang, but the current rule means that settlements in India lack meaningful representation.

Many newcomers whom I spoke to felt that the exile government's policies regarding language and culture led to a false perception of native Tibetan dialects as being inferior or "less Tibetan." They told me that their children were reprimanded in school for being rude if they spoke their dialect, for some lack the flowery honorifics used in Lhasa and exile. Interestingly, Dekyi, who had grown up near Lhasa and was one of my Lhasa dialect teachers at the Library of Works and Archives, taught our class a very different point of view, "In other parts of Tibet people speak politely without using honorifics. You need to know that they are not being rude."

The distinct sub-dialect that has evolved independently in India over the past sixty years contains a lot of Hindi and English terms. Settlers' use of other languages is often not a result of code-switching, as linguists refer to the mixing of languages, but rather an absence of knowledge of Tibetan words, usually for modern things. As I studied only pure Lhasa dialect at the Library, I had great difficulty understanding some of the unique exile pronunciations, although their use of so many English words aided in my comprehension. Many refused to acknowledge new Tibetan words, viewing them as Chinese in origin, although the words' etymologies were clearly Tibetan. Differences in pronunciation were usually put down to Chinese influence.

An interesting example of the confusions about the language occurred in 2011 when a Tibetan in Switzerland released the hip-hop song "Shapale," which became extremely popular among exiles. The rap was performed in pure Lhasa dialect by a young man wearing a shapale—Tibetan meat pastry—fashioned into a necklace, reminiscent of the clocks sported by Public Enemy's Favor Flav. It was interesting to read the comments on Youtube. Many exile-born Tibetans had difficulty understanding what he was saying, and the fact that the singer lived abroad only added to their befuddlement. He was variously accused of using Lhasa street slang, sounding Chinese, or having a confusing French accent or a "super Americanized" one. Later, as word spread of the singer's flawless Tibetan, many of the comments were removed by their authors.[3] Ironically, the song's main theme, aside from urging young Tibetans to respect their elders— shapale is, apparently, a euphemism for a spanking—was the importance of preserving Tibetan language and culture. The Chinese must have felt threatened by the boy and his meat pies because they banned the apparently subversive song and video.[4]

Those from Tibet are immediately recognizable as newcomers as soon as they speak. Most lacked connections within the settler community and the required formal education in exile and, therefore, were the least likely to get good jobs. Tibetan language media, non-accredited colleges, and some research centres hired a lot of newcomers because they needed staff fluent in written Tibetan. Many other Tibetan employers wanted people with university degrees in English, although some of the graduates had poorer English, both written and spoken, than some of the newcomers who had only studied the language informally. As mentioned earlier, opportunities for university education were denied to almost every newcomer above high-school age. The situation was complicated, not least by financial considerations, but many newcomers were extremely frustrated with the status quo.

Most newcomers, of the hundreds whom I spoke to, held poor opinions of exile Tibetans. Among newcomers, "Indian Tibetans," as settlers were often referred to, were seen as bigoted towards people from Tibet, more Indian in their ways than Tibetan, illiterate in their own language, and unable to speak it properly. Most newcomers whom I met coped with the rejection that they faced by rejecting back and being harshly critical of the settlers and their exile society. Thus, the cycle of dislike and mistrust perpetuates itself.

Chapter 7

When I arrived in 2003, some of the newcomers with skills or connections had managed to find jobs, although typically in the service industry, which paid so little that they could not afford to feed and clothe themselves properly, let alone rent a room. Most were unemployed and had no regular income. Many attended English classes for a few hours a day, read, wrote, and studied. Hundreds spent what seemed like half the day walking up and down the three main streets of the town, as one Western friend described it at the time, "like traumatized animals pacing in a zoo." Up and down and around and around they walked, day in, day out, sometimes clowning around or stopping to chat with friends. They had nothing to do and nowhere to go.

What used to be called the bus stand and is now known as the main square was a major point of congregation. Almost every street in town converges there. From late morning until evening, dozens of young men loitered and waited. Many people assumed that they were looking for foreign girls. Certainly, there was a lot of girl watching going on, but the main purpose of hanging around at the bus stand was to run into friends. Very few people had a phone at that time because they were very expensive. Anyone walking through town was bound to pass through the bus stand at some point, so if you were looking for someone, you usually only needed to go there and wait. If they didn't show up, someone else would pass through who had seen them and have an idea of where to find them.

Journalists loved the bus-stand scene and made it out to be far more exciting than it actually was. "The bus-stop delivering backpackers is where the young men first pounce. Competition is fierce so women are hit on from the moment they arrive[1]" wrote Nick Meo. Another journalist was even more laughable in his detailed fantasizing: "The stake-out begins every morning in the dusty town square, a short walk from the heavily guarded residence of the Dalai

Lama, who heads the Tibetan government-in-exile. Foreign tourists clamber out of crowded buses, sleepy-eyed after the 400-kilometre overnight journey from New Delhi to the northern Indian state of Himachal Pradesh. Watching from nearby cafes, the men methodically size up single females coming off the bus: Israeli backpackers are the least desirable, low on cash and skeptical of scams. Single Europeans and North Americans, clutching their Lonely Planet guidebooks, are a better bet[2]," imagined Martin Regg Cohen in the *Toronto Star*.

Women who read the articles and showed up expecting a smorgasbord of potential Tibetan lovers to be waiting to carry their bags to hotel rooms for quick romps before breakfast were no doubt disappointed. Obviously, neither writer had paid a visit to the bus stand to see the busses arrive. This is not surprising, as almost all of them rolled in around 6:30 am, sometimes even earlier, a time of day when certain types of journalists would not likely have stirred from their beds. The bus stand was always deserted at that hour, with the exception of a handful of usually female Tibetan bread sellers setting out their wares on upturned boxes and a clutch of porters, mostly middle-aged Kashmiri gentlemen with full graying beards attired in their traditional dress, not likely to be mistaken for Tibetan youths, hoping to drum up some business by carrying heavy bags. A few Indian taxi drivers competed loudly for fares. The cafés were all shuttered. Arriving on the bus – something I have now done more than a dozen times – was anticlimactic to say the least. Tourists could only stagger, sleep deprived and exhausted from the jolting bus ride, through the deserted streets hoping to find a guest house open at that hour, not a Tibetan boy in sight.

Even McLlo restaurant, renowned for the appallingly long hours the staff is forced to work, was not yet open for business. If it and Hot Spot –at that time a high-end place and the only other restaurant situated within the main square—had been open, their prices were too high for Salai gyals in those days. Most could never afford to frequent them unless they had foreign friends to foot the bill. The bus stand was a place for standing around loitering but seldom before noon.

For Amdo boys, the most popular gathering place in those days was the roof of Tsongkha Restaurant, which straddles Jogibara and Temple Road, and is centrally located a couple of hundred metres down from the main square. Tsongkha was a good place for people watching, and it served up a mean bowl of thanthuk—a hearty Tibetan soup with handmade noodles. I knew people who claimed to have eaten thanthuk there every day for more than a year. If they couldn't afford a thirty rupee bowl of thanthuk or put it on credit, they could get a glass of milk tea for five rupees. They then kicked back in grubby plastic chairs, chatted with their friends and watched the world go by, trying to pretend that they didn't have a care in the world. A lot of young men spent hours sitting up there every day. When I walked past and looked up, I was usually greeted by a row of familiar smiling faces.

Another place to hang out—which was a lot better for meeting, rather than just watching girls—was outside the chai shops, Moonlight and Sunrise, near the Tibetan Welfare Office on Bhagsu Road. The chai shops sat side by side. They were open-air wood and tin structures, only about four feet wide and about ten feet deep, each with a narrow table and two benches in the back. The Indian owners stood at the front next to the narrow doorways where their small stoves were located, boiling endless pots of tea.

In those days, there was little traffic in the narrow street, so most customers hung-around outside unless it was raining. Across from the chai shops, there was a metal bench, with a worn wooden seat—polished to a bright shine by thousands of buttocks—that held a few people. If the bench was full, you could sit on the steps outside of the neighboring shops with your legs spanning the open sewer and your feet resting on the pavement or just stand around as most people did. There was only one coffee shop in town back then, and it was frequented only by the well-heeled. Instead, crowds of backpacker tourists and Tibetan boys hung around in the street drinking sweet, cheap chai.

The Salai gyals were not nearly as slick as people imagined. "Pauline, can you talk to her?" I was often asked after a Tibetan had spent several days watching a girl but was too shy to speak to her, "She will talk to you because you are a foreigner. Then I'll come and you can introduce me." I always complied, although none of my introductions led to the serious relationships that the Tibetans were looking for.

Many claimed to their friends that they were only after sex, but often admitted to me that they were really hoping for more. An "I just want to get laid" attitude protected them from disappointment and the humiliation of failure, but sometimes led to patterns of behavior that were hard to let go. As much as some were untrustworthy in relationships, their promiscuity seemed rooted in a lack of ability to trust and have meaningful relationships with women. Almost a decade later, many of the hard-core Salai gyals have failed to form enduring relationships.

The chai shops attracted a mixed bag of people, especially foreigners. A lot of hippies hung around smoking dope, giving the spot a bad reputation, but most of the tourists were ordinary people just looking to make new friends. Most of the settler Tibetans and a lot of the newcomers shunned the places as if they were dens of sin, but the crowd was harmless. In any event, most of the Tibetans didn't do drugs, although some of the tourists tried to coerce them. Three young newcomers did; they were almost always stoned. They were nicknamed "The Babas" in reference to India's dope smoking holy men.

It became boring meeting tourists who were often in town for only a few days–"I'm going to Manali next. Where are you going?" Nor did I enjoy hanging around with arrogant students and volunteers who failed to understand Tibetan culture—but thought they did—or were condescending. But I was often forced to do so for the sake of my Tibetan friends. "Let's go and hang out with them," Tibetans would say. I couldn't very well say "No, they are awful and boring. I don't want to," for at the very least it was a chance for my friends to practice their English. Going home wasn't an option for me because I was their "wingman."

At that time, it was much harder to be up-to-date on Western pop culture. To be fair to the snickering students, it was rather amusing to have seemingly hip men in their twenties tell me that their favorite music was performed by boy bands, the Backstreet Boys and Blue. During that year, I developed an unlikely fondness for the popular boy bands of the time that has endured to this day. Macho guys also held hands, sat on each other's knees, and danced together – usually to the Backstreet Boys – shirtless. By 2011, no one sat on each other's knees anymore or held hands. Word must have got around that it made them look gay.

Dance parties were expensive and didn't happen very often. Sometimes "Rock 'n' Roll," the bar that hosted them, was closed for months on end if the police tired of the trouble that sometimes occurred. During the tourist season, it was not a nice place for women. At that time, many tourists from Punjab were extremely sexually aggressive. I always went armed with a very large pair of sharp scissors, which I kept tucked discreetly in my waistband. "Sorry madam! So sorry," the Punjabis would cry in surprise when their attempts at physical contact were halted by my discrete but swift and menacing display of a weapon. I wasn't over reacting: on one memorable occasion, two Western hippy girls came bounding in joyously only to leave minutes later in tears, after being groped and fondled by Indian tourists who had pounced on them.

Not surprisingly, dance parties did not attract a lot of foreigners back then, so the Salai gyals often found foreigners to party with at their rooms or on the roofs of guest houses. Before I finally rebelled against the repetitive nature of such soirees and came up with excuses not to attend, I spent many nights sitting around with Salai gyals and foreigners drinking beer and listening to Bob Marley. I can't hear "No Woman No Cry" without remembering the Salai gyals and their often doomed love affairs.

"Hotel California" was the unofficial McLeod Ganj theme song. As I walked about half a kilometer from my room to the centre of McLeod Ganj one day in 2003, I heard it playing in five different locations. Not a day would go by when I didn't hear the tune floating through the air from somewhere. The song's appeal has continued, which was never more apparent than one memorable night at McLlo in 2011 when an extraordinarily drunken customer—a foreigner who was inexplicably wintering in town—had the staff play it non-stop in the almost deserted bar for several hours one week night. He had finally seemingly passed out in his chair and the music had stopped when my son walked in. The customer's eyes opened and he slurred, "Can you put on Hotel California." Oblivious to the hilarity of the situation, my son obliged. Aspects of McLeod Ganj are represented by the references to hedonism in the lyrics, and there is something dark and sinister about the song, evocative of the stranded refugees, yet it speaks of the hold the town has had on the hearts of so many, "You can check out any time you like, but you can never leave."

A few of the young Tibetans displayed their insecurities by telling foreigners outrageous tall tales. Someone, who will remain nameless, would tell people that in Tibet he owned a car entirely made out of wood—including the engine. Guys that I knew who had grown up as monks in Tibet would claim that they had been champion horse riders who could swing from the saddle at a full gallop and pluck katas (white silk ceremonial scarves) off the ground with their teeth. Others claimed that their families were wealthy, but the photos that I had seen proved otherwise.

Most of the Salai gyals were honest about their lives back home in Tibet, and their stories made me sad. I heard so many detailed stories of friends' lives in Tibet that I felt almost as if I would recognize their homes and families if I saw them. I can almost picture Jigme's bicycle rides along the Yellow River and his kind-hearted grandfather full of intelligence and good advice. Other friends missed helping their mothers or sisters with cooking and other "women's work." They worried that there was no one helping now. Sometimes, they would hear that a beloved relative had died. It was impossible to fully relate to their grief. They couldn't even call if they wanted to because in those days almost no one in Tibet had a phone. Most of the newcomer youths had come alone and had no family in India. In nine years, I met only one who had come with his parents, although there must have been more. Some had come with a brother or sister or a cousin. Even fewer had an uncle or aunt in India.

Friends became family. Years later, almost all newcomers told me that they never had friendships like those in McLeod Ganj when they were young, poverty-stricken, and single. Foreign women and sponsors came and went. Tibetan girls were illusive. Family was usually non-existent, but friends were there for them through thick and thin. Friends, even when they had almost nothing, shared food, rooms, and clothing and gave one another endless support and encouragement and forgave most bad behavior.

If one young man had enough money for a small room, he usually shared it with anywhere from one to three friends. It was usual for two young men to share a narrow single bed, a pillow at either end. One friend was so generous with his tiny room that he was evicted after he allowed a large group of Tibetan Transit School students to move in because they had nowhere to go for their holidays. Tibetans were really easy-going about these crowded conditions. Their homes in Tibet had usually been very small or they had grown up in nomad tents, so most of them were used to it. Still, sharing a tiny room with penniless friends didn't look easy. If you put four modern Western youths in a tiny room with two hard beds, no T.V., and nothing for dinner except a few cups of flour, some moldy onions, wobbly carrots, a black-spotted green pepper, tiny cloves of garlic, and a hunk of pork fat, they would be foul tempered and depressed by the second day if not sooner. The Tibetans were usually laughing and telling jokes.

If a guy got a girlfriend and she slept over, the roommates were out on the street for the night. People would go home, sometimes in the middle of the night, with no idea that a girl was in the room. They would leave without questioning, even if it meant that they had to spend the night sleeping in the jungle. I never saw anyone get angry about this. Sometimes, people would show up at our place in the middle of the night and ask if they could stay because their roommate had gotten lucky. If the romances carried on for too long, they had to look for new places to live, but most of the lucky young men moved into their foreign girlfriends' more comfortable guesthouses. Over the years, I met only a few foreign women who had moved in with their Tibetan boyfriends.

I had always been a bit of a hermit at home, but I quickly became used to the living conditions. At our place, we had two rooms shared by five people. I felt very lucky on the rare occasions when I was alone for a couple of hours. I was fortunate that my husband usually studied tailoring during the day or hung around with friends. Everyone left the house for at least a few hours for cham cham, the Tibetan term for strolling. Our bedroom doubled as a living room. The floor was carpeted, and we had cable T.V. I'd read and go to sleep while my room was full of people who were talking or watching television.

Most friends were very nostalgic about Tibet. They spent countless hours watching music videos from their homeland featuring musicians in beautiful traditional dress lip-synching as they wandered through lush grasslands filled with herds of yak and blanketed with wild flowers. Riders galloped by on horseback. There were sparkling streams and waterfalls. Smiling women joyously milked their herds. Rosy-cheeked children capered. The sky was always blue. I don't know why they were produced to make life look so idyllic, probably because anything else was dangerous. Certainly, some of the musicians ended up in Chinese prisons for writing "splittist" lyrics.

During that year, I spent most of my time talking to Tibetan friends. I must have drunk hundreds of gallons of tea, for no matter how poor the people were, they usually had a thermos on the go. I felt very frustrated because the problems of Tibetan refugees were immense and complicated. Solving most of them involved money and power, neither of which I had. Instead, I helped people with their English if they couldn't go to classes because they had jobs or small children. The rest of the time, I hung around with my Tibetan friends and tried to learn as much as I could by listening. Over time, I made friends with a diverse range of people from respected scholars and human rights activists to the most disreputable of the Salai gyals.

I remember how skinny most of the young newcomers were. Of course, this was and still is true of most poor people in India. I think it was one of the first things that I noticed in 2003. I was surprised because I had read historical accounts written by visitors to Tibet in the early 20th Century that mentioned how big the people of Amdo and Kham were. Of the hundreds of young people whom I knew, almost none were stocky. A settler neighbor who was a nurse at Tibetan Delek Hospital told me that anemia and malnutrition were huge problems in the entire community.

Their slenderness wasn't surprising. Most Tibetans that I knew lived on thanthuk or thukpa—noodle soups made with vegetables and sometimes meat. Usually, the meat was little more than pork fat with the rind attached and a sliver of meat clinging to the opposite edge. Most of my friends ate nothing but soup or chow mein except on special occasions. Breakfast was often handmade bread cooked in the frying pan or the remains of the previous night's soup.

Everyone spoke longingly of their mother's home cooking in Tibet. Perhaps some of the stories were exaggerations or based on memories of the best of times because most people in Tibet were very poor at that time. Discussion of food was an obsession. As I dreamed of steaks and bacon, the newcomers talked of tables laden with mountains of yak meat and the joy of carving off slice after slice with a large knife. They spoke of delicately flavored tsampa, roasted and ground barley, which is usually mixed with butter, cheese, and hot water to form thick dough and then pressed into flattened balls with the fingers before being eaten.

They reminisced about fresh Tibetan butter and cheese, completely unlike the dried or rancid tasting versions available in the McLeod Ganj market. ("Yak butter" or "yak cheese" are incorrect and unfortunate terms because the yak is the male of the species.) They spoke of mountains of meaty momos (steamed dumplings) dripping with juices and made with ingredients unobtainable in India. The conversations made mouths water, and the reality of the endless starchy soup dinners made almost everyone depressed.

Nights were usually spent hanging out in someone's room. It wasn't difficult to find a group of friends to spend the evening with. Virtually everyone was unemployed, so many would stay up late drinking tea, talking, and playing cards. Next door to us lived several young intellectuals. Once they had exhausted intelligent discussion, they often played a card game that I nicknamed "moustaches." Each time that someone lost, the victor drew an enormous and often ridiculous black moustache on the loser's face with a permanent marker. This continued until all but one had a moustache. The game, which was often accompanied by much shouting and taunting, often went on until 3 am or later. Because I couldn't understand Tibetan, the first few times that I heard them playing, I became concerned that a fight was in progress. I would stumble outside bleary-eyed and listen attentively. Sooner or later the door would open, and a grinning Tibetan sporting a humiliating moustache would emerge.

The rooms were 9' by 9' or even smaller. Most looked more or less the same. For some reason, they were usually painted in nauseating pastels: pink, blue, or green. The walls were typically smeared with grime and sported large patches of mold, the paint peeling and bubbling from water seepage. Two single beds with thin hard mattresses lined the walls. Blankets were neatly folded back against the walls so that the beds could double as sofas. Traditionally, carpets are laid upon beds for seating, but most made do with a colourful sheet. Between the beds was sometimes a small table. Almost everyone had a least one poster of a female Indian movie star or an idyllic scene taped to the wall.

Most of my friends did not have a kitchen. At one end of the room was a simple two-burner stove that sat on a small narrow table with a gas cylinder next to it. Nearby was a small, free-standing, usually grubby, plastic or metal shelf with containers for flour, sugar, oil, and spices. Often, they were empty or almost so. A plastic basket contained a few vegetables. Plastic bowls, their designs faded with use, several glasses for tea, chopsticks, spoons, a cleaver, two pots, a wok, and a few cooking utensils were typical kitchen ware. Chopping was done on a cutting board on the floor. Everyone had a large bucket with a lid, as water had to be collected when the tap was flowing and saved for the times – they were many – when the tap was dry.

Simple health and hygiene practices did not seem to have been taught in exile schools or in Tibet. Most Tibetans believed that upset stomachs and associated illnesses were caused by "bad meat" and "rich food." On warm days, most people drank unboiled water from the tap or bucket. Hand-washing practices were abysmal. Cutting boards were never washed properly. While making momos and other meat dishes, the cooks would taste the raw meat, including pork and chicken, to see if it had been salted correctly. When we ordered several kilograms of meat for Losar (Tibetan New Year), the package that arrived contained a penis. Fortunately, despite their apparent lack of interest in not getting food poisoning, Tibetans shared many similar ideas regarding food with Westerners: Jigme threw it down the hill in disgust. But rotten meat was sometimes served in restaurants. There was no point in worrying, and, fortunately, we seldom got sick. Happily, food preparation practices have improved somewhat in recent years.

Tooth brushing, however, is still something that is usually done in the morning, but almost never before bed, so a lot of even young Tibetans suffer from dental problems, although the damage is not always obvious. Most Tibetans are blessed with dazzling smiles, although the teeth of small children are often black with decay, the wisdom being that they will fall out. I was told that bad teeth were caused by genetics or "India," not by poor dental hygiene and a modern diet which includes sugar and bread. Many of the young newcomers told me that almost everyone in Tibet had perfect teeth. I wasn't convinced, given that photographs from Tibet often featured toothless old people.

The neglected toothbrushes usually lay on shelving molded into the concrete walls, which also contained a few books, notebooks, pens and other odds and ends. Most people had a metal trunk under their bed where they stored clothes and a small stack of well-thumbed photos and other small keepsakes often brought from Tibet. Often, most of the clothes in the trunk were too threadbare and torn to be wearable, but they were kept, possibly to be worn under more presentable garments when it became unbearably cold in winter.

During that first year, I had very few friends who had their own bathrooms. Most affordable apartment buildings had shared toilets, while some had no toilets whatsoever. The few who had a bathroom were married couples, and they had only cold water. I didn't have even one close Tibetan friend who had a hot shower, and unfortunately nor did we. Many people bathed once or twice a year or even less. On a hot summer day, men might swim in their underpants in the icy mountain spring water of the Bhagsu pool or take advantage of the cold showers there. Women would have a bucket bath in the toilet, but the shared toilets were usually too filthy to properly bathe in, and even in the heat of summer, the glacial water stung the skin and prompted haste.

Thankfully, most Tibetans do not smell. This sounds impossible but it is true. I've spent hundreds of hours in tiny rooms with them, not to mention crammed into taxis and jeeps, but I never smelled body odor. If you looked carefully, you could see that many had arms that were darkened by a film of dirt, the buildup creasing near their elbows. There must be some science behind their lack of body odor, but formal studies have eluded me. Tibetans often spoke of how awful some Indians and Westerners smell. This made me very paranoid. "Smell my armpit," Tibetans would sometimes urge disbelieving tourists, even girls that they were trying to impress. I would watch in amusement as the girls clamped their own elbows to their sides just as I did.

It wasn't that Tibetans didn't like bathing. Whenever I visited India and had a hotel room with a hot shower, many of my Tibetan friends would immediately begin asking if they could use it. Tibetan friends who go to the West seem to have more showers than anyone I know. "Can I have a shower?" was often one of the first things that Tibetan visitors in Canada said when they arrived at my home. "Have a shower," they would immediately offer if I stayed with them. I visited one friend whom I hadn't seen since he left India. His once brown skin was now lighter than mine. He hadn't developed a skin condition; I was much tanned from working outdoors. "You must be tired from your journey. Have a shower and then we will have some tea," he suggested.

Although body odor wasn't an issue, one smell was unforgettable. Many people had such horrifyingly stinky feet that you prayed that they didn't find a reason to remove their shoes. The smell must be caused by some sort of bacteria because at one point I began to suffer from it. Thankfully, I was able to eliminate it with a powder from the pharmacy. Back then, a lot of people were too poor to buy such powder or didn't know of its existence. I was too shy to suggest it or give it as a gift. Fellow Tibetans good humouredly tormented offenders because of the stench or forced them to wash their feet, socks, and shoes. Dugkar told me that when Shawo and Zonthar Gyal—two once notorious offenders—visited his home, he made them wash their feet before they were allowed to enter.

My ex husband, whom I will call Lhapal Kyab, spent some months studying tailoring with our friend Dhondup, who was a gifted tailor, a respectable gentleman, and fastidious in his habits. Across the hall from the tailor shop, in a small room, lived several young bachelors. Over a period of weeks, the tailors started noticing a smell emanating from the neighbors' room. The reek became more and more pungent and even crossed the hall to invade the tailor shop. They implored the boys to get rid of the smell, but nothing was done. Finally, the repulsive stench became too much. Lhapal Kyab and Dhondup entered the room like police detectives, conducted a search, and busted the culprits. A large quantity of reeking socks was discovered under the bed. They then forced the occupants to wash the offending articles—standing by to ensure that the task was completed properly.

"Remember all of the broken shoes?" Sangye asked. Newcomers who had been in McLeod Ganj in the 90's and early 2000's often mentioned it. Tibetans who were extremely poor wore broken old shoes. It rains a lot in McLeod Ganj, and the winters are very cold, so wearing shoes that are cracked or have holes in the soles is miserable. The most popular and worst quality shoes were made of brittle plastic, so although they looked like fancy sport shoes at a glance, they developed splits and tears easily and were usually impossible to repair. Sometimes their toes stuck out the sides.

Before I knew people's names, I identified them by their clothes. Despite their poverty, most, who cared to, managed to have one set of stylish clothing. I remember the guy in the yellow shirt, the guy in the blue t-shirt, the guy with the green shoes... Poor Tibetans often wore the same outfit day after day and month after month, but somehow they usually managed to keep it immaculate and look hip. "Sometimes I think that they are their own worst enemies," said a foreign activist friend. "Tibetans who live in poverty put so much effort into not looking poor that people don't understand how bad their situation is." It was true. On the street, it was often almost impossible to differentiate between wealthy Tibetans and poor ones.

Chapter 8

Many newcomers had no resort but to solicit what is called sponsorship money from foreign visitors to fill their bellies or pay rent. Most receiving sponsorship used the money well, attended English or other classes regularly, paid their bills, and looked for work. A few wasted all or most of it on partying and eating out. I knew several people who showed no remorse and seemed to have no conscience. The minute that they stepped out of the Western Union, their pockets bulging with rupees, it was party time. When the funds ran out, they shamelessly called and e-mailed their foreign "friends" or "girlfriends"—sometimes they had more than one—for more and hit-up visitors around town. People in the community noticed the bad boys squandering money, but they didn't notice the majority who lived quiet, frugal lives, asking only for what they needed to survive or using sponsorship money to become independent by starting small businesses.

Part of what led to irresponsible spending was that the newcomers were mostly young people in a town full of tourists who were having a good time, not that Tibetans need foreigners as an excuse to party. Parties and indulging are a big part of the culture. Losar (New Year) lasts for two weeks in Tibet. Still, watching tourists enjoying themselves non-stop didn't help.

Especially during my first few visits, most Tibetans had little sense of the reality of life in the West. Although the tourists explained that they had worked hard to save money for their vacations, the Tibetans were skeptical. Aside from watching the tourists and volunteers indulge themselves in various ways—spending time in the bar, doing yoga, sitting around in restaurants, or reading—the Tibetans mostly got their views of Western culture from watching television. At that time, little in terms of quality Western programming was available on Indian T.V. Aside from B-movies, which belonged to a genre that could be called "Teen Sex Beach Party," "Friends" was the most popular and, sadly, the most realistic program. Even if one assumed that "Friends" did not depict life in the West with a high degree of accuracy, it was still natural to conclude that day-to-day life in the West did not involve a great deal of hard work and that money was easy to come by.

Foreign visitors usually complained about what locals considered to be small things or even non-issues: the cleanliness of toilets, the quality of mattresses, and noises such as the barking of dogs. When they complained about how hard they worked back home, it was difficult to take them seriously. Many of the tourists also liked to go on about how money couldn't buy happiness and the emptiness of life in a consumer society. The refugees knew very well that money could buy a lot of happiness and contentment, so if it didn't make the foreigners happy, they would gladly spend it for them.

Typically, the Salai gyals were big spenders, and although some felt badly about blowing money, most were young and like many young people around the world, having fun was their main priority. They also had friends, and friends expected them to share what they had. Peer pressure sometimes spelled disaster for well-meaning young Tibetans. Word of a windfall spread like wildfire. Suddenly, friends appeared expecting food and drink. In many cases, the friends had shared money that they had received in the past, so it would have been shameful not to reciprocate.

Most of the young newcomers did manage to hang onto the sponsorship money that they received. The problem was that even a generous donation did not usually last long. Rent had to be paid and food bought. Realistically, for most, it took years of study to acquire the language and/or computer skills needed to find gainful employment. Often, a sponsor was willing to help out only once or twice, and the Tibetan had to find someone new.

Tibetans usually met their sponsors in restaurants or language classes. Finding sponsors required self-promotion and nerve. I would see my friends deep in conversation with tourists, helping them to shop for handicrafts and acting as tour guides for free. From their over-the-top pleasing demeanor and from the look in their eyes, I could tell that they were hoping for financial assistance.

Starting up conversations with tourists was easy, for almost all wanted to talk to Tibetans and hear their stories, but, despite appearances to the contrary, most Tibetans hated asking visitors for money. Even if they had previously been monks who had lived off donations, monastics had high status and usually received money for services rendered or the spiritual significance of their work and study. Tibetans told me that befriending foreign tourists for the sole purpose of gaining personal sponsorship or asking genuine foreign friends for money was humiliating.

In order to find sponsors, they had to talk to a lot of people and carefully gauge when it was the right time to ask for money. Some tourists expressed a great deal of sympathy for their plight but then became angry or dismayed if the Tibetan asked for help. "He seemed like such a nice young man. I couldn't believe that he had the nerve to ask me for money," a scandalized tourist told me after one of my poorest friends had asked her for help. "I know him. He's really poor and he has no family," was my reply. "Well I'm poor too," she snorted, "I could hardly afford to go on this trip."

Fortunately, foreign visitors were often generous, since many Tibetan refugees faced hunger and homelessness. Many of my friends confessed that they had often gone a day or more without eating. When they could find nowhere to stay, they slept in the jungle. One shudders to think how much worse things could have been had McLeod Ganj not become a tourist town. There were no aid organizations to help them, no soup kitchens or homeless shelters.

Many of the settler Tibetans expressed disdain towards newcomers who received sponsorship. I discussed this with Clive, who had spent the better part of a decade in McLeod Ganj. He laughed, "I know, it's ridiculous. This whole town was built on Western sponsors." He was right in many ways, and the money wasn't just given to individuals. Aside from receiving money from the Government of India, the Tibetan Government in Exile, T.C.V. and other schools, and N.G.O.'s all receive much of their funding from foreign sources. Tibetans who practically spat when they spoke of newcomers getting money from sponsors seemed to ignore the fact that foreign sponsors effectively wrote their paychecks. Many employed by these organizations worked very hard, but plenty were lazy and inefficient.

In any event, the settlers seemed to have short memories. Back in the 1970's and 80's, before newcomers began arriving, the quest for individual sponsorship had been their domain. Paul Christiaan Klieger wrote extensively about sponsorship in his PhD thesis for which he conducted research in Dharamsala twice: first in the late 70's and again in the late 80's. He documented institutional sponsorship on a massive scale, as well as the prevalence of personal solicitations and an "almost cradle-to-grave welfare system."[1] Unfortunately, he did not explain how this welfare system functioned or what standard of living it provided. However, he clearly stated that some form of financial assistance was available to almost every Tibetan, at least in Dharamsala.

According to Klieger, as in my time, many of the people who requested assistance from foreigners were extremely poor, particularly during his first visit. Some became financially independent as a result of help that they received. Some were not destitute, but they wanted foreigners to give them cash or things that would improve their lifestyles. Many of the requests were familiar to me: stylish clothes, popular music, sponsorship for education, sponsorship to study abroad, and, the most difficult request to fulfill—marriage to a foreigner. Several of the people who asked for his help were con artists or simply dishonest. He wrote an amusing account of how he was tricked by a ne'er-do-well, with an entirely concocted yet believable tragic life story, into bringing him along and apparently paying all expenses on a research trip overland from Dharamsala to Lhasa.[2] This was in the 80's during a brief period when settlement Tibetans were able to return to Tibet for visits.

As I hunted for information on assistance available to newcomers, I came across a comment from a Tibetan exile government official that I found puzzling and disturbing. A team of researchers studying mental health had interviewed an unnamed official at the Reception Centre on the topic of services available to newcomers in 2001: " So we take care of them and, in that, what we do is we mainly try to rehabilitate them and that includes both social and health rehabilitation. And, eh, from the social aspect we provide guidance, provide housing (. . .) And then like we also try to find jobs for these people and train them in the local trades that they are interested in."[3] Based on this statement, the researchers had concluded that "various forms of organizational support are available."[4]

I had arrived in Dharamsala two years later and found no evidence of any such support in the recent past or the present. That year, I spoke to hundreds of new arrivals about their situations, and I fruitlessly attempted to find opportunities that were available but that they might have overlooked. I did not know of anyone who had been offered housing or training in trades that they were interested in, except for the few who were interested in sewing and making handicrafts. That market was saturated. The provision of housing was limited to accommodation in dormitories during their stays at the reception centre and school. In eight years, I didn't talk to any newcomer who had received assistance from the exile government in finding a job, except for a few that I heard of who had arrived more than a decade earlier.

Because there was no help available to them, over the years I sponsored a number of friends. Sonam is a good example. When I first met him, he was a seventeen-year-old monk. I tried to avoid tutoring monks because so many foreign women seemed to be obsessed with them. I didn't want to join the ranks of the creepy. A friend who had been a famous poet back in Tibet, but who was at that time working as a not-so-famous dishwasher, asked me to teach Sonam, who was desperate to improve his English. Apparently, his monastery had cracked down on English study after a monk had had an affair with a female foreign volunteer teacher. I was relieved when a small boy showed up at my house. No one would get the wrong impression if they saw him coming and going. His goal was to improve his English so that he could read literature, but he could sneak away from the monastery only once a week.

When I met him, Sonam knew little more than his ABC's. He also had the unfortunate Tibetan habit of pointing at things with his middle finger. I started by teaching him the words for common household items. "Fuk," he said, giving a fork the finger. Fortunately, over the years, his English improved, but very slowly because he did not have much chance to practice.

One day I received a message—Sonam had decided to leave the monastery. He wanted to study English in Varanassi, where the cost of living was lower than in McLeod Ganj. He needed money. I didn't hesitate. I knew that his language skills were woefully insufficient to get a typical ex-monk job such as working in a restaurant. He attended school for six months and then found work as a dishwasher, fortunately in a nice café. It paid decent wages compared to most other restaurants. The staff worked only eight hours a day and had one day a week off. The owners even found English tutors for their employees. Sonam could now support himself, and by talking with customers, he continued to improve his English. When I next visited India, we had our first proper conversation. Unfortunately, he was still a long way from having a real career.

Finding jobs wasn't easy. One problem was and to a certain extent still is that many unscrupulous employers in the service industry preferred to exploit more pliable workers—often children and teenagers—from Bihar and other impoverished regions. Some were purchased from their parents for a few hundred rupees a month, while others were so destitute and uneducated that they accepted any wage and working conditions as long as they could sleep in the restaurant and get fed. The employers, both Tibetans and Indians, would sometimes go so far as to pretend or perhaps imagine that they were providing the jobs out of charity; meanwhile, they enjoyed comfortable or even opulent lifestyles without improving conditions and wages for their workers.

Sangye pointed out another major problem for the new arrivals: "In the early 2000's when I came, there were almost no jobs available. There were sometimes jobs in restaurants, but even those run by friends didn't want to hire you. If they did, your unemployed friends would all come and hang around. They would all try to get free meals if the boss went out because they had no money and nothing to eat. No wonder restaurants didn't want to give us jobs! Who could blame them?" This wasn't a small concern for employers in that there were always hundreds of unemployed newcomers in McLeod Ganj through the 1990's and into the late 2000's. The demand for free food was high, and the behavior of the young men was often not good for business.

In 2003, several of my young newcomer friends were able to raise the funds to open restaurants. My friend Tenzin Kyab, who was a great cook, found a foreign sponsor to help him open a two-story restaurant on Bhagsu Road with a roof-top patio. It was a nice place in a good location, but it was doomed from the beginning. Tenzin Kyab was a kind-hearted individual who allowed his many destitute friends to order food on credit. Most of the bills were never paid, for the friends had no way of obtaining money, or if they did, they usually spent it partying.

Tenzin Kyab also made the mistake of installing a T.V. on the ground floor. Almost no one we knew could afford a T.V. at that time. Typically, close to a dozen Tibetan men in their early twenties packed the ground floor watching T.V., clowning around, talking loudly in Tibetan, making a mess, and chain smoking. Potential customers, most often tourists, would peer in the door and usually not enter. I wasn't surprised. The scene was intimidating, especially because the tourists couldn't understand the noisy conversations. The young men reminded me of the groups of harmless but boisterous teenagers who hung out in the food courts at malls in Canada when I was growing up. Most of the so-called friends were not aware or concerned that their behavior was ruining the business. This pattern constantly repeated itself. Most restaurants at the time that were started by young, inexperienced, or even just overly kind-hearted newcomers went out of business.

Chapter 9

In the 2000's, more than 60% of new arrivals were monks,[1] and I suspect that percentages were the same in the previous decade. Many left the monastic community after arriving in India. Official data are not available on the numbers who chose to disrobe, but at least half of the newcomer men whom I met were monks when they arrived in India. In 2012, a reliable and conscientious monk friend—some may be surprised to know that some monks are neither reliable nor conscientious—was kind enough to check the records at his monastery for me. Of the 580 monks who had escaped into exile over the years, approximately 250 had stopped being monks. His monastery has very strict rules, so the number that chose to leave may be higher than average, but clearly large numbers end up on the streets of Dharamsala looking for work and wives.

Most became monks as children or teens; this holds true for nuns as well. In Tibet, monasteries were often the only schools available. Some joined the monasteries because they were extremely religious, while many others joined because they wanted to become educated, they were sent by their parents, or they believed that it was a "cool thing to do." However, many decide, often in their late teens or twenties but sometimes when they are far older, that they are not cut out for a lifetime of monasticism. Although family and even friends are sometimes shocked or very angry, it is considered important to stop being a monk rather than become a bad or insincere one. In India, far from the sometimes disapproving gaze of family, many monks choose to disrobe.

The ex-monks joined the competition for jobs. Although many of them were proficient in Tibetan, they usually lacked office or other work or business skills. And there were other problems. Monks have traditionally been held in high esteem in Tibetan society. But after leaving the monastic community, many, especially those who were intellectuals and therefore were accustomed to a higher degree of respect than ordinary monks, had difficulty adjusting to work life, the reality of their job prospects, and taking orders from lay people. Tsegon told me: "I tried giving a number of friends who were ex-monks jobs in my shop. Some of them were very educated. They did not like to do work that they saw as beneath them. If you asked them to do things like sweep the floor, they would get red in the face and be very insulted. They would take days off without asking or even telling. They just didn't show up. They weren't used to working yet, so they were terrible employees."

The ex-monks were better off, though, than the young nomads who had escaped. Most of the monks had shared cooking and cleaning duties in their monasteries, so they had skills that were somewhat transferable to the restaurant industry. The young nomads often had no skills that were useful in India. In most households back in Tibet, jobs were divided into men's and women's work. Although some were very adaptable or had obviously helped out at home, others saw cooking and cleaning as beneath them. From the wretchedness of their homemaking skills, it was obvious that they had never helped their mothers or even paid attention to what it was that women did. Some of the nomads had been sent to school, but among my friends, those likeliest to have attended school were the children of farmers and business people. They also tended to have more housekeeping and other skills, which didn't help them much because only a few dozen restaurants and guesthouses existed at the time.

Some founded or found work with N.G.O.'s (charitable organizations) that provide services such as English classes to the community, but running an N.G.O. is tough and fundraising is hell. Many of the N.G.O.'s barely got off the ground or had problems with mismanagement. Despite all, over the years, an increasingly large number of Tibetan N.G.O.'s thrived and made tremendous contributions to the community, but back then there were not many, so they, too, did not provide enough work.

Many newcomers, including monks and nuns, were intellectuals or wanted to be. They had escaped from Tibet because they wanted to express themselves freely and contribute to Tibetan culture and society. Some became intellectuals in exile after becoming educated.

As mentioned earlier, Tibetan language media, Norbulingka Institute, Sara College, and The Library of Tibetan Works and Archives hire many newcomers because they need staff fluent in Tibetan, but not many positions become available in those places either. Many of the intellectuals were interested in publishing books, magazines, and newspapers. Unfortunately, the Tibetan population in exile is small, and many settlers can barely read Tibetan. The newcomers who did enjoy reading were mostly unemployed or worked in restaurants, so they didn't earn enough money to buy much reading material. I was told that a Tibetan language book was considered successful if several hundred copies were sold.

Another source of meaningful work was with human rights organizations that needed staff who could speak Tibetan dialects. A number of my friends worked interviewing new arrivals about human rights abuses and cultural and environmental degradation or conducted the often even more stressful task of using phones and internet technologies to gather information from people inside Tibet. Sometimes, their contacts in Tibet were discovered by the Chinese and were arrested. Human rights work appeared to be far more stressful for the people who had grown up in Tibet than it was for others. A number of friends who were employed in the field became alcoholics or indulged in severe binge-drinking. Still, many people coveted the jobs because they wanted to do something meaningful for their country.

Of course, besides jobs, most of the young men were also desperate for girlfriends. A lot of tourists and volunteers were usually in town, many of them single women. What better way to find both wives and jobs than marry foreigners and move abroad? Most had families who lived in dire poverty. Western wages could do a lot to help, while the jobs that they could get in India usually barely provided enough to survive. They would also no longer need to live in fear in India, with expiring or false documents. Once abroad, they could become citizens and travel back to Tibet safely to visit their families. Under the circumstances, for many the choice was obvious.

Most told me that they would have preferred to marry Tibetan women and live in a Tibetan community, but they were not willing to go back to Tibet, and there was nothing for them in India. Some friends were adamant that they would not marry foreigners and go to the West. They had meaningful work and wanted to stay in India and work for their country. But that was not always to be. Some never found Tibetan wives. Eventually, they fell in love with foreign women and moved abroad. Others were willing to go either way, but they wanted to marry just the right woman regardless of her nationality.

When I first arrived in McLeod Ganj, many were not terribly discerning although they sometimes tried to pretend that they were. They wanted out, and from their choices in dating and the haste with which they proposed marriage, it was obvious that they were willing to go out with almost anyone. I repeatedly saw young men attach themselves to any foreign woman who would have them. They were often mocked by their friends and looked down upon by the rest. In a small town little goes unnoticed. For some, this path inexplicably led to true love and enduring happiness. Unfortunately, many moved from one inappropriate relationship to the next. Even if they did meet someone whom they truly cared for, often the relationship did not work out. Their quest for marriages and careers was fraught with enough pain, humiliation, and disappointments to damage them, in some cases seemingly permanently.

A small minority of the young men had arrived in India already damaged. From what I could read into their stories, it appeared that their families had sent them as a last resort, in hope that meeting the Dalai Lama and getting some education would straighten them out. Their teenage years in Tibet had been devoted to drinking, fighting, and otherwise getting into trouble. Once in India, the troubled youths had big ideas and big plans but seldom got out of bed before two in the afternoon. They would then roam around town all day looking for something entertaining to do. Even though their English was poor, they stopped going to the free English classes provided by N.G.O.'s. Usually, they claimed that classes weren't advanced enough for them even though they could barely write a coherent sentence. Instead, they loitered around, goofed-off, or played cards. At night, if they or their friends had money or a foreigner was willing to pay, they would get drunk. Some were very rude to locals. They would purposely bash into settler Tibetans in the street or bar and sometimes try to start fights. They were surly with Indian shop keepers and would loudly use foul language. They were hostile towards those from other parts of Tibet. They strutted around town as if they were royalty, but I suspect that deep down inside, they felt like losers. They had nothing to be proud of and nothing to offer the world except attitude.

Sadly, most of the young newcomers appeared to have been doing well in Tibet and had been encouraged to flee to India because their families wanted a brighter future for them, but for some, the trauma of their escape, the isolation from their families, and, most of all, their miserable situation in exile had taken its toll. In Tibet, India had been whispered of as a land of freedom and opportunity, not as a place where they would face only poverty and rejection. Bright young people with great potential also often hung around aimlessly wasting their days.

One problem for the youths was a lack of mature adult newcomers and parental guidance. As we know, mature adult refugees were mostly allowed to stay only a short time in India as pilgrims. In Tibet, most of the youths would have been living with their parents or their wives' parents. Even those in their late teens were often married in Tibet. In India, there was no one to tell them to get out of bed, no one to remind them to mind their manners, no one to chew them out for drinking too much or for not going to class.

The pursuit of love and marriage in Dharamsala was fraught with difficulties, for some worse than others. Unfortunately, I could not get my hands on definitive data to illustrate what I knew to be true: men outnumbered women by a wide margin. I visited the exile government's Department of Information, but the staff wouldn't give me any. "We are no longer releasing information on the people that escape from Tibet," I was told when I asked if I could obtain the number of males and females who fled Tibet since the 1980's, broken down by year, region of origin, age, and sex. I was disappointed, but I had enough information to make my point. As mentioned, I had the 1998 Demographics Survey, which told me that in the previous four years, 85.6% of new arrivals from Amdo had been male, while the numbers for Kham and U-Tsang were 86.3% and 61% respectively.[2]

I cobbled together more recent data from a myriad of other reports. Some of the information was illuminating. The International Campaign for Tibet reports told me that three quarters of the new arrivals who came between 2001 and 2006 were from Kham and Amdo.[3] This was not surprising; men from those regions were, in my experience, the most likely to seek foreign women for sex and marriage. I looked for sex ratios in studies conducted at T.T.S. where all young adult newcomers who were neither monks nor nuns were obliged to study. A 2001 study recorded the student body as being 80% male,[4] while a 2006 study indicated that 71% of the students were male.[5] I examined another study conducted at the Reception Centre where the researchers had interviewed all of the new arrivals over the age of 16 who were planning to stay in India and who had arrived between November 2003 and September 2004. 84.7% of them had been men.[6] Although sex ratios were recorded in reports, they were never remarked upon, but obviously, the quest for love and marriage presented severe challenges for newcomer men.

Clearly, there were not enough settler Tibetan women to go around, and in any event, settler Tibetans often don't approve of their children marrying newcomers. At the Tibetan Centre for Conflict Resolution, Sonam discussed some of the issues with me. She told me that it was difficult for newcomers to be seen as suitable marriage partners: cultural differences made Indian-born women hesitant to get involved with newcomers, and there were other issues. One of Sonam's newcomer friends had fallen in love with a settler girl: "The mother refused the marriage because she was worried that he would leave her daughter and return to Tibet. It was sad to see that they were not allowed to start a life together. She [the Tibetan girl] was forced to go somewhere else. Later, he met a Western woman and went to France. It was a real relationship not for gains or anything." Dorje Wanggyal, the newcomer scholar, had mentioned similar problems, blaming the reputation of newcomers as unreliable husbands on a small number who had conducted themselves shamefully or even criminally and then fled back to Tibet.

Friends spoke of other issues, "Girls and their parents are looking for someone with a university degree and a good career. Newcomers often don't usually have either." Others bought into stereotypes: "They are rough and they beat their wives," an employee of Tibetan Women's Association told me in casual conversation. I didn't talk to any settler Tibetan girls who expressed interest in dating newcomers, and among my dozens of friends and acquaintances, only one newcomer married a settler woman.

Indian women were almost entirely off limits. I knew of only one Tibetan man who was married to an Indian woman. They are the husband-and-wife film-making duo Ritu Sarin and Tenzin Sonam, who, as I understand it, met in the United States and later moved back to India. I did meet a few Tibetan women who were married to Indian men, but they were exceptions. Reports that I came across told me the same thing that I observed: marriages between Indians and Tibetans are rare.[7]

Because newcomers' dating options were so limited and, most importantly, at that time their financial situations were usually very desperate, it is fair to say that in 2003, any woman, no matter how repulsive her personality and regardless of her beauty or age, could hook-up with an attractive young Tibetan. Some of what went on was essentially prostitution. For Tibetan men who couldn't find jobs or sponsors and who didn't have friends who could provide food and places to sleep (or felt that they had already asked for too much), there was no choice other than turning to crime. Despite the criticism that they have endured, newcomers are almost without exception essentially good, law-abiding people. Rather than doing what could have come easily—breaking into rooms, mugging people in the dark streets, or stealing purses and backpacks—they chose to sleep with women. If they got lucky, they could stay in the women's rooms and be bought meals. They might also receive gifts of cash and clothing. Some became talented and relatively successful gigolos who could attract the more desirable women, but many of the couplings were a depressing sight to behold. Outside of the peak tourist season, even the most successful Salai gyals often had to lower their standards if they had no other way to get by.

Although newcomers always talked about how others engaged in such behavior, few would share their own experiences or discuss their feelings. I never pushed anyone to tell me anything, for as much as people made light of what went on, I knew that memories of personal experiences must be painful. I was surprised when, many years later, as the two of us sat in McLlo Bar discussing Salai gyals, one friend mentioned what it was like for him. He had been a teenager when we first met more than seven years earlier, a very bright boy with a gift for languages who was often in the company of Western women far older than he was. Now, times had changed. He was buying me beer. He was often guarded in his conversation, but that night he said what no one else had been willing to say: "You had no money and nothing to eat so you would go out and try to meet someone. When you did meet someone, you wanted to be in love with them, but you knew in your heart that you weren't. It was a horrible feeling."

I couldn't find anyone who would admit to having sex with gay Western men, but I had heard enough stories from reliable sources to know that it happened. This was not a case of gay Tibetan men sleeping with gay foreign men. My sources were certain that the Tibetans involved were not gay. I was quite sure that one of my friends had done so, for he had received large amounts of money from a gay Western man with whom he had a suspiciously close relationship. This volunteer teacher in his forties was also suspected of having taken advantage of other impoverished Tibetan youths—highly suspicious activities had gone on at his apartment. There were other rumors, but no one who might have had personal experience was willing to talk.

At any given time, several bossy women in their forties, fifties, and sixties were seen around town in the company of Tibetan men in their twenties. (Bossiness wasn't exclusive to that age bracket.) From their behavior and gossip around town, it was obvious that they were in relationships. Some of these unlikely pairings seemed amiable, but I often overheard the women chastising their Tibetan boyfriends or instructing them on appropriate behaviors and habits. Some of the women seemed so disrespectful toward their Tibetan boyfriends that it was difficult to understand why they were attracted to them in the first place. They reminded me of mothers nagging their children. Conversations that I overheard in restaurants frequently involved the Tibetans' overuse of salt and sugar, discussion of fat intake as it related to heart disease, and the importance of flossing one's teeth. The Tibetan boyfriends, like twenty-something's in the West, were too young to care about their health in middle or old age. They tried to appear interested, although in some cases they looked annoyed or embarrassed. They usually listened in stony silence, punctuated by an occasional grunt of acknowledgement.

Not all of the Tibetans dating much older women were insincere. I heard a number of stories from Tibet in which young men had happily run off with much older, often divorced Tibetan women, and I did hear of a few marriages between young Tibetans and much older foreign women that were successful. Sonam Tsering had an interesting Salai gyal story. He is in his late twenties and successfully married to a Western woman whom he met in India. He has lived in the US for a number of years and was visiting India on holiday when I ran into him in 2011. One of his friends, Lhamo, had married a woman about twenty five years older than he was and also gone to the States. They divorced, but Lhamo hadn't started dating younger women. "He likes old ladies," Sonam Tsering told me with glee, "We'll be in the bar [in America] and there are lots of young girls. He isn't interested at all. He just looks bored. Then some lady in her fifties or sixties walks in and his face lights up. Sometimes he is dating two old ladies at the same time."

It was common to see strikingly handsome Tibetan men with unattractive-looking foreign women. Of course, physical beauty loses its importance quickly. One of my friends had dated a woman whom he admitted that he at first found very physically unattractive, but as the months wore on, he became very fond of her. They had similar interests and much in common intellectually. "Even though she wasn't beautiful, she was so cute in her own way. I felt really sad when she left. I still think about her."

What was depressing was seeing nice young men with women who were unpleasant, mentally disturbed, or condescending. Many of the Tibetans had poor English, so I wondered if they were aware of their girlfriends' shortcomings in terms of personality. There were women who regularly bossed and scolded their "pet" Tibetans in public or fawned foolishly over them. There were young students and tourists who referred to their boyfriends as "cute" because they weren't up-to-date on Western culture or because they had a limited vocabulary and therefore didn't understand what the women were saying or asking, "Oh my god, he doesn't know what a high-rise is! Isn't that cute!" I often heard Tibetans say, "I don't know," when what they meant was, "I don't understand." There were also foreign women who thought that their Tibetan boyfriends were geniuses; unfortunately, it became apparent that they weren't as their language skills improved.

Many of the newcomers were in a tremendous rush to get married. Those in their early twenties often told me that they were failures because they weren't married, with kids and careers. This was partially because in Tibet, people typically married and started families when they were very young. I also think that their attitudes may have been due to skewed perspectives. They had left as teens, and their memories of what those in their twenties were doing in Tibet were probably clouded by teenage judgment. I remember as a teen thinking that many of my friends who were in their twenties were really successful and had beautiful homes. Looking back, I realize that my older friends were little more than kids themselves with bad jobs and seedy apartments. Life for the average family in Tibet at that time was far from opulent. I recall reading statistical data that showed that the per-capita income in Tibet at the time was virtually the same as that of Rwanda.

Not all of the relationships were anticipated to end in marriage. A lot of casual sex was going on as well; the young men craved affection and sex. Newcomers told me that exile-born or raised Tibetans were strangely conservative about sex. But in Amdo, most people started secretly dating and having sex when they were teenagers; this may be true of other regions as well. Everyone spoke of "night hunting," especially in nomad areas. A boy would go to the tent of a girl that he fancied, and if she was alone, sneak in for sex. If she wasn't alone, he would coax her into going outside where they would have sex on the grass using their chubas (traditional cloaks) as blankets. Perhaps surprisingly, over the years few women told me that they disapproved of night hunting— some even giggled gleefully when discussing it — although most would not admit to being involved; some, it should be mentioned, had terrible experiences. Even if I discounted the most outrageous stories that I heard, it was apparent that many indulged in casual sex.

Back in Tibet, most young people had had serious or somewhat serious but often secret relationships. These would frequently end when one of the pair's parents set them up in an arranged marriage, often with virtual strangers. Sometimes the girl was pregnant with her lover's child when she was made to marry someone else. Although it was apparently deeply frowned upon and single mothers had difficulty finding husbands, most spoke fondly of their step-fathers. A number of people informed me that they had been told that their fathers had died before they were born and their mothers had re-married. But several strongly believed that their fathers had not died, and some were even pretty sure who they were.

Sometimes, the parents had their children's best interests at heart when they planned arranged marriages, but they could also be more akin to business deals. Kelsang Gyal told me that his family wanted to marry him to "a stupid, ugly girl because her family was rich. I felt like I was being sold." He had refused, and his family allowed him to go to India to study. Over the years, I met a number of people who had fled Tibet to escape arranged marriages. Some had run away with their lovers.

Arranged marriages were also common among the settlers in India. A settler Tibetan neighbor fell in love with a man from New Zealand. He desperately wanted to marry, but her parents refused to allow her to marry a foreigner. "They can't be trusted. They all get divorced," said her mother. For months, the young woman played "White Flag" by "Dido" at full volume every time that she was alone at home. I always hear the song playing in my mind—"There will be no white flag above my door. I'm in love and always will be"—when I remember sunny afternoons in my former apartment. Later, she went abroad and her parents arranged her marriage to a Tibetan.

In Amdo, love marriages were not unknown but were far less common. Among my friends was one such couple. They had been together almost twenty years and were still in love. The husband emigrated abroad, and it was some time before the wife could follow. Losar (Tibetan New Year) could have been a depressing time for her. Shortly beforehand, a large box from her husband arrived in the mail. My mouth hung open as she joyously unpacked and tried on the perfectly fitting, stylish clothes and shoes that he had sent. Other love marriages, much like those in the West, ranged from highly successful to disastrous. Among newcomers, divorce was an option, but because many refugees are poor and rely on two incomes, it was not often affordable.

Settler Tibetans seem more opposed to divorce than their countrymen from Tibet: they often disapproved when I said that I was divorced. Two young brothers told me with confidence that it was crucial to stay with one's "life partner" and have "salad on the side" rather than consider divorce. Their view was not unusual. Clyde told me of a well-known businessman who would openly brag about his infidelity. Dechen, a middle-aged friend, was often in tears because her lover wouldn't leave his wife. The wife knew all about the affair and tolerated it as long as her husband visited Dechen late at night so that neighbors wouldn't notice. Many settlers told me that divorce was against Tibetan custom, but from information that I located, it appeared that extremely conservative values in regard to divorce had developed during sixty years of exile, likely due to Indian influence.

Visitors such as Sarat Chandra Das (1880's) and Ekai Kawaguchi (1900's) wrote of the prevalence of divorce in old Tibet. Kawaguchi's statements are rather outrageous: "From the highest to the lowest they [wives] are allowed to have their own savings, more or less, according to their position and circumstance, and fortified with that source of strength they receive a decree of divorce from their husbands without any sense of regret."[8]   The scholarly explorer William Rockhill mentions the prevalence throughout Tibet of "contract marriages"[9] which lasted as little as a week. Rockhill, who had travelled extensively through Eastern Tibet in the 1890's, mostly in areas where polyandry was uncommon, also notes that "children are spoken of as of such and such a woman; hardly ever is the father's name mentioned."[10] Although marriages were arranged, the women didn't seem to be chattels, for Rockhill further states that "as soon as the woman has entered the home of her husband she assumes control of nearly all his affairs; no buying or selling is done except by her or with her consent and approval."[11] Somewhere on-line, I had read two fairly different accounts of divorce practices written by exile women who had grown up in Lhasa prior to the Chinese invasion, one stating that divorce was accepted, the other that it was not, but I was unable to locate the sources again. The preponderance of evidence suggests, though, that divorce was more prevalent and accepted in old Tibet than many settlers believed.

Newcomers would often insist that divorce was uncommon and unacceptable in their homeland and then go on to tell me of their brothers', sisters', parents', or grandparents' divorces. Choepa Dondrub told me that his brother had been married five times. Each time, the family held a wedding ceremony and prayed that it would last. More usual were arranged marriages breaking down and those involved later marrying the partners of their choice. The same happened with love marriages. Most mentioned domestic violence and infidelity as the main reasons the marriages fell apart. People often told me all of the intimate details and dramas of their relatives' divorces, much the same as friends in Canada would. The main difference seemed to be that in Tibet, families worked harder to convince the couples to reconcile.

My search for information on divorce in Tibet met with little success, but I did come across many studies that focused on polygamy and polyandry, practices that obviously captivated the interest of some Western scholars but that were not in style in Dharamsala and did not seem popular among most Tibetans. The lack of studies surprised me since I found the combination of pre-marital sex, arranged marriage, divorce, and love marriage interesting and seemingly unique; of course, getting honest answers on such sensitive topics would be extremely difficult for a foreign researcher. Most of my friends from Tibet had grown up in families with two parents. Only one, Shawo Gyal, had grown up in Amdo with two dads. They visited him in India on separate occasions. The family seemed at ease, and he spoke lovingly of both of them, but I didn't ask a lot of questions. Apparently, polyandry and polygamy are uncommon in Amdo, but no one seemed to disapprove of the family.

In Kathmandu, I once stayed in the home of a woman whose husband had a second wife in Tibet. The husband was a wealthy businessman who had residences in Lhasa and Kathmandu—one wife in each house. This practice likely came from a time when traders were gone for months or even years. Tibetans to whom I spoke thought that one partner was the ideal. They felt that polygamy and polyandry were caused by poverty or engaged in by the rich to keep family property intact. No one whom I spoke to had any desire for more than one spouse at a time, although some would have been happy to replace their current one.

Once I had an understanding of the unique and varied nature of sex and marriage in Tibet, I started seeing the seemingly outrageous behavior of some Tibetans in a different light. Sleeping around with tourists wasn't that different from night hunting. Marrying women whom they weren't in love with wasn't morally reprehensible if you considered that they were essentially arranging their own marriages. If they asked someone to marry them after two weeks of courtship, it wasn't necessarily strange in that back in Tibet people often married complete strangers.

At any given time, no more than a few dozen newcomers, out of the several thousand who lived in Dharamsala, were regularly chasing and dating multiple foreign women. It seemed that there were more because they were very noticeable in such a small town, and they seldom went out of their way to hide their activities. None had elders or parents holding sway over them, and most of the settlers despised them already. Friends were often disgusted, but they seldom voiced their disapproval—it wasn't worth creating friction when people were so interdependent. Foreigners came and went, and most didn't know each other, so it was difficult to gain a bad reputation among them.

Realistically, many of the women who slept with and dated Tibetans were more than willing victims. Anyone who thinks that women are morally superior to men when it comes to sex would have learned otherwise if they had spent time in McLeod Ganj from the late 1990's until the late 2000's. Some of the women were as shallow as the worst Salai gyals. Many Tibetans are good-looking, and a lot of foreign women used them for holiday flings. Some of the women had boyfriends or husbands back home. Even if the Tibetans knew that they were being used for sex, most of them couldn't afford to walk away, and many of them wanted sex and needed affection, even if the experience was sometimes demoralizing.

Some of the women were blatant about their sleaziness and spoke in the presence of their "boyfriends" as if they were talking about a piece of meat, "Oh my god, isn't he hot. I love his hair. Can you take a picture of us together? Here's my camera." Most of them took lots of photos of their holiday conquests to show to their friends back home. The Tibetans were refugees and they were from Tibet. Some of them had even been nomads. They had met the Dalai Lama. That was all so "cool." Tibetan boyfriends were usually ready and willing to do whatever the women wanted, whenever they wanted, as long as they paid all expenses. How could girls resist flings with men so exotic, so cooperative, and so available? It was so much more fun than being with guys back home. Unfortunately, some of the Tibetans, particularly those with poor English, fell head over heels for these women and believed, at least for a time, that the relationships had a future.

Some older women even behaved like predators. "You know that guy? He's hot. Can you introduce me to him?" a very attractive woman in her fifties asked me. The object of her lust was a really lovely person in his late twenties. I knew that he was looking for a serious relationship. I suggested that having an affair wasn't a good idea because she was leaving town in a few days, "What's wrong with sex?" she admonished me with a smile. "I am friends with these people. I won't be involved in something like that," I replied sanctimoniously. She made a humorous pouty face, "I want him!" She didn't get the object of her desire, but a lot of similar women succeeded with other men.

Not all of the women having flings were just in it for the sex. Many of the women enjoyed the company of the handsome young men. It felt good to feel more desirable than back home. Even in the streets and restaurants random Tibetans often made flirtatious eye contact. Finding lovers was easy. Some older women were very pragmatic. "It feels nice, even if it is meaningless," one told me.

Some of the women were essentially sex tourists. One in her twenties was quite amazing. Within several days of arriving, she had scored one of the hottest guys in town. They dated for a couple of weeks, and to all intents and purposes, it appeared that she was serious about the relationship. She and the Tibetan were glued together. But she left with a group of Western friends for a trip to Ladakh and returned about a month later with a Ladakhi boyfriend in tow. He, too, she treated like a boyfriend. Before she left town, we exchanged e-mail addresses. Weeks later, she bulk e-mailed me and all of her other friends pictures of her next conquest—a very attractive and muscular Sri Lankan.

Many of the sleaziest Salai gyals started innocently and with good intentions. Some fell deeply in love with their first foreign girlfriends, only to have their hearts broken when the women returned home and ended the relationships. Many of the foreign women were not entirely insincere: sometimes they wanted to return to India, marry the Tibetans, and bring them to their country, but once they got home, the idea seemed crazy or the complexity of the immigration process and the costs involved led them to reconsider their plans. Others were dissuaded by their families, and some simply got cold feet.

Some of the Tibetans became hardened by these realities. Honest and kind-hearted young men whom I found to be wonderful friends would often be ruthless and cold hearted in relationships, probably indicating severe emotional problems. Some would shed tears of genuine sorrow when they saw their girlfriends off at the bus, only to head straight back into town and begin looking for new women only minutes later. The same men would often e-mail the women who had left, sometimes daily, expressing their undying love and regularly asking for money. The women usually eventually found out if they were not the only ones. Some felt used and were devastated; others were simply disgusted.

Many of the hardcore Salai gyals had very confused notions of romantic love. Love was a never-ending topic of conversation, but their actions seldom fell within what would be defined as loving behavior towards women. Others claimed to be in love with women with whom enduring relationships were unlikely. I had an interesting conversation with Sherab, a newcomer who arrived as a teen. He was a regular Dharamsala visitor whom I have known for many years. He was well acquainted with the Salai gyal lifestyle and witnessed the poverty of many newcomers, "Some of them were sleeping in the jungle because they couldn't afford a room. They were so poor that they couldn't afford to eat." He went on, "What does love mean any way? Sometime people love someone because they help them. Maybe that is different from romantic love, but it doesn't mean that it isn't real love."

"I want to fall in love with a woman from Canada, America, Australia, or England," Tibetans would often tell me. Although it sounded rather calculating, English-speaking countries were naturally the most desirable, for the thought of having to learn yet another new language was a major worry. Canada was at or near the top of most people's lists, so a lot of Tibetans asked me if I could find them wives. Unfortunately, I wasn't successful.

Few Tibetan women dated foreign men, although many, in private, expressed interest in at least trying one out. Many people both Tibetan and Western told me that Tibetan women were very conservative when it came to sex, but that was not my experience. Conversations with newcomer and settler women were often bawdy, but only in private. Tibetan women, of course, had no trouble finding Tibetan boyfriends and husbands, and there seemed to be more pressure on them to conform. Over the years, I met only a handful who married foreigners. Some argued that given the shortages, they should marry Tibetan men, but that seemed rather dehumanizing.

Huge numbers of Israeli tourists visit the area, but even back then when so many Tibetans were desperate, very few married them. On arrival, most Israelis made for Bhagsu, a picturesque village two kilometers up a dead-end road from McLeod Ganj, or Dharamkot, a rural village spread over the hill above Bhagsu. Most were fresh from serving their compulsory military service. Some were deeply traumatized. Many chose to lose themselves in a haze of marijuana smoke and look for peace and solace in the company, and often the arms, of their fellow former soldiers. The hippy drug scene that many Israelis enjoyed wasn't to the taste of most Tibetans. Military service also appeared to have made many Israelis aggressive, suspicious, and argumentative.

For those single Israeli girls who did join the rest of the tourists in McLeod Ganj, dating a Tibetan was definitely an option. I knew a number of Tibetans who dated Israelis; a few of them married and emigrated. Israel, though, was not a choice destination because Tibetans were well aware of the terrorist attacks, military conflicts, and tensions with its neighbors. Israeli women whom I met also spoke of racial discrimination against non-Jews in their homeland and therefore dissuaded their Tibetan boyfriends from the possibility of marriage.

Settling in India has never been a viable option for the vast majority of foreigners married to Tibetans. The R.C. (Registration Certificate) that Tibetans receive does not provide refugee status or pave the way to citizenship nor can their foreign spouses become permanent residents of India. Indian citizenship is extremely difficult for Tibetans to achieve, and in any event, newcomers do not meet the requirements.[12] Of the small number of foreign wives and husbands who do live in India, almost without exception, their Tibetan spouses have high-ranking positions or they themselves have specialized skills. The only options that I am aware of for long-term stays in India, other than marrying an Indian citizen, are business and student visas, both of which are temporary and must be renewed regularly. The only durable solution was to go abroad.

Chapter 10

Although I have heard plenty of gossip and imaginary statistics quoted, how Tibetan marriages to foreigners really fare is little known. It is often presumed, especially in India, that Tibetans marry foreigners only for personal gain, but in my experience many who dated and married foreigners were entirely sincere. Over the years, I have kept in contact with almost all of the couples that I met in 2003 and since then. Over half of the marriages have been successful—some extremely so. This may seem an abysmal success rate, but according to the Canadian census, four out of ten first marriages in Canada end in divorce,[1] and typical Canadians do not have to face the culture shock that Tibetan émigrés do.

There was more to surviving as a couple once the Tibetan emigrated abroad than just maintaining a healthy relationship. At that time, culture shock was much worse than it is now. Most Tibetans that I knew in 2003 had never used a bank machine, driven a car, operated a washing machine, taken a subway, knew what street signs were, or even owned a phone, and very little authentic foreign food was available in McLeod Ganj. When they arrived in the West, they felt like children. Even a visit to a restaurant was an exercise in humiliation, with menus full of unknown foods and drinks and men's and women's toilets, often with confusing signs—"Dudes" and "Dudettes" or "Buck" and "Doe." Even the international symbol for "women's toilet" could create confusion for it resembles a man in a chuba (traditional cloak). My husband got lost the first time that he visited the tiny shopping mall where we lived because once inside, he completely lost all sense of direction.

In India, even if Tibetans were poor, they were the experts on the culture and customs: they translated, they gave directions, and provided advice. My ex-husband spoke of what it was like for him in Canada at first, "I didn't know how to do anything. You were always telling me what to do. I felt like you were always bossing me around and trying to control me. I knew that you had to teach me how to live here, but I hated it." He spent the better part of two years depressed and seemingly always in a foul mood, but slowly his spirits improved. Feeling like an equal was a big part of his transformation. He became an extremely talented and well-paid carpenter, got his driver's license and a credit card, and learned thousands of new words that he needed to thrive in his new world. He memorized the entire citizenship textbook and would often explain Canadian history to those born in Canada.

"Where are you taking me?" he had asked in despair as the Greyhound bus drove through forested mountains for hours, following our arrival in Vancouver with its small but vibrant Tibetan community. Although he, like others who lived in areas with no Tibetans, was later delighted by his relatively swift integration into Canadian society, he initially felt completely lost without Tibetan friends. But slowly he befriended many Canadians. Even rednecks – poorly-educated, narrow-minded white trash who tend to be racist – loved him. They eyed him suspiciously, for he was a slant-eyed foreigner with long hair and a funny accent. "How's it going eh?" he would say in his best Canadian slang and then launch into a conversation about something dear to their hearts such as ice hockey scores or the merits of some particular power tool. Later, after he mastered English, he watched documentary films and memorized information obsessively; Alexander the Great and Genghis Khan became two of his favorite subjects.

In the West, most people have little interest in Tibet or understanding of what it means to be a refugee. In India it had been easy; Tibetans could endlessly make friends with foreigners on the sole basis of their country of origin. Tourists and visitors were fascinated with refugee stories. They had gone to India because they wanted to experience the exotic and unknown or because of knowledge of or interest in Tibetan culture. In the West, most people were more interested in talking about things that they already understood. Friendships in the new country were long-term. The foreigners weren't just passing through town; they lived up the street. The novelty of long hair and the story of escape from Tibet got old after a week. The average person just saw a Tibetan as another Asian immigrant—nothing special. Those who did have some idea often thought that Tibetans were all extremely religious. "I'd love to meditate with you some time," was one of the first invitations to friendship that my husband received—the closest that I had ever seen him come to meditation was a really bad hangover. Most women weren't flirting and fawning. "So what do you do for a living?" everyone wanted to know. The adjustment was difficult.

Eventually, my husband and I separated. In India, he had suffered from a serious inferiority complex and possibly from PTSD, which, among other things, manifested itself in dramatic mood swings and severe headaches. In Canada, he was better, but spent much of the first two years lying on the couch in a sullen depression when he wasn't at work, and he drank too much. By the time he became easy to get along with and self-confident, it was too late for our marriage. He apologized many times for his past behavior, but whatever we had had was gone. We lived apart for a number of years, hoping that our relationship could be salvaged. He was one of my best friends, earning more than I did. It would have been easier for us to get back together, but instead I asked for a divorce. He was reluctant, but finally agreed. I never felt that our marriage was a mistake; I respect him in many ways, and my relationship with him has given me a life that I could never have imagined. I remain friends with him and especially his family.

In 2003, newcomers in Dharamsala were mostly unconcerned about the difficulties of adjusting to life abroad. They had little real idea of what life was like in the West, but they were certain that their situation would be better than it was in India. In those days, when Tibetans left and went abroad, communications between friends back in India slowed to a trickle. Phone calls to the West cost ten rupees (about twenty five cents) a minute and calls from the West to India were usually even more expensive, so friends rarely if ever spoke on the phone. Internet cafes were plentiful, but most newcomers could not read or write English well enough to communicate effectively, and Tibetan and Chinese fonts were not readily available, so e-mails and chat messages usually stated only that the person abroad was well and happy and often included photos of him with an expensive new car—

typically not his own—or with a backdrop of a modern city skyline. It looked like paradise. Throughout 2003, I do not recall anyone receiving messages from Tibetans abroad that stated that they were deeply unhappy, although some did mention that they were lonely. Tibetans abroad later told me that they didn't like to complain about their good fortune of being in a free country with opportunities, and they didn't want their friends in India to worry about them.

Although most newcomers wanted to leave India for a more promising life, the thought of what that would mean was a source of stress. Many worried about being isolated from their countrymen and cultures. Parting with their friends, who had been their only dependable source of support of any kind since they had escaped into exile, filled many with anxiety, even if they didn't often show or discuss it. One rare incident does come to mind.

On Amdo Losar, a party was held at my friend Tsering's restaurant; I stayed very late and staggered home like a newborn giraffe learning to walk. When I awoke near noon, I discovered that my husband hadn't come home. I had coffee and then headed back to the restaurant. As I climbed the stairs, I could hear heart-wrenching sobbing. My heart raced. Upstairs, I found my husband and several of his closest friends, their bodies shaking as they wept in despair, hugging each other. They were obviously very drunk. "We are crying because we love each other. Soon we will be gone to different countries. We might never see each other again," my husband explained as he cried. His face was red and his eyes were almost swollen shut. Later, I practically carried him home. He passed-out with his face hanging over a laundry bucket, vomiting onto his long hair.

Most of the time, newcomers were more concerned about having a viable future than imagining what it would really mean to leave. They knew that acquiring English-language skills was imperative to their success both within India and abroad. A small number could earn a living working entirely in the Tibetan language, but they could usually only rise so far in their careers if they could not communicate effectively in English. Except for the fortunate few who were able to find Tibetan wives, learning English was essential to dating, marriage, and, for those who hoped to go abroad, their lives in new countries.

Tourists and volunteers were sometimes puzzled that Tibetans, including monks and nuns, were studying English or saw such studies as frivolous. Some thought that Tibetans' time would be better served by studying Hindi. Although Hindi is the official language of India, the 2001 census recorded 122 languages with more than 10,000 speakers.[2] Needless to say, in many parts of India, Hindi is not the mother tongue. As a result of this diversity, English has become the de facto common language. Without knowledge of English, travelling throughout India and completing simple business transactions such as shopping are difficult and using devices such as computers is almost impossible.

As a result, the demand for English instruction is huge, and fortunately many volunteers gladly oblige. McLeod Ganj is arguably one of the easiest towns in India for foreign visitors to live comfortably in thanks to it is small size and the large number of furnished rooms that visitors can rent by the night or month, many complete with small kitchens. In 2003, facilities for tourists were more rudimentary than they are now, but there was a Japanese restaurant, an Italian restaurant, and several places that specialized in pizza. Dozens of restaurants ranging from the small and grubby to the more elegant and pricy served up pancakes and omelets along with Tibetan or Indian fare. Guide books seldom failed to mention the numerous bakeries and cake shops. There were yoga studios and Buddhism classes. At almost 2000 metres above sea level, the climate is moderate, and the views of the mountains spectacular. The streets were full of potholes and collapsing in some places, but that kept speeding to a minimum. The colorful inhabitants distracted the eye from the open sewers and the garbage-strewn streets and hillsides. Tibetans are not usually aggressive sales people, and unlike in other tourist destinations where visitors were harassed endlessly, the Indian and Kashmiri shopkeepers mostly adopted their more laid-back sales techniques. The cost of living was a fraction of that in the West. Volunteers flocked to McLeod Ganj. Many tourists were so enamored with the place that rather than moving on, they lingered and often took up volunteering.

Some organizations required skilled volunteers, but most were looking for English teachers and conversation partners, no qualifications necessary. Even though some of the schools did not have great curricula and some volunteers told me that they did not feel that they were good teachers, countless newcomers transformed their lives through the language skills that they acquired. Years later, former students spoke of their teachers by name and with gratitude.

Most newcomers were not nearly as slick as their detractors believed. There were always a few who would boldly strike up a conversation with anyone and flirt shamelessly, but the rest struggled with meeting women. English-language classes were good places to meet women in a more natural and less high-pressure environment than restaurants or the streets. Except during winter, there were almost always dozens of female foreign volunteers in town, and there were newcomer women in the classes, some of whom were single.

One evening, I was sitting around drinking tea with a group of rather proper intellectual friends. A young Tibetan complained about his lack of success finding a girlfriend. "Why don't you sign up for English classes?" a serious-minded foreign resident suggested, "It's almost like joining a dating club." The Tibetans all agreed and encouraged their friend to follow her advice. The young man seemed unconvinced. Dharamsala's version of speed dating didn't seem to fit his romantic vision. Unlike him, an intellectual friend who spent most university holidays in McLeod Ganj sometimes had a new "teacher" within days of arriving; not surprisingly, his language skills were impressive. He was always up front with the women— a serious relationship was unlikely given his commitment to his education. He made light of the rejection that he faced from most settlement Tibetan girls as a consequence of not disguising his identity as a newcomer, which he could have done. "No need to bother with those Tibetan girls. My great teachers don't care who I am and where I am from," he joked.

For a short time, I was coerced into teaching an English class. I had a horror of speaking in front of groups and no talent for teaching whatsoever. To compound my misery, the students in my class ranged from absolute beginners to the relatively advanced; fortunately, for most volunteers, my situation was not typical. I muddled my way through for several weeks, although I sometimes stayed home claiming to be sick. I couldn't handle standing in front of the class sweating with fear—my mind drawing a complete blank—as more than two dozen students stared at me expectantly. Thankfully, an enthusiastic and skilled pair of Europeans arrived and took over my duties.

Instead, I decided to devote most evenings to tutoring people who had jobs and couldn't attend formal classes. One of my favorite students was the famous poet from Tibet who worked as a dishwasher. Despite his renowned abilities in his own language, he struggled to learn English. He made me feel less of an idiot, although I was worse, struggling to memorize the Tibetan alphabet. At that time, I had yet to master the basics of teaching English, so I was in many ways a liability and a waste of his time. English class consisted of the two of us attempting to have intellectual discussions with the aid of Tibetan-English and English-Tibetan dictionaries.

I soon realized that he was terrified of speaking, so rather than pushing him to talk, we communicated by writing on pieces of paper. His spoken English was limited to several words, usually reserved for saying, "no, no, no" when a definition in one of the notoriously unreliable dictionaries was wrong. I wrote down questions, usually about Tibetan history, geography, or politics, and he wrote down the reply. He was very poor and doubtlessly suffered from malnutrition, so I would sometimes order an entire chicken chili from Mountview restaurant and we would gorge ourselves in secret.

I also tutored the mother of a small baby who worked at a preschool. Part of our lessons involved her keeping a diary in English. It was depressing but illuminating to read of her life. She lived in our building, where water seepage and mold were huge problems. Her baby was often ill with colds and fevers. She documented her life of working, cooking, cleaning, and looking after the baby. I knew her young husband. He drank too much and devoted more than a reasonable amount of time to polishing his motorcycle and playing cards. Fortunately, she was later able to take over a successful business. Many of her customers were tourists, so her language skills paid off.

Another supposed student was a brilliant young man with exceptional abilities in English. Class consisted of my attempting to help him with a book that he was being paid to translate. Unfortunately, the book concerned Buddhist philosophy, and the writing was poetic and rather abstract. He was very popular, so he was constantly inundated with Tibetan visitors. English class became my dropping by to drink tea and hear the latest news and gossip from the Tibetan world or discuss social issues, history, and politics, as he translated. Eventually, we gave up the charade of pretending to conduct English lessons.

Chapter 11

By the late fall of 2003, I had virtually stopped hanging around with foreigners. I had little in common with most of them, and they were just passing through, so, although I was hopeless at Tibetan, I found that I enjoyed hanging out with my Tibetan friends a lot more. Despite the language barrier, I came to know people well, almost completely forgetting that many of them didn't speak English so seamless was the translation of our friends. Our lack of a common language became apparent only when we ran into one another in the street and were reduced to grinning stupidly in lieu of conversation.

One of my so-called students, Rinchen, had a small dark room that I soon nicknamed "The Walk in Cooler" because it was miserably cold in the winter. There, we sat around during the evenings clutching hot glasses of tea to try to keep our hands warm, discussing social issues and politics or telling stories and jokes. There was no heating in most apartments in Dharamsala, and Rinchen's was especially glacial as it was on the ground floor in a particularly congested part of town. The sun never shone on his room, so the concrete never warmed.

Eventually, we often broke down and sought another means of warmth. Only a few metres away lived a man we nicknamed "Dr. Whiskey." Dr. Whiskey was a very young Tibetan doctor; in the summer he made his living treating Western patients, but, as Tibetans preferred to visit more experienced practitioners of traditional medicine, in the winter he didn't have enough business to get by, so he doubled as a bootlegger. Rinchen had a fairly good income, and I had some money. Although most of our friends had jobs, they were usually broke, so Rinchen and I took turns buying bottles. The whiskey drove the chill from our bones and lubricated the conversations. Often, up to a dozen of us were crowded into Rinchen's small room.

Although newcomers had a reputation as drinkers, many did not drink or drank very little; among them were some who wore ordinary clothes but were still, essentially, monks. Several had long hair and looked like stylish party boys, but, though they had left their monasteries, they had not yet stopped keeping their core vows and were more monk-like than many of the red-robed monks in town—they wouldn't even make eye contact or say "Hello" to me. Most were transitioning to becoming full-fledged laymen but had not become interested in drinking, smoking, or girl chasing. One, Zonthar Gyal, could pick up any musical instrument and play it well. He never missed a party and joined the rest of us even when we carried on into the wee hours. He never touched a drop of alcohol; instead, he drank tea and sometimes entertained us by playing a mandolin or harmonica. Rinchen was good at collecting interesting friends and keeping away those who were bad drinkers or annoying. My husband and I ended up there almost every evening, and for a time, there was a party almost every night.

Unfortunately, all good things come to an end. Several days before Losar, when Dr Whiskey's business was at its peak, I was walking down Bhagsu Road when I came upon a sad sight. Dr. Whiskey was sitting in a police truck, and a number of police officers were carrying boxes of beer and whiskey out of his apartment. We all felt terrible, for as his best customers we had been contributors to his demise. Luckily, the notoriously corrupt and drunken police must have been pleased with their windfall of free booze—Dr. Whiskey was released several days later without having been charged. Dr. Whisky left the trade after that, and we resumed buying—albeit less frequently—from the official liquor shops.

That winter as I hung out at Rinchen's, I became more aware of the complexity and diversity of the newcomer world. Many in our crowd were intellectuals and some were ex-politicals. (Tibetans use the term ex-political to describe those forced to flee Tibet because of activism, regardless of whether or not they had been arrested or imprisoned. Some, for example, had been hunted by the police for demonstrating but managed to escape.) I learned many things about life in Tibet, the country's history, and the struggles of Tibetans, but perhaps the most valuable lesson of all was that human beings are capable of great resilience and humor even in the face of tragedy and suffering. This forced me to examine how I reacted to events in my own life; as a consequence, I became more resilient. Some friends had been through horrible experiences and continued to suffer the results, yet they didn't lose themselves to despair. What I remember most was the laughter.

Many, including those who were skilled at working with computers and other technologies, had grown up in nomad areas and villages where there was no electricity. One night, someone mentioned that he hadn't seen a T.V. until he was seventeen. Teasing is a big part of Tibetan culture, so his friends all roared with laughter and began calling him the Tibetan equivalent of a hillbilly. One, who was teasing him the most, suddenly stopped and said, "Oh! I didn't see a T.V. until I was seventeen either!" Soon they were all laughing as they discovered that not one of them had seen a T.V. before he was fourteen.

Lhalung Dhondup then told the story of how his family in Tibet got a T.V. Lhalung Dhondup's dad believed that T.V. was full of garbage and Chinese propaganda. His kids agreed, but they wanted one anyway, so Lhalung Dhondup and his brother conspired. Lhalung Dhondup was only around twenty years old, but he was a monk and very respected by his father for his intellectual abilities and his often dangerous political activism, so when the brothers bought a T.V., Lhalung Dhondup carried it into their home. They connected the D.V.D. player. Their father was seething with anger, but he didn't do anything. Lhalung Dhondup turned on the machines and popped a disk into the D.V.D. player. It was a video of the Dalai Lama. Lhalung Dhondup's father immediately began prostrating before the T.V. He let the machines stay.

Tibetans often use nicknames—some of which are humorous—because Tibetan names tend to be repetitive. I've met dozens of Tenzins, Jamyangs, Tashis, Kalsangs, etc. Most Tibetans do not consider it rude to point out obvious physical characteristics, so nicknames often reflect them, sometimes in exaggerated forms. One friend was nicknamed Popo (Grandfather in Lhasa dialect) because he was prematurely graying. There was a Na (Nose), a Gortuk (Thick Head), and worst of all—to my Western sensibilities—an Amnye (Grandfather in Amdo dialect), a young man so nicknamed because he was balding and wore a bridge—the Chinese had smashed his teeth when they tortured him. After a time, I became accustomed to this sort of moniker, so when I later met men referred to as Gyakpa (Fat), and Naytso (Parrot), I adopted them with relative comfort, although it might have helped that they were in a foreign language. Using people's real names could be frustrating. It might take ten minutes of conversation to figure out, for example, which Tenzin someone was referring to. The problem was worst among those born in India because it is considered auspicious to have your baby named by the Dalai Lama, and every name thus obtained consists of the name "Tenzin," the Dalai Lama's first name, followed by a second name. Although most people go by the second name, you still meet an extraordinary number of Tenzins. To complicate matters, some Tibetans do not have two names, so on their identifications, their first name is repeated. I actually have a friend whose legal name is Tenzin Tenzin.

We had another friend whom my husband and I nicknamed "Undercover Brother" after a character in a movie because his curly hair was combed into an afro. Undercover Brother had a great sense of style. Along with his crazy hair, he wore a Bob Marley t-shirt and stylish necklaces. Many people probably assumed incorrectly from his appearance that he was a Salai gyal, but he was in fact an ex-political who had only recently stopped being a monk. As Rinchen said so well, "His only vice is bubble gum." Among our group of friends, Undercover Brother was one of the most acclaimed for his cooking skills.

I was often told that ex-monks made the best husbands. In the monasteries, they had learned traditional women's work: cooking and cleaning. Some people said that marrying an ex-monk was considered unlucky. Certainly, it is completely unacceptable to go after monks or nuns, although, in India, if they disrobe of their own accord, they don't seem to have any more difficulty finding partners than anyone else. The great thing about having so many friends who were ex-monks was that dinner parties were popular among our group; wonderful feasts were created even from simple ingredients. However, it is best not to make assumptions, for despite their reputations, some of the most dreadful meals that I have ever eaten were made by ex-monks, many of whom were hopeless and lazy housekeepers.

Momos (steamed dumplings usually filled with meat) are arguably the most popular Tibetan meal. Many refugees, however, could afford to make them only a couple of times a year. We were very fortunate that we were "rich," so we were able to make them fairly often. Since momos were labor intensive to make, dozens of them were usually prepared at once. No one I knew had a refrigerator, but I never got sick from eating leftovers that were sometimes more than a day or two old.

Another favorite meal was hogo—a type of Chinese-style hot pot. Hogo required a lot of ingredients; it was, therefore, expensive and best prepared by and enjoyed with a big group. During the coldest weeks of winter, we made it often. Meats and vegetables were washed and cut into bite-sized pieces, and then piled on every plate we owned. The two-burner gas stove was placed in the middle of the table, and a spicy broth was created in a large pot. My friend Lhamo Sham's husband, an ex-monk, made the tastiest broth with a multitude of herbs and spices. A big pot of rice was prepared and a dipping sauce was created with garlic, oil, salt, and the key ingredient– MSG.

As the big pot of broth boiled and friends filled the room, the temperature warmed considerably. It sometimes dropped to 1 C indoors during the winter, so this truly was wonderful. We always sat around the table for hours—sometimes late into the night—tossing meat and vegetables into the pot and fishing them out with chop sticks, then dipping the tasty morsels in our little bowls of sauce; I developed a life-long love of MSG that winter. As the steam from the pot and the heat of our bodies warmed the room, we were able to remove our heavy winter coats.

For Christmas, I planned a party, together with Olivia, the Western girlfriend of one of our friends; she was only eighteen but smart and mature. (They later married. Eight years later, she is a lawyer and, thanks to the support of her parents, he, too, was able to earn a university degree and has a good job at a school. They go on more exotic international holidays than anyone I know.) People in

Dharamsala are mostly under the impression that at Christmas, Westerners go to church and then go to the bar and get drunk because that is what most tourists do. Although we couldn't host a truly traditional Christmas, we wanted to do something special. We decided to serve Tibetan and Chinese food and introduce our Tibetan friends to a gift "stealing" game. My small son took charge of decorating; he collected evergreen branches, creating a small Christmas tree in a pot, complete with hand-made decorations, and he cut snowflakes from paper and hung them around the room and on the windows.

Olivia and I pooled our funds and bought what we hoped were useful gifts—one for each guest. After our friends arrived and the game started, initially, the Tibetans refused to steal each other's presents. Instead, they chose one, opened it, and said, "Thank you." I was feeling rather worried that the game was doomed to failure until one friend opened a present containing a large package of Gold Flake cigarettes and the next received a pair of plates. With a cheeky grin, the plates were exchanged for the cigarettes and the game was on.

Some of the Tibetans had either dreaded or been excited by the idea of participating in Christmas religious rituals, but we completely disappointed them in that regard. They had to make do with a smorgasbord of Tibetan-style Chinese food—there were neither turkeys nor home ovens in Dharamsala. Undercover Brother was the chef because Olivia and I feared that we lacked the ability to impress with our culinary skills. Long after midnight, our guests left with their stomachs full and smiles on their faces. I had never imagined that one of my happiest Christmases would be spent on the other side of the world from "home" with a room full of Buddhists.

Little over a week later, it was my son's birthday. Birthdays are not traditionally celebrated by Tibetans. Instead, they become one year older on the first day of Losar. Still, many, including young adults, like the novelty of hosting a birthday party if they can afford to; in India, the one whose birthday it is pays for everything. Our friends were excited to hear that my son would be celebrating his birthday, so I knew that I had to plan something more elaborate than was usual for a ten-year-old in Canada.

I invited his child friends over to play and have lunch before heading to the main event. We had met a little girl around his age who had just arrived alone from Tibet: although she was easily distracted, her face often bore a wistful expression, so I invited her as well as his close friends. I mentally prepared myself for a great deal of mess and noise created by five children, four of whom spoke little or no English. My son had a lot of toys that we had brought from Canada. The Tibetan kids instantly mastered Lego and constructed houses and cars, painted pictures, and played with his miniature cooking set. They removed every toy from his trunk, playing with them all. I was happy to see the kids enjoying themselves so much, but I dreaded cleaning up the mess. When it was time to leave, a surprising thing happened; without being asked, they carefully packed all of the toys back into their respective boxes and containers and neatly organized them in his metal trunk.

Because there were so many adults interested in attending my son's birthday party, I had arranged a buffet dinner at Tsering's restaurant. Soon, the room was packed with almost two dozen people. As they arrived, they placed their gifts in front of him until he almost disappeared behind a pile of presents. As he began opening them, I felt overwhelmed by the generosity and sacrifice of our friends. For almost everyone present, their gifts represented several days' wages, sometimes more. There were toy cars, a small train set, a soccer ball, and so many others that they almost filled an entire suitcase when we returned to Canada several months later. Many guests suffered from obvious under nutrition and had scant possessions. All that we could do was smile and say "thank-you."

Every Sunday, a dozen or so Amdo guys got together and played football or sometimes basketball. Early in the morning, they would head to lower Dharamsala or Upper T.C.V. and not return until after dark. Many were intellectuals in their mid to late twenties who had been monks—not all of them were what one would describe as "sporty." Nonetheless, they put all of their efforts into playing the best games possible. Most owned only one pair of ill-fitting dress shoes or cheap sneakers, so broken toenails, pulled muscles, and other injuries were common. It didn't help that the sports fields were mostly gravel.

Most of the players worked, so they were able to practice only once a week. Still, over the course of many months, their skills improved, and they concocted a plan to play in the Tibetan National Football Championships. They knew that they couldn't possibly win; the rest of the teams were composed of players who were younger and fitter and had been educated in exile schools where sports were part of the curricula. Their only hope was not to disgrace themselves. I contacted my sister's former husband who had been passionate about "footy" during his youth in Australia. He and his mother immediately agreed to put up the money for uniforms and shoes for the team.

One team member had a motorcycle, so he and another player set off and scoured the Kangra valley for matching uniforms, socks, and shoes. Once the uniforms had been assembled, the pressure was on. A meeting convened at Tenzin's restaurant, and a serious discussion ensued. The original plan had been that the team would be comprised of only those who participated every Sunday. They played with passion, but some were quite dreadful, doomed to cause the team to lose. "The settler Tibetans will say that we suck because we are newcomers," they explained to me. They decided to recruit several newcomers who had played football at schools in Tibet and a player's younger brother who had been a goalkeeper at a T.C.V. school. The very worst athletes would only play for a short time during the match, but everyone would participate.

From then on, the group met as often as they could to practice drills, even at night. When the big day came, we all walked up to T.C.V. The match was a preliminary one, but the crowd was still large. They felt that the dignity of newcomers rested on their abilities, so everyone was apprehensive; their chances of winning were slim to none. What they lacked in experience, they made up for in guts and determination, but as the game wore on, I could see that the players were becoming exhausted. Even my usually optimistic husband was grave. Rinchen had taken on the role of coach; from the moment the game started, he exuded stress and concern. By the end, he was sweating and lighting cigarettes one after another. Despite all, the players did not give up but fought on to the bitter end and miraculously managed to win by one point.

It was as if they had won the championship. The team and their many supporters in the crowd were jumping up and down and cheering. The goalkeeper was carried through the air. The now rejuvenated group practically floated down the hill back to McLeod Ganj and celebrated with endless bowls of thanthuk (handmade noodle soup) and as many piping hot tingmos (steamed buns) as anyone could eat at Tsering's restaurant. Several bottles of whiskey were produced, and toasts were made. Even though, as expected, they lost their second match several days later, they still felt like winners.

Finding a job or a wife or winning a football match is not the biggest concern of many newcomers. What most people do not realize is that Tibetans are not protected as refugees in India. India is not a signatory to the United Nations Refugee Convention, meaning that India creates its own rules for dealing with refugees.[1] Tibetan refugees in India are not entitled to the same status that they would enjoy in any of the 144 countries in the world that are signatories to the convention. In some cases, this distinction is meaningless since it must certainly be much less unpleasant to be a refugee in India than in, say, Kenya, which is a signatory. Details of discussions between the exile government and the Government of India are kept from the public, but what is known is that newcomers do not enjoy the same privileges as the settlement Tibetans. They are expected to return to Tibet.

The Government of India Bureau of Immigration website lays out the somewhat baffling rules that apply to Tibetans. Essentially, the system is two-tiered. Tibetans who arrived in India in 1959 and those who were born in India are allowed to stay—presumably indefinitely. They receive a Registration Certificate (R.C.), which must be renewed periodically. Most newcomers who arrived prior to 1994 received R.C.'s as well. In September of 2011, the Tibet Justice Center released a groundbreaking, comprehensive report which was often quoted, but it seems that certain sections were either ignored, not comprehended, or went unread: "Beginning in the early 1990s, however, the C.T.A.

(Tibetan exile government) and the Indian Government abandoned the policy of absorbing the new arrivals into the existing Tibetan communities and instead adopted a policy of voluntary repatriation."[2] This is a polite way of saying that newcomers are essentially forced to return to Tibet by being denied the documents that they need to remain in India.

Most people I know who, in the past, managed to get R.C.'s paid huge bribes and went through great trouble to obtain them, but many others were unable to do so. In 1998, a volunteer who had spent six months at Tibetan Transit School was disturbed by the discovery that many of her students would not get R.C.'s and "would undoubtedly be tortured or even killed" on their return to Tibet. She heard the same plea that I so often did, "Is there no country where we can be free?"[3]

In 2003, the situation became even worse; newcomers who fled Tibet were essentially given the choice of declaring themselves as either students or pilgrims and were admitted into India via Special Entry Permits (SEP's).[4] Unless they were monks or nuns who would study in monasteries or nunneries, adults—I could not find the age limit but it seemed to be anyone over the age of twenty five—were given permission to visit only on pilgrimages, so they could remain in India for only one to three months, and buying R.C.'s soon became impossible. As I read the report from the Tibet Justice Center, I learned that even most former political prisoners and victims of torture had been classified as "pilgrims" and "students." Dozens of newcomers whom I spoke to over the years told me that they felt utterly betrayed by the exile government when they discovered that they could not legally remain in India. Many had no intention of returning to Tibet. Most had not even fully understood the implications of the documents that they had been forced to sign following their escapes.

The official line from the exile government was that newcomers should go back to informally teach people in Tibet their country's true history.[5] Samdhong Rinpoche, the prime minister of the exile government from 2000 to 2010, stated that he did not want refugees going abroad: "This is very bad for the Tibetan community and it will affect adversely the Tibet movement. Inside Tibet there is genocide, there is enforced birth control and enforced intermarriage. So to protect a pure Tibetan race is also one of the challenges which the nation is facing."[6] Rather than being seen as refugees or human beings who might wish to make their own choices, they seemed to be considered as little more than tools and breeding animals to be sacrificed for the cause. Rules were changed to prevent Tibetans who arrived on SEP's from reuniting with their families abroad.[7] Who was responsible for the changes is unclear, but what is abundantly clear is that Samdhong Rinpoche's exile government did not object publically, and no one asked human rights groups based outside the country to raise objections if there were concerns of offending India. The newcomers were betrayed by their own people.

Of course when it was still possible to buy R.C.'s, many newcomers refused to co-operate with their imposed destiny and stayed in India, some of them hoping to find a way to the West. The Tibet Justice Center reported exactly what I observed and what my friends and acquaintances without documents experienced:

Tibetans residing in India without R.C.s live in a state of fear and insecurity. They must keep a low profile and avoid contact with the Indian authorities. Many do not travel outside their communities or remain outside after dusk. Tibetans without R.C.s also find it difficult to secure housing because landlords, guesthouses, and hotels alike tend to require the production of evidence of legal status. Many Tibetans without R.C.s therefore move in with friends or family in very overcrowded accommodations. Tibetans without RCs also cannot open bank accounts and have trouble finding employment because most businesses, including those run by the C.T.A., condition employment on possession of an R.C. Finally, Tibetans without R.C.'s face difficulties obtaining benefits or services, including education and medical treatment that the C.T.A. often supplies to Tibetans with R.C.'s.[8]

Once it was no longer possible to obtain proper R.C.'s, few newcomers lasted long in India once they finished school. By 2010, it was almost impossible to find recently arrived newcomers who had completed their educations and stayed on. Monks who decided to disrobe were also no longer eligible to remain in India. Many newcomers would have returned to Tibet regardless, but others desperately wanted to stay. For them, there was no mercy. (At the time of writing, the shameful policies continue.)

Untold millions of dollars have been raised by various parties through highlighting human rights violations in Tibet and publicizing the escape of Tibetans; in a sane world, there would be a move to find them somewhere to go if India won't accept them, but I am unaware of any countries being asked to accept newcomers as refugees over the past decades, although Australia does take a group of ex-politicals each year. Of the tens of thousands who returned to Tibet, it is unknown how many died enroute or were arrested and tortured on their return or how many of the women were raped. No human rights organizations publicize their plight. No petitions have been drawn on their behalf. The almost two decades of silence from Tibetan organizations speaks volumes about the status of newcomers in exile.

Most settlement Tibetans whom I spoke to made light of the newcomers return to Tibet. "They can study here and then they should go back," I was often told. The people telling me this spoke in a dismissive tone as if going back to Tibet were no more arduous than a shopping trip to Delhi. Usually, the speakers had soft, smooth, pale skin and didn't look as though they had ever carried anything heavier than a parasol to ward off the sun or a shopping bag. It was difficult to imagine them walking to Triund, the ridge above the McLeod Ganj, let alone surviving the month-long trek back to Tibet though the Himalayas with all of their food and possessions on their backs or surrendering themselves to Chinese authorities as some newcomers did. It was impossible to imagine them coping well under torture, although it might have jolted some sense into them. They reminded me of mindless sheep when they bleated, "They should go baaack."

I knew a number of people who went back but seldom heard from or of them again. Contacting the outside world could be dangerous once they returned to Tibet—if they survived the journey. Several friends went back around 2006. They had never been involved in political activities during their time in India, but on their return to Tibet, they were arrested and tortured. The Chinese hoped to extract any useful information that they could, so torture was standard fare. People were sometimes very afraid to go, and some were never heard from by anyone again. They may have died on the journey or in prison.

I had direct contact with only one person after he had walked back. His reason for returning was rather unusual. He left school in India to follow a girlfriend back to Tibet—she had somehow come to study in India on a Chinese passport. They were in love, and they had a plan. She would take the bus back, and he would walk. They would reunite in Tibet and get married. He would attend university.

His Tibetan friends and I implored him not to go, but he was in his late teens and thought that he knew everything. He did extremely well in school and was very popular; he had never known failure. We all knew the fate that awaited him. When we told him that he would never be able to continue his studies in Tibet and that he would be arrested and tortured, he smirked at us knowingly, "Those are the unlucky people. I am a lucky boy. Anyway, I have never done anything political." No one could obtain his parents' phone number in Tibet or even knew if they had a phone. They were the only ones who could have stopped him. Even when we had respected elders from the community attempt to talk sense into him, he was unmoved. We were forced to see him off at the bus, dressed in his best clothes, his bag packed with his essays and poetry that he was so proud of. Even as he boarded, we implored him to change his mind, but he only smiled confidently.

No one heard from him for many months. Almost a year later, I ran into him on-line. As expected, he had been detained and tortured for months, "The Chinese beat me but I had nothing to tell them. They kept trying to get information from me, but I was just a student. I didn't know anything." All of his possessions had been taken from him—his precious writings destroyed. His girlfriend's family had refused their marriage. Who would want to marry their daughter to someone considered a criminal by the Chinese? He was unable to continue his education. I was glad to see him on the webcam. He was smartly dressed, looked healthy, and had most of his old confidence. Something had changed though; his attitude of invincibility was gone, "I'm so sorry," he told me. "I should have listened to you guys." I never contacted him again, for I didn't want him to get into trouble with the Chinese authorities who are suspicious of contact with the West.

At night in McLeod Ganj, the police, often stinking of alcohol, would roam around town asking Tibetans for their R.C.'s. If those without R.C.'s were caught, they usually had to pay bribes to be let go. The bribes were generally every rupee that they had in their pockets. If they didn't have money, they were usually manhandled. During an informal community meeting in 2007, Phayul reported: "According to some persons who spoke during the gathering, on failure to produce the book, which is not mandatory for Tibetans to carry it all the time, the officers would then beat them at their own discretion and would charge pecuniary fine or even in some cases they have reportedly snatched away cell phones too."[9] Sometimes, they were arrested and threatened with deportation.[10] One of my friends had been part of a group that was imprisoned for three months for failing to have an R.C.

One friend had an amusing yet pathetic story of extortion. One night, he was making his way home when he was confronted by a policeman who demanded to see his R.C., which he was, of course, not carrying on his person; R.C.'s are fragile booklets not conducive to longevity if carried in one's pocket. The policeman demanded a fine. My friend emptied his pockets in front of the officer, but being desperately poor, he had only ten rupees (about twenty-five cents). The policeman tried to take the note, but my friend held on. Keeping a firm grip on the money and making a sad face my friend said, "Chai?" A minor tug of war ensued between him and the policeman as he continued his plaintive plea, "Chai? Chai?" The policeman finally reached into his own pocket and produced a very dirty five rupee note which he exchanged for my friend's ten rupees. Five rupees was enough to buy a tea.

Many Tibetans that I knew had to run from the police regularly because they didn't have R.C.'s. Fortunately, they often got away, since they were usually faster and more athletic; at that time, the police seemed to come in two sizes: too skinny and too fat. Although unsympathetic critics said that newcomers could solve their problem by staying off the streets at night—the only time when police usually demanded R.C.'s—many worked in restaurants that stayed open late or had other good reasons—as if a good reason were needed—to be on the streets.

In 2003, a young couple that we knew held a party to celebrate their son's first birthday. They had invited almost 100 guests, so a team of young Tibetan volunteers helped with the cooking. The preparations began early in the morning and continued throughout the day. By the time that we arrived near dusk, a feast had been prepared and the hall decorated. The tiny celebrant was dressed in a silk chuba (traditional costume) and flanked by his parents. As guests arrived, they draped a white kata (ceremonial scarf) around the baby's shoulders and presented him with a gift or a decorative envelope containing money. As is custom, the presents were opened later at home.

Tea was served along with the large meal. Then the time came to sing songs. Tibetans grow up singing at social events, but I am a truly horrifying singer from a culture with no such tradition. Each guest sang a song in turn; when I knew that mine was approaching, I went and hid outside until the singing was over. Fortunately, everyone later became aware of my phobia of singing, and I became exempt from being asked. After the singing ended, the guests chatted and the children played until it was time to go home. When we left the party around 11 pm, the volunteers were still hard at work washing a mountain of dishes and cleaning up.

As a group of about six of us walked home on a deserted street, we were confronted by two policemen. "R.C.'s," they hissed and tried to block our path. We ignored them and pushed past pretending that we hadn't heard—only one person in the group had an R.C. Because they may have been put off by my presence, they did not follow us. We breathed a sigh of relief when we got home.

Some of the volunteers were not so lucky. Around 1:00 am, we were surprised to hear knocking at our door. Several of the volunteers entered, sweating and breathing heavily. The police had confronted them, but fortunately they had managed to get away—the police in hot pursuit. They had made for our place because it could be accessed by cutting across the pitch dark hillside, thereby avoiding the streets in town. It was a painful reminder to everyone present that even the most hardworking and community-minded newcomers were second-class refugees. What had been a lovely evening full of song and celebration was tainted.

After I had been in Dharamsala for a number of months and had become well-known in their community, newcomers would often bring foreign visitors to me who they were hoping would help them financially for bribes to obtain R.C.'s. The foreigners were incredulous; some even thought that the Tibetans were lying, for as they understood it, Tibetans had been given refuge in India. I would carefully and patiently explain that this was not the case for most newcomers. I always urged the foreigners to pay for the documents if they could, explaining that they might literally save the Tibetans' lives. I'm sure that some of the foreigners thought that I was lying to help the Tibetans with a devious scam. I'd had trouble believing it myself when I first arrived.

Because people who didn't have R.C.'s didn't like to be on the streets at night, if they had to work late in restaurants, they often slept there. Employers generally understood this, and in any case, many staff, both Tibetan and Indian, slept in the restaurants since they didn't earn enough money to pay for a room. In 2003, most restaurant jobs didn't pay much more than eight hundred rupees a month (about twenty dollars). Even a tiny, dingy room cost five hundred rupees to rent. To put it further in perspective, a pair of shoes or a winter jacket cost four hundred rupees and a beer at McLlo Bar cost eighty rupees— not that they ever went there. It was best to sleep and eat in the restaurant where they worked. Once the restaurant closed, usually at

10 pm or later, mattresses were rolled out onto the floor and the staff slept. Often, by 6 am they were up and preparing the restaurant for the work day. If they didn't quit their jobs, their lives went on like that for months or even years on end.

Chapter 12

How could the problems have gone on for so long without being analyzed or addressed? The situation was so bizarre that, at times, I felt as though I must be hallucinating. As I devoted hundreds of hours to research, I looked for any commentary on the newcomers from those who knew them, studied them, reported on them, and were responsible for their well-being and safety. While researching Tibetan Transit School, I came across an article in *Outlook* magazine that was very illuminating regarding the opinion of Samdhong Rinpoche, the exile prime minister from 2001 to 2011. During that time, he was the most powerful Tibetan exile, second only to the Dalai Lama, whom he advised. While discussing problems between Tibetans and Indians in Dharamsala, he made the following statement:

> It's a major achievement that we've lived here for 50 years without any major incident. It's natural for small differences to crop up and the reason why more of this is happening now is that the old Tibetans who came in the 1960s were the true Tibetans, reared and imbued with genuine Tibetan cultural and social ethos. But the new arrivals, who began coming after 1988, are products of a harsh Chinese regime. They have known only violence and life under the red flag, and are intolerant. Under our own census, which we conducted in 2009, we have estimated that roughly 30 per cent of the population in Dharamsala comprises new arrivals.[1]

Before discussing violence and intolerance between Tibetans and Indians, it is important to first examine the black and white picture that Samdhong Rinpoche paints of Tibetan exile society. On investigation, his statements lack credibility on many fronts. Although no expert on Tibetan history, I have conducted research and engaged in conversations with those who are. No credible historian has ever described Tibetan society as the utopia of virtue described by Samdhong Rinpoche.

Although there was much to be admired in old Tibet, the accounts of visitors in the 19th and 20th centuries were riddled with as many observations of violence, dishonesty, and cruelty as they were with tales of compassion and tolerance. Old Tibet, particularly in the Lhasa region, had done its best to keep foreign visitors out, often imprisoning, torturing, and mutilating Tibetans who, even unknowingly, assisted them. Many of the ruling elite, including monks, were deeply suspicious of outside influence, closing schools that offered modern education and even going so far as banning the game of football. Just prior to the Chinese invasion of Lhasa, the great scholar and artist Gendun Choephel was flogged repeatedly and essentially lost his mind during his imprisonment on questionable charges. When the Tibetans fled into exile, the current Dalai Lama set about creating a modern and democratic society in the face of opposition from some influential Tibetans who wanted neither.

I came across a wonderfully articulate article written by Tenzin Sonam, a settler-Tibetan filmmaker and writer who had lived abroad and is one of a small minority of settlement Tibetans to have visited his homeland in recent years. His writing mirrored many of my thoughts to an uncanny degree:

> Our sense of self-importance and moral superiority was also shaped by the growing fascination of the West with Tibet and Tibetan Buddhism, and its expectation of what Tibetans were supposed to represent as a people. By this measure, we were an almost otherworldly race, spiritually evolved, naturally compassionate, peace-loving and with the good of all sentient beings always at heart. We began to take this idealised view of ourselves seriously, and remade our history in its image. The wars we had fought in the past with our neighbours, the factional infighting, the court intrigues and political assassinations, the system of cruel punishments sometimes meted out by the state, the banditry that was commonplace in many parts of the country, even the fact that many thousands of Tibetans had not so long ago taken up arms against the Chinese invasion—these were all airbrushed out in favour of a

reinterpretation of Tibet as a mythical Buddhist land of peace and harmony, governed by compassion and inhabited by the morally upright and ethically pure.[2]

Of course, the settler Tibetans were as much of a mixed-bag as the newcomers. The youths were just as prone to be aggressive and surly, even if they didn't actually fight as much. Many times, settlement Tibetans, both young and old, shoved in front of me in line-ups in shops or made rude or racist comments about foreigners thinking that I couldn't understand. Foreign friends had similar experiences. One overheard a mother telling her child, "If you don't behave, I will give you to the foreigner." On a number of occasions, drunken settler Tibetan youths, almost young enough to be my children, became sexually aggressive in the bar and were hard to get rid of, reminiscent of the obnoxious variety of unsophisticated Indian tourists common in the town. Of course, worst of all, to my mind, most of them were disrespectful and indifferent towards their own people who had fled Tibet.

Many problems were common to settler Tibetans and newcomers, as well as Indians. Most had little sense of social responsibility. Some owned child slaves and exploited their employees. Others spoke of local women as if they were whores if they drank a glass of wine or a beer, smoked a cigarette, or even went dancing. Stereotyping was endemic. After spending almost a year and a half in McLeod Ganj when he was a teenager, my son had greater and greater difficulty coping with the injustices. He practically had a meltdown shortly before we left for Canada, "I hate the way that people here treat each other. They are prejudiced against each other and foreigners. They are so sexist. I can't stand it anymore. I want to go home."

There seems to be a head-in-the-sand attitude towards social problems in exile. For example, domestic violence is a problem in Tibet and the newcomer community, as it is among those born in India. One day, I was talking to an American volunteer who had spent most of the past three years in the community. The topic of the Tibetan Women's Association came up, "They are out of touch with the problems of the women in Tibet and are in denial of the problems with domestic violence in the exile [settler] community. It is a serious problem, but there isn't even one women's shelter."

In 2011, a bizarre incident occurred in the very remote Tibetan exile settlement of Tenzinghang in Arunachal Pradesh, reminiscent of something from the Dark Ages or a backward village in Pakistan.[3] Horrible isolated events happen around the world in every society, so it would not be important to mention if it were not for the way that the situation was handled. A Tibetan woman, Choeyang, accused of having an affair and a child with a married man, was dragged into the street by the man's estranged wife, Kunsang, and her relatives. There she was stripped naked, had her long hair shorn short and black dye poured over her. Kunsang attempted to cut Choeyang's nose off with scissors but failed. Choeyang was then beaten so badly that the nurse who treated her stated: "She was beaten black and blue. I had to give her injection and I couldn't find a single spot which wasn't bruised and it got very difficult to inject her."[4] Choeyang remained bed-ridden for two weeks.

Despite investigation by the exile government and the TWA, Kunsang and her relatives—who demonstrated no remorse—were charged with no crime, although two of the men lost their jobs. One of them, Kunsang's brother—who, ironically, had two wives—was President of the Tibetan Freedom Movement (also referred to as President, Local Tibetan Assembly). Only one of the perpetrator's real names was published in the TWA report on the incident, understandable in a certain sense, as TWA endeavored to protect the victim.

In the course of the isolated settlement's justice process, which involved the perpetrator's paying for expensive religious rituals "to appease local deities upset with the incident, who might cause harm to the village," the husband somehow ended up agreeing to build his ex-wife—a woman who, from what is written about her in the TWA report, clearly belongs in a prison or a psychiatric institution—a house and pay her 5000 rupees a month until his retirement, at which point he would also give her half of his pension.

The Tibetan Women's Association then stepped in and appeared to have done its best to help the victim, but it had difficulty getting past the feudal mentality of the villagers and the local exile Tibetan administration. To complicate matters, there were no exile government policies to attempt to enforce. The police were not involved. TWA paid the victim's medical costs and offered to relocate her and even try to get her to Canada through the Tibetan Resettlement Project. The offers did not include her lover/soon-to be-husband, who is the father of her child, and were, not surprisingly, turned down. One wonders why he was not also offered assistance, as he was also a victim of his ex-wife's madness. Although the child was a result of an earlier affair with Choeyang, he and his wife had been separated for a year at the time of the assault. Members of the community involved clamored for punishment for adulterers and were upset at being embarrassed by media coverage, which, as is typical of controversial events in exile, was not reported on by any high-profile, English-language Tibetan media, but they were apparently unconcerned about such extreme violence being perpetrated against women in their community.

Despite campaigning for women's rights in Tibet, after sixty years in India, the exile Tibetans had no policies of their own. According to their report on the incident, the Tibetan Women's Association, which was formed in 1959, finally took action in this regard:

> The Kashag / Executive is requested to ensure the effective enforcement of the host country's laws and acts on dealing with any forms of violence against women. To this end, the Kashag / Executive is requested to provide a directive and a proper guideline to the settlement officers in India, Nepal and Bhutan, and the overseas representatives, on the effective implementation of the laws and acts protecting women's rights. This will bolster the confidence of women.[5]

Another incident involving exile women's rights occurred around the same time, but not in a remote village. A volunteer I met, who had been working on a large project for the Tibetan Institute of Performing Arts in McLeod Ganj, had discovered that adult female students were confined to their rooms after 7:30 pm and were expelled if they were known to have boyfriends. The volunteer said he was particularly disgusted because an administrator was "shacked up with a former student," and male students were allowed to do as they pleased. According to the volunteer, he was punched in the head by a member of the TIPA administration when he objected to the policy, pointed out that it went against the United Nations' Universal Declaration of Human Rights, and threatened to take the matter up with the exile government. According to the volunteer, an administrator told him that he didn't care about the U.N. or the exile government. Apparently, he considered locking up women to be a part of "Tibetan culture." The volunteer showed me a copy of a letter that he had submitted to the exile government, but he left the country shortly afterward, and I never heard whether the matter was resolved. I didn't have much faith. The exile government later substantially reduced the number of women who would receive scholarships to study farming in Israel because of "undignified behavior by earlier female participants." [6]

Some of the unacceptable behavior of settlers was more innocuous, but also worth mentioning in light of Samdhong Rinpoche's comments on the superiority of settler Tibetan values. When my son was nine, he spent weeks gathering wood from the forest and built a small play fort; it is illegal to cut wood in Himachal Pradesh and villagers are quick to gather fallen branches to use as fuel, so finding materials to build a fort was no small undertaking. Entirely unmoved by my son's feelings, our settler Tibetan landlord intentionally destroyed the fort and stole all of the wood to bake cookies for his New Year's celebrations, but he didn't offer my son any. We would have moved, but the awful man was just visiting from America where he had recently emigrated, and his daughter, who usually acted as the landlord on his behalf, was a lovely young woman.

My only other settler Tibetan landlord was a young man who told me that he had a university degree in business; he certainly had a degree in monkey business. We made a verbal agreement on the price of rent because when I asked to sign a contract, he commented that foreigners were untrusting, dissuading me from doing so. A month after I moved in, he decided to charge me for electricity on top of the inflated special-foreigner rent that I was paying. Because he had demanded three months' rent as a deposit, I was powerless to do anything. I would never have agreed to such a large deposit, but the apartment was everything that we had hoped for, and we had unreasonable hopes by McLeod Ganj standards.

Fortunately, electricity meters were installed in the building because the sour-faced old settler woman who lived below us and who, ironically, was always holding religious rituals in her home, told the landlord: "The Injis [foreigners] should pay more." Thanks to the meter readings, we paid less than she did. Just before I moved out, the landlord extorted more money for water use over the past fifteen months. I had never heard of anyone being charged for water, and we used very little: we often ate out, and we showered quickly because the water pressure was so poor that bathing was akin to being urinated on. I was glad that I left, for almost certainly, the landlord would have found some excuse to charge me for the air that I was breathing. My Tibetan friends laughed at his dishonesty and greed—he was far from poor—telling me that they preferred to rent from Indians, who tended to be up-front about ripping people off.

The apartment was, essentially, a small cabin on the rooftop of a building located only about one hundred meters from the heart of downtown. The economically constructed building was, like most in town, precariously perched on the edge of a steep hillside. Death would have been almost certain in the event of a major earthquake—Dharamsala is in an extreme earthquake risk zone—but almost every building in town was a deathtrap and mine happened to provide a great deal of privacy and have one of the best views. We looked down on the tops of tall trees which grew only a few metres away and had a panoramic view of the forest-clad hillsides. We could see the Dalai Lama's compound and Namgyal Monastery about a kilometer to the south, the village of Forsythe Ganj on a hillside to the north, the golden roof tops of a monastery far below, and, far off in the distance, the Kangra Valley and Shivlak Hills. It was the closest that you could come to solitude in the heart of McLeod Ganj.

My neighbors, who were mainly monks, nuns, and families with babies and small children, for the most part lived in small ramshackle rooms and shacks, sharing decrepit toilets and an outdoor water tap. They were pleasant, kindly neighbors. The monks and nuns at the bottom of our stairs lived in a row of tiny, dark, damp meditation cells. The meditation cells would have once enjoyed spectacular views, but an apartment building had been constructed only a few feet from their doors, so the windowless rooms were accessed by a dank passageway.

Other neighbors lived in an apartment constructed on the roof of the meditation cells. Their floor and roof were made of tin sheeting. They had two cute babies who were only about a year apart in age. The babies must have been colicky, for they cried almost continuously. From my desk in my room, I could hear the parents patiently soothing them with gentle words. Once, the guest of an old monk who lived in a derelict looking shack made from tarps and wood scraps took up playing the guitar. Over the course of several weeks, he practiced almost continuously; what began as tuneless strumming evolved into surprisingly melodious music. Everything: every cry, every word, the shrieks of monkeys and the chirps of birds, I could hear from within my room, for there was no insulation, my windows did not seal, and my roof was made of tin. When it poured rain during monsoon, it sometimes pounded so hard on the roof that we couldn't hear each other speak unless we were in the same room, and even then we practically had to shout. Despite the noise, our rooms were otherwise very private. I kept my curtains open continuously, since the only ones who could see in were the birds.

In the midst of the tiny neighborhood, a monastery was constructing a large opulent hotel or centre of some sort. From dawn until dusk for months on end, the building site produced a cacophony of screams from concrete and marble saws, pounding that made my building shake, and incessant hammering. Concrete dust and an occasional stray brick rained down on the neighborhood. None of this really bothered me, but the builders kept cutting off my water supply and made a filthy mess in the jungle and on our neighbor's roof, which had once been a place where residents relaxed in the sunshine.

When my landlord— to his credit he was very conscientious about making repairs—complained after my water had been cut off more than a half-dozen times in six months, the building owners were quick to go on the offensive. "Newcomers in your building were fighting," he was told. I was puzzled, but after several days, I finally figured out what they were talking about. I had heard people arguing once, about four months previously, in one of his other apartments, which didn't share my water line. Apparently, this was enough for the "Church of the Poisoned Mind"—as I secretly nicknamed the ostentatious building and its inhabitants—to justify cutting off the water supply to my room repeatedly, including prior to the fight. Perhaps I was guilty because I had newcomer friends; the only frequent visitor was a tiny woman from Amdo who seldom stayed after dark. I never had a party or noisy guests. We were always quiet and respectful. The other neighbors liked us. I had no idea where their animosity came from.

Each day as I made my way past the new building, it became more and more grand. From where the impoverished neighbors gathered at the tap each morning to collect their day's supply of water, I could see skinny Indian laborers polishing the hardwood and moving the gilded Buddhas into position. Needless to say, I was not always impressed by Samdhong Rinpoche's "true Tibetans" and their "ethos."

If it is beginning to appear that I despise the settlement Tibetans, that is profoundly not so, although I do despise some of the behavior that I have seen. Settlers are human beings like the newcomers, as diverse as any people on the planet. I could fill a book with stories of pleasant interactions, but that would be very boring. However, I will give some examples. I volunteered in my free time with an organization that works with Indian slum dwellers. My settler Tibetan and Indian colleagues were, with no exaggeration, among the finest people that I have ever met. Certainly, some of them could have made a lot more money in other fields. They chose social work because they wanted to make a difference by changing lives, which they actually do. Working with slum dwellers can be extremely frustrating and disappointing. My heart fills with love and respect when I think of their perseverance, compassion, humor, and friendship.

A settler monk of my acquaintance took it upon himself to do social work in his free time. He travelled to remote Himalayan regions and taught English. He also initiated various fund-raising efforts over the years on behalf of the poor who couldn't qualify for other assistance. He arranged funding for a hip replacement operation for an old man who could barely walk. Another project involved raising money so that a poor girl could study hair dressing, thereby becoming independent and contributing to her family. I looked forward to receiving his requests for funds, knowing how much thought went into choosing each project.

Over the years, I met many lovely settlement Tibetans from every walk of life although I did not make as many close friends among them, partially because when they are not at work, they are often busy with their families or their lifelong networks of friends. Most newcomers lacked a family life, so they had much more free time. Another major impediment to friendships with settlers was my friendships with newcomers; as mentioned earlier, the two don't usually mix.

Aside from meeting many good people, I heard stories of settlement Tibetans who had taken risks to help newcomers obtain R.C.'s and worked hard to help them in other ways. I knew one woman who experienced a great deal of trouble with the authorities because she assisted one of my friends. She did not give up or back down, and he succeeded in obtaining an R.C. She, like many others, helped out of concern, not for payment. Settlement Tibetans who worked together with newcomers often lost many of their prejudices, although some developed respect only for their colleagues, whom they saw as different from the rest.

Once, when large numbers of pilgrims came from Tibet for the Kalachakra (religious teachings) in Bodhgaya, I spent several nights down at the bus station watching Tenzin Tsundue and other settler activists devote countless hours to anonymously assisting the pilgrims to board their busses. The pilgrims would have fled in terror of Chinese reprisals had they known who their helpers were—especially if the activists had begun discussing politics—but despite their passions, the activists put politics aside for the duration of the Kalachakra. Instead, they read off passenger lists and kindly and tirelessly rendered assistance to the pilgrims for close to a month: no flags, no slogans, no mention of a "Free Tibet," just Tibetans helping Tibetans in need.

Chapter 13

Samdhong Rinpoche also claimed that newcomers are "violent" and "intolerant." I heard many similar assertations over the years, but they didn't correspond with most of what I witnessed. I've known hundreds of newcomers and observed thousands of them. The vast majority were peaceful toward Indians, although many were fearful and suspicious of them. The precarious legal status of newcomers is a major contributor to this problem. True, some conflicts and misunderstandings occurred, and it really didn't help that the newcomers were not taught Hindi. It was the settler Tibetans that many newcomers resented. Interestingly, by 2010, when Samdhong Rinpoche participated in the interview in which he voiced his condemnations of newcomers, I had witnessed a sharp decline in hostile behavior among them—more on that topic later. But even when I first arrived in Dharamsala, newcomers had been very aware of the importance of maintaining good relations with Indians and endeavored to conduct themselves accordingly.

One incident in particular stands out. When I first met my ex-husband in 2003, we lived in an apartment at the bottom of the Yongling Stairs. The building was entirely inhabited by young newcomers from Amdo with the exception of me, my son, and a young Canadian woman who also lived with her Tibetan boyfriend. The Indian landlord lived with his family in a spacious apartment which was separate from those of his tenants and provided a great deal of privacy. There was never any trouble, and the landlord had a good reputation among the tenants. One night, we arrived home to find the landlord's brother—who did not live in the building—extremely drunk and belligerent, hanging around in front of the rental units. He began shouting, but no one could understand what he was saying, so we went inside our room.

He continued shouting and kicked our door repeatedly, so my husband and our roommate went outside and tried to calm him down. All of the other tenants came out and tried to talk him down as well.

He continued yelling and shoving people. Around a dozen Indians from the neighborhood then appeared wielding sticks. Instead of attempting to control the drunk, they began shouting at and threatening the Tibetans. The landlord did not join in, but he also did nothing to calm the situation. The drunk smashed our window and tried to get into our room, but he was prevented from damaging other rooms by the crowd of Tibetans. The Indians continued shouting and threatening. The Tibetans did not lose their cool. Instead, they slowly defused the situation.

After it was over, our roommate came inside and punched the concrete wall in frustration. I put my arms around him so that he wouldn't hurt himself more and tried to soothe him. He began to sob, "We are helpless here," he cried. "We have no rights. They can do anything that they want to us." I didn't know what to say. It was true, and there was nothing that I could do to help them. Although I offered to go to the authorities and contact overseas human rights organizations, I was implored not to, for many in the building lacked R.C.'s; they were terrified that bringing attention to problems might make their situation worse. Given what I now know, I'm glad that I made no such attempts.

Everyone in the building was very angry about what had happened, for Indians often abused Tibetans with no repercussions. The next morning, unbeknownst to me, the Tibetans held a meeting. My husband returned home with some surprising news, "The Indians need to learn that they can't treat us this way just because we are refugees. We are all finding new places to live and everyone is moving out today. It will teach the landlords a lesson." It wasn't just talk. By the end of the day, all but one of the tenants had found new rooms. Word of what had transpired spread among the Amdo community. Dozens of young people arrived and helped everyone carry their belongings to their new homes. By noon the following day, only one tenant remained. He was extremely poor and rented a room not much bigger than a closet. He couldn't find anything for the same price – 500 rupees a month.

Word must have spread throughout the Tibetan community; for months after, the building stood vacant. It was little better than a slum with a single toilet shared by all residents, usually around twenty two people. Only the poorest refugees lived in such accommodations, and the poor were most often victimized. No one wanted to live in a building where they could be confronted by stick-wielding thugs because they knew that neither the police nor the exile government would come to their aid if they were attacked. The vacant building stood as testament to everyone that refugees were not entirely powerless. Since the landlord was not a bad man, eventually newcomers returned. There has been no trouble there since.

That year, I witnessed another disturbing incident during Diwali, the Indian festival of light. The lack of unity between Tibetans and Indians was often on my mind. I was encouraged by any mutual appreciation—even very small things. During Diwali celebrations, I was pleased when a number of Tibetans joined Indians in setting off fireworks at the bus stand (now known as the Main Square). My son was nine years old and very enthusiastic. My then husband purchased a small quantity of fireworks. He and my son, along with several Tibetan friends, joined in the revelry. Being an up-tight Western mother who, at that time, shuddered at the idea of children playing with fireworks, I went along to keep an eye on things.

Several dozen Indians and a few Tibetans were scattered throughout the square. Child and teenage restaurant workers set off small crackers, while wealthy Indians put on impressive, albeit somewhat dangerous, displays. My husband began setting off his crackers and small fireworks. A very new car made its way through the bus stand past the Indians and their more volatile displays. It lurched to a stop in front of my husband and son. The driver—from his dress obviously an Indian businessman—leapt from the vehicle and approached my husband, "You go home now." he shouted, "Know your place." He poked my husband in the chest. I was ready to confront the man, but one of our Tibetan friends made gestures not to. My son looked scared, and the Tibetans stood silently as the businessman continued to verbally abuse them. Once the man completed his tirade and left, we tried to regain our spirits, but it was not the same. "I fucking hate Indians," one of the Tibetan said as we were walking home.

Although they didn't usually direct their anger toward Indians, a minority of newcomers, mostly very young men, were quick to anger, especially during the bleakest and most poverty-stricken period that I witnessed in Dharamsala—the early to mid 2000's. People told me that violence among youth was a problem in Tibet; many of them had scars as proof. Still, my observations of newcomers, both in Dharamsala and among those who emigrated to the West, led me to conclude that many of their social problems were a result of the challenges that they faced, not necessarily the result of their upbringing in Tibet or Chinese influence. Sonam of the Tibetan Centre for Conflict Resolution told me that her centre now conducts workshops at Tibetan Transit School. I can't help but wonder whether those workshops are partially responsible for the dramatic reduction in negative behaviors that I have noticed in recent years, although as we will later see, there are other reasons.

Newcomers had come from a bad situation in Tibet to, for many, a worse one in India. I became interested in the impact of trauma on men and youths and also wondered what services were available to newcomers and settlers with emotional and mental health problems. I had never heard of such services, which was strange as Dharamsala is essentially a refugee camp; emotional problems are common and should be expected.

A few seconds of searching on-line immediately told me that direct links exist between trauma and anger issues. Indeed, direct links occur between trauma and almost every social problem that I had witnessed among newcomers in Dharamsala: overreactions, including sudden unprovoked anger, general anxiety, insomnia, substance abuse, depression, guilt feelings, compulsive behavior patterns, self-destructive and impulsive behavior, an inability to make healthy professional or lifestyle choices, feelings of ineffectiveness, shame, despair, and hopelessness, an inability to maintain close relationships or choose appropriate friends and mates, sexual problems, and hostility and/or arguments with family members, employers or co-workers.[1]

A report on youth and trauma in America explains that youth responded more extremely to trauma than adults: "These young people report exhibiting much more anger and ventilation; avoidance and passivity; and aggressive, antisocial behavior. They describe yelling, fighting and complaining; drinking, smoking and using doctor-prescribed drugs more frequently; and sleeping, riding around in cars and crying more often. They are less inclined to do things with their family or to go along with parents' rules and requests."[2] These descriptions almost perfectly described what I had witnessed among many of the young Salai Gyals during the first year that I lived in Dharamsala. Newcomers, fortunately, tended to be anti-drugs, but they were a problem for T.C.V. kids. Riding around in cars corresponded with "cham cham," as Tibetans call strolling and loitering. Parents were represented by the established Tibetan exiles, including the older and more successful newcomers who attempted to provide guidance. Many of the settlement Tibetans exhibited similar behaviors. According to the reports, coping strategies can be taught and, as I also observed, the problems often go away on their own once the causes of stress and trauma are removed.

"Depression??? What are you talking about?" my ex-husband had practically screamed at me one afternoon in Dharamsala. "We don't get depression. Only you foreigners do. We are Tibetans. We don't have your stupid Western problems." He chortled maniacally and rolled his eyes. Years later in Canada, he spoke openly of suffering from depression and "problems" both in India and during his first years in Canada. His headaches, anger, and obstructive behavior had mostly melted away after a few years in Canada as he became a more confident man who excelled in his career. "I have so many regrets," he told me. I didn't see his problems entirely as his fault.

In 2007, one Tibetan counsellor provided services to the entire refugee community, this at a time when an average of 2,500 people a year were escaping from Tibet and mostly ending up in Dharamsala.[3] According to an extensive and informative report and what people told me over the years, the Western approach to mental health was considered to be needed only by "crazy people" or psychotics.[4] Meanwhile, I watched Tibetans struggle with and sometimes become almost completely debilitated by treatable mental-health problems.

A study at Tibetan Transit School in 2001 reported:

> Approximately a third (35%) of the respondents met the criteria for "substantial emotional distress." Twenty-five percent had excessive scores on anxiety, with an even higher proportion over the cutoff point for depression (42%)."[5] Physicians for Human Rights reported that one in seven new arrivals from Tibet, in their study group of 258 people, had been subjected to torture. "Fifty eight percent of all torture survivors we interviewed were less than twenty one years old at the time of their reported torture, and 15% were sixteen years or younger at the time of their reported abuse.[6]

According to another study, in 1998, 11.5% of the children at Upper T.C.V. suffered from Post Traumatic Stress Disorder.[7] Ten years later, a study on mental health in children and teens who attended Upper T.C.V. and T.C.V. Suja reported that 82% of students born in Tibet and 61% of those born in exile suffered from depression and anxiety.[8] A lack of contact with family was pointed to as a potential contributing factor. However, I was told by numerous students that as of 2012, pupils at T.C.V. schools—which are boarding schools—are forbidden from owning phones and computers, increasing their difficulty in keeping in regular contact with their families. I was also told that students from Tibet at Suja—I don't know about other T.C.V. schools—are repeatedly told that they must return to Tibet once their education is complete.

Since the 1980's, thousands of children have been smuggled out of Tibet to receive educations in exile.[9] Students from Tibet are not taught in the dialects of their regions that they are apparently expected to return to, nor are they grouped or housed with other children from their home regions. The children are intentionally mixed up, presumably so that they will lose their distinct cultures and dialects as quickly as possible and become the exile's version of "Tibetan." The youngest children from the dialectically different regions quickly lose the ability to communicate with their parents.

In 2005, I met a mother from Amdo who had managed to go to India to visit her young son. She was distressed that one year after she had sent him to study at T.C.V., he was already losing the ability to communicate with her. Friends in India, though, convinced her husband that it was critical to leave their son in the school because of problems among youth in their community in Tibet and limited educational options. Several months after going home to Tibet, the mother managed to return to India behind her husband's back. She shocked her family by returning to Amdo with the child. I couldn't help but sympathize with her.

Sending children alone to India did not always end well. A report from Kunphen, a Dharamsala-based N.G.O. which offers services and treatment to Tibetan substance abusers, described the tragic death, from a drug overdose, of a former T.C.V. student who was sent to India to study as a small child. He had not spoken to his mother in four years because he had lost the ability to do so.[10] I met a number of other T.C.V. "orphans" who suffered from mental-health and substance-abuse problems; what part their loss of language plays in their problems is unclear.

Life as adults is often difficult for the "T.C.V. orphans." They frequently have no families in India, and many have, understandably, not wanted to return to Tibet and stayed on. A study involving 319 students between Grades 7 and 12 at Upper T.C.V. and T.C.V. Suja reported that those from Tibet were 69% male.[11] Although I could find data from only the one study, friends who had attended the schools observed similar discrepancies, indicating that they are at a substantial disadvantage when it comes to marriage. Some try to befriend newcomers from their regions, with varying degrees of success, but for the ones that were sent to India when they were very young, integration can be difficult because they have often lost their cultures and the ability to communicate in their mother tongue and have also absorbed the prejudices against newcomers that are so prevalent. For this reason, the newcomers usually see them as settlement Tibetans. If they go back to Tibet, they have trouble fitting in. Worse yet, they can face stigma and persecution from the Chinese due to their exile education. I could not find out what, if anything, is done to help them deal with these realities.

The lack of mental health services was shocking. Many in the community believed that counselling was available to newcomers and students even though it was not. No mental health services were provided in any of the other fifty one Tibetan settlements. From the reports that I read, it appeared that officials at the highest level were dismissive of and resistant to improving mental-health services. Most people in the community had little or no understanding of the causes of mental and social problems or any understanding of the benefits of "Western" treatment. Currently, the Central Tibetan Administration's Department of Health website does not mention counselling except for a small program for former political prisoners.[12] Almost an entire year after Harvard-educated Lobsang Sangay was sworn in as the new exile prime minister, a much anticipated health insurance plan was launched in 2012. Among other vital measures, it excludes "any treatment related to alcohol and substance abuse" and "treatment after attempting suicide," leaving one with the impression that little if anything has improved in terms of access to care for those who need it most.[13]

Another new program was announced in the same year that points at delusional backwardness: "The Tibetan government in exile has maintained that alleged infiltration by Chinese is reportedly being done to tarnish the image of Tibetans in host countries by dragging the youth towards drugs and sex abuse." To combat problems imagined to be caused by its Red Menace, "it plans to deploy special teachers, probably monks, in Tibetan offices and colleges, who will work to integrate human values among Tibetan youths."[14] After reading the article, I felt that perhaps some in the exile government would especially benefit from improved mental health services.

A Tibetan friend wasn't surprised at all by the exile government's reasoning. He pointed out that what could be perceived as illogical responses were not just confined to social issues: "Many times, the

Tibetan government has organized mass ritual events for getting freedom soon and for solving Tibetan political problem. They claim that we lost independence because we are short of common good deeds. If anyone questions this view, they are seriously considered anti-religion and marginalized from the society."

The consensus seemed to be that Buddhism was the best possible treatment for mental health problems. Buddhism is obviously very beneficial, for considering the obstacles that they face, most Tibetan refugees, including newcomers, are remarkably resilient and stoic. They tend not to obsess over events that happened in the past, as is too common in my society. Unfortunately, needless to say, religion can't be expected to solve everything. I tired of hearing treatable problems being blamed on "poor Buddhist practices," "karma," or "Chinese influence," and it was extremely depressing to watch Tibetans flounder and often fail as they attempted to solve their sometimes very serious problems with nothing but religion. Interestingly, the only Tibetan that I became aware of who used medication over the long-term to treat his mental illness was the Dalai Lama's youngest brother. [15] The resistance to medical treatment, it seemed, didn't originate at the top.

Chapter 14

As we know, tensions between Indians and Tibetans have been blamed on newcomers. They make convenient scapegoats, but, on examination, the problems have other causes and far deeper roots. Samdhong Rinpoche seemed to have somehow forgotten the rioting and extreme violence perpetrated by local Indians against Tibetans in Dharamsala in 1994, following the killing of an Indian youth by a young Tibetan who was born and raised in India. Later, in 1995, the state of Arunachal Pradesh mounted an anti-outsider campaign and attempted to expel the approximately 12,000 Tibetans living in the state. In 1999, an Indian mob burned 140 Tibetan shops in Manali and looted Tibetan homes following a fight between a Tibetan teen and three Indian boys during which one of the Indian boys was killed.

I could find no evidence whatsoever that newcomers had anything to do with these incidents or that there was a sizable newcomer population in Arunachal Pradesh or Manali. In the case of the Arunachal Pradesh event, the 1998 Demographic Survey reported only 143 Tibetans who had been born in Tibet and who fit the newcomer demographic by being under the age of fifty living in the eastern part of India where the state is located. It seems unlikely that those few individuals caused such irreparable damage that residents would have wanted to expel more than ten thousand settlement Tibetans.

In Dharamsala, a lot of mutual appreciation exists between Tibetans and Indians, but so does a lot of bad blood. One Western friend who has spent much of the past three decades in the Dharamsala area noticed tensions when he first arrived in the early eighties and believes that the problems began when the refugees first arrived, "There were many aristocrats who fled Tibet in 1959 and settled around Dharamsala. Even though most lost everything during their escape from Tibet, they saw themselves as sophisticated people and looked down on the poor and uneducated Gaddi farmers. Things got off to a bad start from the beginning." It seemed likely that there was truth to what he said. Many once powerful monastics had fled as well, and they, too, likely weren't humble—by most accounts they hadn't been so in Tibet. Still, my contemporary experience pointed toward another cause of tensions—the Tibetans' perceived economic prosperity.

When the settlement Tibetans first escaped into exile, they were, for the most-part, impoverished and suffered tremendously. They were put to work building roads and struggled to clear jungle in order to create farms on land that they were given by the Government of India to create settlements in far-flung and often remote parts of the country. Many died as a result of illness. The conditions of Tibetan children at Upper T.C.V. and other schools were appalling.[1] Many of the early refugees built small shacks, some of which can still be found in McLeod Ganj and remain inhabited by Tibetans.

Of course, extreme poverty was endemic in India, and the Tibetans received a lot of aid. That they desperately needed it and continue to do so is undoubtable, but the assistance that they receive has created resentment among local Indians. Although the exact figures are unknown, Paul Christiaan Klieger documented millions of dollars in aid during the early years of exile.[2] While many Tibetans are now self-sufficient, funding continues to be needed by many Tibetan organizations and individuals. Aid from the Government of India and abroad does provide many Tibetans with incomes, but the lifestyles that the jobs afford are far from extravagant. Both Indians and Tibetans who have become wealthy have mostly done so through business ventures: restaurants, shops, hotels, etc.

Most of the money that Tibetan exiles earn and receive is spent in Indian businesses, many of which thrive. Tibetans buy food, goods, and services. They eat in restaurants. They stay in guest houses. They rent rooms. They take taxis. If foreign sponsorships of all kinds were removed, the results would be catastrophic to the local Indian economy. Still, one can't blame some Indians for being jealous and resentful. Unfortunately, little is done by the local Indian community to capitalize on the many potential foreign donors who visit the town by highlighting the difficulties that poor Indians face and raising funds that would help them.

As an aside, I also heard numerous complaints that visitors show no interest in the local Gaddi and other Indian cultures. They probably would if there were some sort of museum or information centre which taught visitors about the indigenous local cultures, products, and handicrafts. Unfortunately, in McLeod Ganj, I could find nothing, not even a small book or a pamphlet. Doubtless, many Tibetans would be interested, too, for despite inhabiting the same community, little interaction occurs between the cultures. Although I have listened to close to a decade of complaining, I have yet to see any efforts made to market local Indian culture in the tourist hub that is McLeod Ganj, whereas Tibetans, both settlers and newcomers, are adept at doing so.

Much is made of the disparity between many Indians and Tibetans in terms of noticeable material possessions. Both Indians and Western tourists told me that Tibetans were wealthy compared to Indians. Tibetans often told me that Indians were wealthier. Rich Indians tend to live down in the valley or up in the hills and therefore go unnoticed by many people. As one friend noted, wealthy Indians in Dharamsala also often conduct themselves as though they are not. As an example, he pointed out that the rich owner of a large apartment building wore old clothes and plastic sandals even in winter. Journalists, too, remarked on the apparent disparity and consequent animosity, but they didn't necessarily recognize the biggest reasons for the Tibetans' perceived affluence: "It does not help either, that the average Tibetan in Dharamsala, flush with foreign aid, is today well dressed, and has plenty of money to spend."[3] A photograph of a moneyed-looking young Tibetan was included with that article. Ironically, he wasn't terribly representative, because he was just visiting his old home, McLeod Ganj. He is married to a foreign diplomat who was at that time stationed in Delhi.

It is true that nowadays most Tibetans in Dharamsala have new shoes and stylish t-shirts and jeans—mostly cheap fake name brands. Some have lap-tops, motorcycles, and even cars. One thing they don't have is huge weddings to spend years saving for. Weddings in the Tibetan exile community are low-key. Most newcomers heartily approve of this exile Tibetan development, whereas, in Tibet, expensive, pretentious weddings are still the norm. In exile, Tibetans are free to spend their disposable income on other things.

Indian weddings are no small affair. In 2004, in Himachal Pradesh state where Dharamsala is located, an average Indian wedding cost the groom's family 94,327 rupees and the bride's family 114,839 rupees. The bride's family usually gave a dowry as well.[4] At that time, the per capita income in Himachal Pradesh was 9,942 rupees and average annual total household earnings were 46,684 rupees.[5]

In contrast, my wedding in Dharamsala in 2003 cost 16,000 rupees, excluding the wedding clothes which were a gift from my sister-in-law. We had 150 guests. We served a buffet meal, which included plenty of expensive meat dishes and a reasonable, although not excessive, amount of alcohol. We also rented a sound system and held a dance party. By the standards of the Tibetan community, the wedding was considered extravagant.

My friend Clyde has spent the better part of a decade in McLeod Ganj. He has been to a number of local Indian weddings. He told me of one: "They are pretty typical villagers. They own a handful of sheep, a buffalo, and have a few square metres of corn. No one in the family earns more than a couple of thousand rupees a month. At that time, one son worked in an Internet café and the father was working part-time in construction. [Construction workers earn less than Rs140 a day.] For the wedding, they renovated their house. They had hundreds of guests. It was insane. This was just the groom's family. The bride's family held their own huge party. I have no idea how they paid for it. But everyone has to do this, because if they don't, they think that everyone will look down on them."

Another long-term Western resident told me a similar story. Antonio's landlords were inviting 1,000 guests to their daughter's wedding, which, as was typical, would last for several days, "They have been saving for this thing for years. They are putting on this big event that will go on for a few days, and they will have nothing to show for it after. It's a complete waste of money. They could improve their lives so much with the money. It makes no sense at all."

Tibetan weddings were almost always modest. Some people with no family to object simply moved in together. Generally, there were fewer than 150 guests, sometimes only a few dozen. In the morning, a hall or restaurant was cheerfully decorated with balloons, streamers, and a hand-made sign. In the afternoon, tea and dinner were served. There were speeches and singing and sometimes a small dance party with drinks. There was no dowry.

Another reason that Tibetans have more disposable income is that they can't legally buy real estate in Himachal Pradesh or elsewhere in India for that matter. In the 1960's, the Tibetans were given land to build settlements mostly in remote areas, but further acquisition of land has been difficult. A small number of Tibetans owned homes and buildings in Dharamsala, but their status is precarious. At the time of writing, a mysterious individual from Rewalsar called Pawan Kumar, who is using legal means to make life in Himachal Pradesh as unpleasant as possible for Tibetans—among other things, he went to court to have the flying of Tibetan flags from buildings and flag poles banned[6] and the painting of mani stones and the hanging of prayer flags from trees outlawed[7]—is before the courts to have the properties confiscated.[8]

As a consequence, most refugees in Dharamsala rent apartments or live in staff quarters. Often, the rooms are small and unappealing. When I first went to McLeod Ganj, I was surprised when well-dressed Tibetans brought me to their apartments, and I discovered that they lived in small, dingy rooms often with a shared toilet or even no toilet at all. The wealthier among them might paint once a year, but repairs and renovations are the responsibility of the landlord. The Himachalis tend to be anti-outsider, and many fear being overrun with Tibetans. Complex rules prevent most non-Himachalis from buying land, with exceptions of course made for the powerful and influential.[9]

Himachalis and Indians in general get no sympathy or understanding from me when it comes to their policies regarding land ownership. Himachal Pradesh has a population of around 6,856,509 Indians[10] and only 27,542[11] Tibetans, representing 0.04% of the population. Conversely in British Columbia, Canada, where I live, the population is 4,561,040 of which 232,270 people are of Indian origin[12] or 5% of the population. It might shock some Indians to know that Indian immigrants and "outsiders" from other parts of the country are allowed to buy property anywhere in Canada. Of course, Canada's population is vastly smaller, but when one looks at the tiny numbers of Tibetans and other "outsiders" in Himachal Pradesh and elsewhere in India, the policies seem draconian.

Indians sacrifice a great deal to buy and develop property, but, of course, real estate is usually a sound investment that can be passed on to their children or sold. Tibetans do have more pocket money in the short-term, but they end up with no investments. In McLeod Ganj, you see a lot of elderly Tibetans working in shops or selling curios in the street to pay for their "retirements."

Tibetan women, unlike their Indian counterparts, almost always have jobs outside the home. Gradually, more Indian women can be seen in the workplace, but typically only women, especially married women, from very poor Indian families work. Throughout the state, only 37% of women in urban areas have jobs, and elsewhere in India the number is half that.[13] Conversely, many Tibetan women run businesses and hold management positions, and, in fact, Tibetan women are employed in almost every profession. If I met a Tibetan woman who did not have a job, she was looking for one. What I observed is backed up by data: the 2009 Demographics Survey showed that Tibetan women were only two percent below men in terms of being equal participants in the workforce.[14]

Within the Indian community, the average woman marries at the age of eighteen and has her first child at twenty.[15] Only 21% of Tibetan women marry before the age of twenty, and many wait until they are over twenty five. More than half of Tibetan women do not have their first child until they are older than twenty five.[16] Tibetan children are usually sent to baby-care centres when they are only a few months old so that their mothers can return to work, and, therefore, marriage and parenthood do not usually greatly impact the income of Tibetan families in India. I never met a Tibetan woman who was a housewife although I am sure that there must be a few.

Tibetans also have much smaller families. Indian families average 2.6 children, although Himachal Pradesh residents have fewer—1.9.[17] Exile Tibetan families averaged only 1.18 children.[18] This is a tremendous drop from the late 1980's when the average Tibetan family had 4.9 children.[19] Having very few children has freed Tibetans from the often crippling cost of raising large families, although it does raise concerns as to who will support them in their old age in a society mostly devoid of pensions. According to the 2009 Tibetan Demographic Survey, high educational levels and the popularity of contraceptives were responsible for lower fertility rates.[20] I imagine that the uncertainty and instability of refugee life plays a part, too.

As long as priorities and lifestyles remain different, the discrepancies between Indians and Tibetans with similar incomes will remain. Obviously, the answer isn't for Tibetans to hold big weddings and remove women from the workforce or bankrupt local businesses by always eating at home and wearing old clothes. Perceptions need to be carefully and realistically assessed and discussed by all parties.

Despite having more disposable income, many Tibetans remain incredibly poor and helpless. In 2011, a newcomer bread seller from Tibet with a disabled daughter was brought to my attention in hopes that I could do something to help the family. Lucy, Tsering Tso, and I entered an apartment that resembled a cave. Monsoon was just ending; the floor and walls were heavy with moisture and dark with mould. There was a fetid smell. But it was a tidy family home. The mother made us tea and explained, through Tsering Tso because she didn't speak English, that the family had to live where they did because they couldn't carry their daughter far—she was almost four—and they needed a large room in order to bake their bread. They had gone into debt trying to do their best for their daughter. They had approached the Tibetan exile government many times for assistance but had always been told to come back the next year, although they were reimbursed for medical bills.

The family had travelled to see specialists but was told that the girl could not be treated without a lengthy stay at a physiotherapy clinic in a town far away. They had already missed a great deal of work seeking treatments, but they still didn't even know what was wrong with her. We raised funds to pay off their debt, and Lucy met a foreign doctor who immediately diagnosed the girl's affliction. She had cerebral palsy and could learn to walk through simple exercises. (Later a friend with a similar case of cerebral palsy had better exercises designed by an expert in South Africa and e-mailed them to a translator friend.) A few weeks later, the little girl took her first step, but the family's problems were far from solved. They still earned a pittance making and selling bread, they lived in the "cave," and their daughter would likely require treatment from a specialist to achieve her potential.

Vinayak Sharma, a local Indian lawyer who studied at T.C.V. and speaks fluent Tibetan, provides legal aid to Tibetans in his free time: "'There is a big misunderstanding among Indians that Tibetans are receiving donations from foreigners and are well off,' Sharma says. 'Reality is totally different. ... Their incomes are very limited.'".[21]

Chapter 15

Occasional eruptions of anti-Tibetan violence have been on my mind for many years. In these incidents, settler Tibetans have been as likely to be the victims of injustice as newcomers. Samdhong Rinpoche seemed to believe that the problem would go away if the newcomers did, but from what I knew that seemed highly unlikely. That some Tibetans do instigate fights is undoubtable, but they tend to fight one-on-one—man-to-man so to speak. What I am referring to is something entirely different, the mindless horror of mob attacks— often on innocents. Because nothing was ever done about it, I became a collector of articles on the subject in hope that one day they could be useful.

Certainly reliable reports are now often hard to come by. The English-language Tibetan media seldom cover incidents anymore, and the human rights organizations based in Dharamsala report on abuses only in Tibet and Nepal. If it isn't already painfully obvious by now, international human rights organizations didn't have anyone independently monitoring and reporting on the Tibetan refugee situation in India. From what I have been able to gather, the powers that be within the Tibetan exile establishment don't want anti-Tibetan violence to be mentioned for fear of hurting the feelings of the Indian community and potentially angering volatile state politicians. Thus, they muzzle the Tibetan media. It is unclear what if any part is played by local, state, or national Indian authorities in hushing up events, but certainly they now seldom receive coverage in the Indian or international press.

The situation is pathetic, foremost because the majority of local Indians never behave violently towards Tibetans and with the right measures, the situation could be improved. In many instances, including ones which I witnessed, local Indians have protected or helped Tibetan victims. Of course, some Indians are afraid of retribution from goons, while others are ambivalent. As guests in the country, Tibetans seldom retaliate; in some cases, they don't even defend themselves so as not to further anger their hosts. The exiles are in a tough position, but what is clear is that allowing potentially murderous thugs to rampage without consequences only contributes to mistrust and instability.

The earliest published reports I found of anti-Tibetan violence in Dharamsala came from 1994. As mentioned earlier, in April of that year, a settler Tibetan student from the Arts and Metal Crafts Centre in Lower Dharamsala stabbed and killed a Gaddi youth during a knife fight that was precipitated by a disagreement over a sporting event. The Tibetan ended up in hospital with stab wounds, so it would appear that the deceased wasn't an unarmed innocent. An article in *The Independent* described some of what happened next:

> During the funeral Krishan Kapoor, a politician belonging to the right-wing Hindu Bharatiya Janata Party (BJP), yanked the shroud off the corpse, reached into the cadaver's open stomach, pulled out a length of intestine, and held it high. 'This is what the Tibetans have done!' he yelled. The mourners went berserk. Shouting 'Death to the Dalai Lama!' and 'Long Live Deng Xiaoping!' the mob stormed the compound of the Tibetan government-in-exile, smashed windows, set fires and destroyed furniture. They then looted Tibetan shops and beat up refugees. Not to be outdone by Mr Kapoor, the rival Congress politician, a shrill ex-princess named Chandresh Kumari, helped circulate a petition calling for the Dalai Lama and the Tibetans to get out of India.[1]

I was unable to ascertain if the part about the corpse and the intestines was correct, but everything else was corroborated by other reports.

A thoughtful overview and analysis of what transpired appeared in the *Tibetan Review*, which at that time still covered contentious issues. Following the funeral, a mob had first attacked the Arts and Metal Crafts Centre, then stoned the building and set the studio on fire. The students fled as best they could. At risk of great peril from the mob, some Gaddi (indigenous Indians) families assisted and hid students. The mob then attacked a Lower T.C.V. school building where five to seven-year-old Tibetan children were housed. Over 2000 window panes were broken at Lower T.C.V. The mob looted, cut off the water supply, and tried to light the buildings on fire. Although the police apparently attempted to intervene, they were outnumbered. Fortunately, no one was killed. According to the article, "It was only six days after the rioting that some Tibetan officials paid a visit to the school on their way from somewhere else. After all that the school had gone through, the only thing the bureaucrats did was publicly admonish the students and the staff for indulging in a flashy or colourful life-style which the locals disliked."[2]

Tibetan offices and residences were attacked at Gangchen Kyishong, the exile government headquarters. Only the hospital was spared. Up in McLeod Ganj the violence continued:

Around 3 pm, a lone Tibetan boy ventured out towards Surya Hotel. From nowhere an Ambassador car stopped. Five local boys got out and started beating and kicking the Tibetan boy while other Tibetans watched in horror from rooftops. Then they heard shouts and slogans. The rioters came in groups of 15, 10, five and even three, and ran amok in McLeod Ganj. On the way there, at Jogiwara, they had beaten and robbed a Tibetan businessman from Nepal. At Kotwali Bazar in Lower Dharamsala, Tibetans reaching Dharamsala by bus or taxi were pulled down and beaten up. A young boy, a woman, and a monk were the three unlucky arrivals who had to bear most of the beatings before some policemen saved them. In McLeod Ganj, the looting and pillaging went on till five in the evening. Some Westerners who came out were manhandled, their cameras snatched and their film rolls taken out. Two shops were broken into and looted. While some rioters threw out the merchandise from the shops, others leisurely selected the things they wanted and set fire to the rest. There were a few policemen in attendance but they remained mute spectators; some even joined in the sharing of the loot. Those Tibetan families who lived outside the market-place had their money robbed; some even had their bed sheets pulled and snatched away. In all about 15 Tibetans were injured.[3]

The author, K Dhondup, went into detail discussing the social environment that influenced the attacks and mentioned other incidents that had occurred in India as far back as the 1960's, holding little back in naming names and laying blame where blame was due: Indian politicians who had whipped up anti-Tibetan sentiments and Indians who made their livings off Tibetans had attacked them. Meanwhile, the exile government had resisted efforts to enlist the help of influential Indians from outside the area and had opposed a media tour organized from Delhi. Interestingly, the author mentioned that some exiles wanted to blame "the entry of anti-social and criminal elements, sent by the Chinese [meaning newcomers] to destabilize the exile society and tarnish the Tibetan image," but he pointed out that "the Tibetan boy involved in the recent incident is not a fresh arrival from Tibet. He is from the exile community in India itself."[4]

More than a decade later, it seemed that little had changed, although the media were no longer so free. This became apparent in 2007 when Phayul reported on a fight at the McLeod Ganj bus stand. A taxi driver had hit a Tibetan man with his vehicle; taxis frequently speed through the streets and are often driven carelessly, endangering and annoying residents and tourists because sidewalks are nonexistent and the streets are narrow. The Tibetan became angry. Rather than apologizing, the driver assaulted the Tibetan. According to reports, upward of thirty five taxi drivers joined in and beat the Tibetan and a friend who was with him. The Tibetan men were punched, kicked, and had their heads stomped on. Two Tibetan women tried to stop the assaults; they, too, were beaten and then tossed down the hillside. When the assault ended, both men required hospitalization. No charges were laid, and none of the attackers was arrested, although the event was witnessed by dozens of people, including the police, who stood by watching.

The next day, an informal gathering of Tibetans took place in the Tsuglakhang courtyard (the main temple). Tibetans voiced their grievances against the police and the notorious Taxi and Auto

Rickshaw Union. Tibetans were united in their frustration with the status quo. Those born in India as well as newcomers shared personal stories of abuse and persecution, most often at the hands of police and taxi drivers. Those assembled made a commitment to boycott taxis and auto rickshaws. Tibetan shops in McLeod Ganj closed for a day in protest.

On May 4[th,] three articles appeared on Phayul. A staff journalist reported on the event, describing what had transpired.[5] A visiting Bangladeshi photo-journalist and human rights activist who was spending several months in the town wrote of the legal protection and rights which Tibetans and others holding R.C.'s in India are entitled to under United Nations guidelines. She chastised the Indian government and local law enforcement for not enforcing the directives and condemned the Indian media for biased and dishonest reporting on what had transpired.[6] Topden Tsering, former editor of *Tibet Bulletin*, wrote a scathing op-ed piece discussing the event that had just occurred as well as incidences of violence, including rapes, in the past. He criticized the spinelessness with which the Tibetan exile administration handles such issues.[7] None of the writers pretended or imagined that the problems were caused by newcomers. It appeared for a short time that Tibetans were finally going to stand together and confront the problems head on.

Several days later, all three articles were removed from the Phayul website. Instead, Phayul posted a groveling apology for publishing the articles.[8] Numerous comments were posted chastising Phayul for giving up its integrity by bowing to pressure, which, as many pointed out, undoubtedly came from the exile government. The Phayul discussion forum that had been home to debate on the topic was then disabled, and its entire archive of discussions of hundreds of topics— going back years—was removed. The forum remained closed until July 7th. When it did reopen, the archive was not reinstated. The first comment posted mentions that the forum was closed due to a "spat" between Tibetans and taxi drivers and a "riot" (?) exacerbated by Phayul!

Fortunately, I had copied two of the articles. I forwarded them, along with a letter regarding what had transpired, to the Canada Tibet Committee's head office. Thanks to CTC's World Tibet News archive, there they remain to this day. The Phayul staff journalist's article, which I had neglected to copy, later reappeared on another website. Fortunately, censorship is not entirely universal in the Tibetan world.

The next development was even more surreal. Phayul posted nothing for several days. It then began posting the usual Tibet-related international stories. On May 11th, a "Joint Press Statement" from the exile government and the Taxi and Auto Rickshaw Union appeared.[9] According to them, the incident "was between a few local individuals belonging to the Indian and the Tibetan communities," nothing more. The beating of the girls was condemned by both parties, but no mention was made of the hospitalized Tibetan men. In apology, Tibetan ceremonial scarves were presented to the girls by the Indian Auto Rickshaw and Taxi Union (wouldn't a gesture representing their own customs have held more meaning?) and the representatives of the Union received the same from the Tibetan delegation. Of course, no charges were laid. Those I spoke to in the community were appalled— the problem had been "solved" with nothing but scarves worth a few rupees—but there was nothing that they could do. The taxi drivers must have been laughing their heads off.

The exile government's handling of the situation was ironic considering what Topden Tsering had written only days earlier: "The blood, the screams and the fear: it happens out there on the streets in the real open world. But if viewed from the confines of Tibetan administration offices or from the Indian municipal centres, it is as if not one straw is out of place in the greater harmony of the world."[10]

In an article on his personal website, at odds with all of the others, downplaying the events, local Tibetan journalist Lobsang Wangyal remarked:

Perhaps this sort of concern was in the minds of exile government officials, but it was a shortsighted one, for of course, the Indians and Tibetans are mutually dependent on each other. Many feared that the exile government's weak response was a grave mistake and felt that the law should have been followed, even if it involved going to higher authorities than the local police, because allowing such violence and cruelty to go unpunished would only encourage more trouble, which it did.

Several months later on August 14th, I saw two photos and a short blurb in the *Chandigarh Tribune* regarding a demonstration by Indians, mostly local women I judged from one photograph, against attacks by Tibetans. There was also a photograph of an Indian man who had been injured, thankfully not catastrophically so, for he was photographed fully dressed and standing outdoors.[11] Nothing was mentioned by Tibetan media.

I immediately contacted a friend in McLeod Ganj, whom I will call Tashi, who was always completely honest and unbiased in his accounts. According to Tashi, the bloodshed had occurred because of a dispute over the use of a toilet; the poorest of the poor rent rooms that lack access to toilet facilities. A newcomer had several guests over for dinner, including a monk and a woman. The female guest, who did not understand Hindi, went to use a communal toilet. An Indian landlady yelled at her and then slapped her because she was not a tenant in her building and therefore not entitled to use the facility. The situation escalated—the Tibetan who was hosting the dinner party slapped the Indian woman in retaliation. A crowd of villagers arrived and broke into the Tibetan's room. The Tibetan tenant produced a knife—not likely a genuine weapon, they were cooking dinner in the room—to frighten the mob off, and three villagers were cut. The tenant managed to escape, but two of his guests including a monk were beaten by the mob of approximately twenty villagers. The monk was taken to the police station and imprisoned, so badly injured that, Tashi related, "he even has no strength to lift his head."

What happened next was predictable. According to Tashi, the next day, following the demonstration reported in the *Tribune*, gangs of Indian men armed with sticks, in groups of ten to fifteen, went around McLeod Ganj beating any Tibetan that they could get their hands on. They broke windows and smashed Tibetan-owned motorcycles. A taxi strike was occurring, which no doubt contributed to the violence.[12]

Tashi reported that at least a dozen innocent Tibetans were severely beaten, including the father of a small child:

"One of them was having dinner at his home that night around 9:30 pm. His boy child, aged 3, went out on the street. On hearing shouting outside, the father went out, thinking that there might be something wrong with his son. While he was looking for his child on the street, a group of local Indian young men approached him, and without a single word, they started beating him with sticks, kicks and whatever weapon they could find. However severely they were trying to beat him, he never fought back, fully understanding that a Tibetan's problem with local Indians would badly affect the whole Tibetan community."

Tashi said that the Tibetan owner of a local travel agency had risked his life by riding around on his motorcycle warning Tibetans to get off the street. A Korean tourist who witnessed the beating of a Tibetan man who was a complete stranger to her had lain over his body to stop the mob from injuring him further. (The mobs weren't about to attack foreign tourists who intervened; doing so would not be tolerated by Indian authorities.) As usual, a relatively small number of Indians were involved in the assaults. An Indian neighbor offered to take the injured father to the hospital in his car.

Tashi sent me photographs of some of the father's injuries. One particularly painful looking wound had obviously been created by a hate-fueled blow from a stick or a bar, creating a five or six inch gash in the father's back. He told me that the rest of the injured that he spoke to were bandaged and didn't want to be photographed for fear of repercussions. In faint hope that something could be done, he spoke to an Indian lawyer who works with Tibetans. As expected, the lawyer's words were discouraging: "In my years of experience dealing with the cases related with the Tibetans, I find that when a Tibetan is engaged with a case, nothing became of it."

Nothing regarding the mob violence was reported in the Indian or Tibetan English-language media. Phayul, perhaps in protest for being muzzled by the exile government, posted nothing on any topic for several days. Its annual article celebrating India's Independence Day was notably absent. Some days later, a thread with a few comments appeared in the Phayul discussion forum. That was it. It was as if nothing had happened. I wrote a detailed report and sent it to Amnesty International but never received a reply.

In some ways, the situation has improved since then. A taxi stand has been built just outside of McLeod Ganj, in the forest. Rather than loitering and often drinking in the Main Square, the drivers now retire there for the evening. Tibetans also now have their own night watchmen who keep an eye on the community and encourage late-night stragglers to move along by blowing loudly on whistles. Mostly, this system seems to help, although, when extra watchmen were employed during the winter of 2012 because the exile government anticipated that offices would be broken into by Chinese spies, one they hired was a young man we nicknamed "Glasses Guy", a mentally unstable youth prone to assaulting innocent people in drunken rages. Fortunately the Chinese menace never materialized, for few were confident that security was in capable hands when they saw a boy with psychopathic tendencies wandering around town at night armed with an officially sanctioned weapon. Glasses Guy, to his credit, seemed to do his job; he remained sober and did not assault anyone—at least not before I left town. Fortunately, most of the other watchmen lacked bad reputations, and the late-night streets seem safer for most Tibetans.

Unfortunately, being Tibetans, the watchmen are vulnerable, and problems with taxi drivers still persist. In April of 2010, I read a fairly unbelievable story in my usual source of tainted Dharamsala news, *The Tribune*. Apparently, Tibetan security officials, including a member of the Tibetan prime minister's security team, had attacked Indian Taxi drivers with "sharp-edged weapons" because the Tibetans objected to taxis being parked near the exile government buildings. All three Tibetans had been arrested. [13]

My suspicions were confirmed by calls to my contacts in Dharamsala and an article by Lobsang Wangyal, who had downplayed the violence in 2007, on *Tibet Sun*, a low-profile Tibetan news website. [14] According to Wangyal, eyewitnesses reported that the fight had been initiated by ten to fifteen taxi drivers and Indian villagers who appeared to be drunk. A taxi parked within the gates of the sprawling Tibetan government in exile compound was found with a wiper blade and rear tail light broken. The taxi drivers accused the watchman of not protecting their vehicles. Two exile-government security officials, who had been drinking beer with friends, tried to stop the ensuing argument. A taxi driver hit one of the security officials with a sharp edged weapon, injuring him badly. One of the Tibetans snatched the weapon, and a violent fight ensued. An Indian received serious injuries, two others minor ones. The Tibetans involved claimed that they had unsuccessfully attempted to call the police during the mêlée. Eight to ten more taxi drivers drove up, but the Tibetans were able to escape. Three Tibetans, but none of the instigators, were arrested. An anonymous source said that attacks on watchmen were commonplace and that the three Tibetans involved were not the sort of people who would instigate a fight.

From time to time racially motivated crimes still occur, but nothing ever seems to be done about them. After he got off work late one night in 2011, my friend Tamdin, a waiter, was walking home to Amdo Village, a bedroom community ten minutes walk from McLeod Ganj. Little did he know that some local Indians had been arguing or fighting with Tibetans—who they were or what had transpired I never heard. The Tibetans had gotten away, so when the group—seeking to exact their revenge on any Tibetan—came across Tamdin walking alone, they jumped him and beat him severely.

For me, this incident was particularly horrible because Tamdin is one of the most gentle and soft-spoken people that I know. He was so badly injured that he had to miss more than a week of work. When he did return, he was sporting a massive black eye—it wasn't entirely gone months later—and a scar where he had received numerous stitches to his lip. Tamdin was proud that he had not fought back, giving his attackers no excuse for more violence. "I just let them beat me," he told me with a sad smile. Some months later, Tamdin gave up on his dream of studying to become an accredited English teacher. He returned to Tibet.

Another disturbing incident happened a few months later at the end of monsoon. My friend Rinchen Dondrub also lived in Amdo Village.

One evening he heard shouting outside. Apparently there had been a disagreement between one of the Indian landlords and a Tibetan. Rinchen Dondrub didn't know what had occurred, but when he arrived at the scene, a Tibetan man was on the ground being kicked by Indian villagers, including small boys and girls. The Tibetan was begging them to stop. "Stop saying that. You are only encouraging them," Rinchen Dondrub shouted when he saw that the villagers were enjoying the man's suffering. When the Tibetan stopped crying for mercy, the villagers lost interest in beating him. Rinchen Dondrub was extremely disturbed that Indian children had participated in the violence, "They are teaching hate to their children."

Chapter 16

In January of 2011, an incident occurred that could have potentially led to violence: India, especially Dharamsala, was rocked by a scandal involving the Karmapa, the third-highest lama in the Tibetan Buddhist world. The Indian media had a field-day with the story, which involved the admittedly shocking discovery that the Karmapa's Trust had been storing cash, with a value reported to be up to $1.5 million U.S., in several of its offices. The media turned what transpired to be no more than a serious accounting problem into a high-profile national security issue and an opportunity, in some cases, to slander Tibetans. I was immediately concerned because Indians often complained to me that Tibetans are "rich," and a lot of money was involved in the story.

The situation first came to light when two Indian men were stopped while driving from Delhi to Dharamsala at one of the frequent roadblocks set up for India's Republic Day. In the ensuing search of the vehicle, 1 Crore rupees, about $218,000 U.S., was located and seized. It transpired that the money was a down payment for land being purchased by the Karmapa's Trust from a Dharamsala businessman. The authorities were suspicious about the exact nature of the cash and the legality of the transaction. Their suspicions led to searches of the Karmapa's Trust offices and the discovery of even more enormous sums of money, in various currencies, stored in metal trunks.

Initially, most reports in the Indian media focused on the vast sums involved, speculating that the money was being used for illegal land purchases. However, in the days that followed, the speculations shifted to accusing the Karmapa of being a Chinese spy because Chinese currency had been found in the Karmapa's Trust office. Although both the Dalai Lama and the Karmapa's office informed the media that pilgrims from Tibet and Mainland China frequently visit the lamas and holy places of India and often leave sizable donations in cash, the media for the most part refused to acknowledge this fact and continued with their allegations.

Over the years, several factors have complicated the life of the, at that time, twenty-five year old Karmapa. At the age of fourteen, he and several of his aides made a dramatic escape from Tibet. His flight was not without controversy because some authorities were incredulous that such a high-ranking lama could escape Tibet unnoticed, but the explanations given by the Karmapa and his entourage were compelling. It also made little sense that a child lama would be sent by the Chinese to India in order to act as a spy. The situation was further complicated by the existence of a second candidate for the position of Karmapa already residing in India, but the newly arrived Karmapa was welcomed and endorsed by the Dalai Lama, and the Indian authorities allowed him to settle in the Kangra Valley, near Dharamsala, although restrictions were placed on his movements. There he remained for eleven years, mostly confined to a building in the Gyuto Monastery complex, studying Buddhism and giving teachings and audiences to his many followers from India, Tibet, and around the world. The Karmapa avoided politics, and his philanthropic work was low-key. Thus, he avoided major media attention until January 2011.

Very little information regarding the ongoing investigation was released to the media by the investigating authorities, but this did not stop the Indian media from quoting unnamed sources in many highly speculative articles. On January 28th, the *Tribune* reported that "Officials believe the Karmapa is the recipient of huge funds from China and has been using the funds to help Beijing control the Buddhist monasteries spread from Ladakh in Jammu & Kashmir to Tawang in Arunachal Pradesh."[1] The reporter, however, neglected to name any sources, and no such information had been released by the government investigators.

On January 29th, in an article entitled "Himachal Police Grills Karmapa over Raids," IBNLive reported that "During his questioning Karmapa was aided by a translator as he speaks only Chinese. Karmapa reportedly feigned ignorance about the source of money."[2] In reality, the Karmapa speaks only Tibetan fluently—although his

Chinese may be very good because he, of course, grew up in Tibet—and traditionally and possibly unfortunately, Tibetan lamas, particularly those of his age and status, have little if any involvement in the management of their finances. The article goes on to state that "Sources say 1.14 lakh Chinese Yuan recovered from his office on Thursday was in serial number," implying that the money came from the Chinese Government, while following the pattern of not naming a source. On the same day, a headline from NDTV.com boldly stated: "Karmapa money trail: Recovered cash came from Nepal"[3] although it, too, neglected to name the source of its information. This pattern continued in dozens of articles and news reports, many of which appeared to contain only one or two sentences that related factual information from reliable or named sources. The investigators from the Indian government could hardly be blamed for providing little information, for they had been examining what was obviously a complicated case for just over a week; their comments to the media had been understandably cautious and concise.

The Karmapa's supporters, including the Dalai Lama, insisted that he was not a Chinese spy, and the Tibetan community held several events, erroneously described by several media outlets including the *Tribune* and IBNLive as protests against the investigation,[4] in which they implored the media to refrain from speculation and wait for the results of the investigation. Perhaps faulty accounting occurred or perhaps the money had been, as the Karmapa's office stated, accumulating since 2002, awaiting government clearance to be deposited to a bank under the rules governing the Foreign Contribution Regulation Act.

In February of 2011, the Karmapa was cleared by the Government of India of accusations of spying, and in August of that year he was given permission to travel to America. This was only the second time that permission to travel abroad had been granted to him since he had arrived in India in 2000. This move was seen as a clear sign of the Karmapa's complete exoneration by the Indian government.

The Karmapa scandal heightened tensions between Tibetans and Indians in the Dharamsala community. There was much discussion of the wealth accumulated by Tibetans and illegal land transactions. As mentioned earlier, Tibetans and, indeed, non-Himachalis are forbidden from purchasing property in the state, with few exceptions. A positive sign was that other than a lot of grumbling, nothing untoward occurred.

I couldn't help but feel terribly sorry for the Karmapa. Since his escape into exile, he has been living as a guest at a monastery. He has no fenced yard where he can exercise. If he wants sunshine, he is restricted to the roof. If he were to leave the building without bodyguards, he would be harassed by his foreign followers, many of whom stay at the monastery to be near him. He must have been excited to have been buying property of his own where he could enjoy some privacy. Since arriving in exile, he has gained weight; his gait and physique are no longer those of a young man. He seldom appears happy; his apartment seems to me to be little more than a glorified prison. His presence brings huge numbers of pilgrims from around the world to the area, yet he has received no thanks or consideration from the state for this tourism boon, even in the form of permission to build a home. In most countries, his situation would be viewed as a human rights violation, but few seem to care. He is, in a sense, the ultimate newcomer.

Chapter 17

In part, tensions and misunderstandings between Indians and Tibetans can be blamed on the Indian media. India, arguably, enjoys some of the freest media in the region, a claim which is less impressive than it sounds: its neighbors include China and Pakistan. Reporters without Borders ranks India 131st out of 179 nations[1], and I expect that India will begin denying me visas once this book is published; it is known for doing that kind of thing. Even though Tibetan and other journalists in India are forced to practice self-censorship and threats and violence against journalists are relatively common, the Indian press enjoys a great deal of freedom when it comes to reporting on many topics. Unfortunately, to put it mildly, this does not always translate into honest and unbiased journalism. As one friend put it during the Karmapa crisis, "The Indian media are a marvel in Asia. In many neighboring countries, journalists are imprisoned for reporting the truth. In India, they can publish the truth, lies, seemingly whatever they want. It's really quite remarkable." Coverage of the Dalai Lama and political events related to Tibet are generally straight-forward and unbiased, but reporting on issues concerning Dharamsala often has an anti-Tibetan and even inflammatory slant.

The coverage of the following event is a perfect example. On December 1, 2010, a fire gutted eight shops on a narrow winding stretch of Jogibara Road in downtown McLeod Ganj. Around midnight, my son and I heard the wailing of fire engines far below and observed the twinkling of their lights on the long road that winds its way up from Lower Dharamsala. Shortly thereafter, the electricity went off in McLeod Ganj. When we stepped outside onto our balcony, we saw thick black smoke illuminated by an ominous orange glow coming from the heart of downtown. I grabbed my first aid kit, and we ran to the scene, several blocks from our place. Local Indians and Tibetans, both men and women, as well as Nepali workers and a few tourists, had formed bucket brigades and were valiantly battling to put out the flames that had already completely engulfed several businesses. Employees of a roof-top dhaba (road-side eatery), fortunately located in a concrete building, were trapped by the flames, which blocked their only escape route, and efforts were underway to rescue them.

The fire department arrived, but the trucks could not navigate the narrow, winding street. However, dozens of men and women assisted the firefighters to rapidly run hoses down to the scene and pull them into position. No one was asked to help; they just pitched in and worked as fast as they could. At times, the firemen were busy ensuring that the hoses were laid correctly, so ordinary people, both Indians and Tibetans, manned the hoses. That night no one was Indian or Tibetan, rich or poor, a newcomer or a settlement Tibetan. The fire was brought under control, the men trapped in the dhaba were saved, and no one was seriously injured. It was a remarkable example of community co-operation in a time of crisis.

Local news events are most often covered by *The Tribune*; as is typical, it ran a negative article with no mention of how the community had come together on that cold winter night. Everyone involved was blamed in one way or another. The fire department was criticized for arriving late, but there was no mention that it takes time to drive fire engines up the long winding road from Dharamsala. The shorter route is far too steep for fire engines heavily loaded with water, and vehicles of such size would not be able to navigate the hairpin corners. The writer, probably their usual hack Lalit Mohan—the article had all of his hallmarks—blamed street stalls in McLeod Ganj for blocking access, presumably not realizing that the street stalls are packed away at night.[2] After I read the article, I examined the road myself, and in several minutes discovered that electricity poles created the narrowest sections. Electricity lines were another concern. He also blamed development, even though the fire occurred in an old part of town where the roads are wider and better maintained than they have ever been. The town occupies an extremely narrow ridge not more than a few dozen metres wide in many places. Most of the businesses and residences downtown would need to be bulldozed to create wider roads.

But instead of sympathizing with the business owners, most of whom are local Indians, he wrote: "The shops that were destroyed yesterday were illegal structures developed by locals and further rented to outsiders who were running commercial activity." As if it matters that one of the businesses was run by a Nepali and another by a Kashmiri. All of the businesses had lost everything, and the owners, who had no insurance, were bereaved and in shock. Some of them— grown men–were almost in tears when I went back to survey the damage the morning after the fire.

The reporter made one final dig, entirely unrelated to the fire, "A large number of Tibetans have encroached and constructed habitations and guest houses on reserve forest land in McLeodganj [sic]." This statement was interesting because almost every new building that has gone up around town over the past few years has been built by Indians, although Tibetans do rent shop spaces and offices from them. I can think of only one new Tibetan hotel out of dozens. In any event, whatever encroachments were directly involved had been built more than a decade previously. I was later told that the government is loathe to crack down on encroachments in Dharamsala and elsewhere because most belong to Indians and such a move would prove hugely unpopular with Indian voters.

This article was just one of many negative ones in the Tribune and seemingly written by the same journalist. He seems to enjoy using his journalistic license to stir the pot of hate and mistrust, even managing to blame monsoon damage to McLeod Ganj roads on the Tibetans.[3] I couldn't find many articles, other than those about the Dalai Lama or the political situation in Tibet, in which he had anything nice to say about Tibetans, didn't invent some aspect, manipulate the truth, or go out of his way to criticize Tibetans and other "outsiders." One wonders if someone is padding his pocket to stir the shit pot. The sad thing is that many people around the country, from ordinary folks to politicians and other influential people, read what is written and believe it. I've been told that just as much unsubstantiated rubbish is written in Hindi papers under the guise of journalism.

In the end, I realized that I had a complicated relationship with Lalit Mohan of the *Tribune*. On one hand, I despised him for the way that he phrased many of his articles, but on the other hand, he was often the only journalist who reported on situations involving the Tibetan community. For example, no other media and no human rights groups reported that, in 2012 two Tibetans were deported by Indian authorities who dumped them in the Himalayas near the Chinese border. [4] I looked to the *Tribune* for what I often could not find elsewhere. Strangely, an often nasty journalist that I had never met was somehow my ally in my pursuit of truth and justice.

Chapter 18

My first encounter with Dharamsala's finest was in May of 2003 when I attended my first and only out-door dance party at Bhagsu with two Tibetan friends. The event, known as a "full moon party" was advertised, so if the police had wanted to put a stop to it before it started, they had plenty of opportunity. It was held on the only flat piece of land near the Bhagsu waterfall. Perhaps a residence had been there prior to the 1905 earthquake; except by an unlikely freak of nature, such a flat expanse could only have been artificially created. The crowd of about one hundred was very laid-back, mostly foreign hippies, whose greatest crimes besides some marijuana smoking, were terrible dancing and even worse fashion; an enormous industry in India is devoted to making, for the tourist market, hippy costumes of such ridiculous appearance that they would not look out of place in a circus. If anything, the party was boring. We sat on the grass talking, and each of us bought a beer.

At around midnight, close to a dozen policemen showed up. They began shouting at everyone, kicking the Tibetans and Indians and hitting them with sticks. When they arrived at our group, although we were not drunk and were waiting politely for their commands, they dragged one of my friends around by his hair and kicked the other. One officer pulled off my shawl and made a rude comment. I was dressed modestly in a t-shirt with sleeves and jeans. A tourist woman began screaming and begging after they went through her bag and took all of her money and her passport, but they only laughed and pushed her around. They took everyone's personal alcohol as well as that being sold by the promoter, loading it into boxes. They told everyone to leave, but they didn't seem concerned if we did so, for they marched off clutching open bottles and boxes of beer laughing and joking. No one was charged with anything, and no paperwork was written up.

The Tibetans dispersed among the boulders exposed along the river by glacial melt-water in centuries past. Once the police had climbed back up to the path to Bhagsu, the Tibetans began howling like wolves. The eerie sounds rang out from among the rocks up and down the river; Francis Younghusband described hearing similar "jackal-like yells" when Tibetans attacked during the British invasion of Tibet in 1904.[1] The police carried on, no doubt pleased with their prizes, and realizing that if they did return to attempt to punish the howlers, most of the partygoers could escape by fleeing down the treacherous creek bed. Fortunately, the next day, the woman's passport was found lying at the side of the road and returned to her. That was the first and last time that I went to a full-moon dance party.

I witnessed a more disturbing incident in 2006. My then husband, who is of course Tibetan, and I were visiting India from Canada on a holiday. We went for dinner at McLlo with a newcomer and two foreigners. It was a cold winter night, and there were no other customers in the restaurant. We had one beer and left at 10 pm. The square in front of the restaurant was, as was usual in those days, full of parked taxis but otherwise appeared deserted. As the two Tibetans headed down the stairs in front of us, an Indian man appeared and aggressively blocked the bottom of the stairs. "What's your problem?" my husband asked and pushed him aside. The Indian hit him, and he immediately hit back.

It appeared to have been a set-up because within seconds, around two dozen taxi drivers emerged from behind and within the taxis parked in the square and attacked the Tibetans, who picked up stones to try to defend themselves with, but they were immediately overwhelmed. The taxi drivers held the Tibetans by their hair and bent them forward, kicking and punching them in their faces and abdomens. Blood poured everywhere. I was afraid that my husband or his friend would be killed, so, guessing—thankfully correctly—that they would not harm a foreigner, I dove into the fray and dragged the taxi drivers off as quickly as I could, but although they were small and I was pumped full of adrenalin, there were too many of them. They reeked of liquor, but they were smart enough not to beat me, a Western tourist. Several Indians who operated businesses in the vicinity as well as our foreign friends shouted at them to stop, to no avail. The police arrived and stood around watching but doing nothing even though the situation was obviously life-threatening. It was not until I began repeating, "He is Canadian. (He was actually just a landed immigrant.) He is from Canada," that the taxi drivers stopped beating my husband. They all joined in beating our friend for a few minutes, but we were able to drag him away down Bhagsu road. I think it had dawned on them that they may have been beating a Tibetan who was no longer a refugee—that could cause problems for them—so they had lost their enthusiasm.

When we got back to our room, the sight was sickening. Both were covered almost from head to toe in the blood that was pouring from their noses. Their hair was torn out in handfuls. Our friend was the worst injured, with what appeared to be a broken rib; his ear was torn, and his face sported several ugly wounds. I regret that I never took photographs. Thankfully, their injuries were not worse—their attackers were small and drunk and most wore sandals.

Once I knew that the guys were more or less ok, I went back to the square to talk to the police. When I told them that I wanted to file a complaint, they assumed a threatening manner and ordered me to go back to my room. The taxi drivers were cavorting in the square, proudly waving our friend's jacket that they had pulled off him. Back at our room, I vowed to contact the Canadian embassy for support, but our friend implored me not to, "The police will question my R.C. They will make terrible trouble for me." He was almost in tears as he pleaded. I never contacted the embassy, but I did write a report of what had occurred as well as other events that I had witnessed and sent it to the Canadian Minister of Immigration in hope that doing so would help Tibetans with refugee claims. I did receive a personal reply stating that my comments would be taken into consideration and that my letter would be forwarded to the embassy in Delhi.

Other problems with the police have been equally if not more disturbing. One night in 2011, my son was leaving Excite, a local bar, late at night. A Tibetan man who was drunk left ahead of him. Down in the square, the police beat and kicked the helpless man and tied him up. My son was appalled. He didn't know the Tibetan personally, but he had seen him around and knew he was harmless. No one else said or did anything, so my son, who was only a teenager, walked up to the police and bravely said, "Give him to me. We are talking him home." He was joined by several male Western friends. The police untied the Tibetan and handed him over, so obviously he was not a criminal. My son's foreign friends walked him home.

The incidents were not isolated. Around the same time, customers in a bar witnessed another more grotesque beating of my friend Norbu on the street late one night. I had seen Norbu that evening, as I had on so many occasions, quietly drinking himself into oblivion at another local bar. Although he was an alcoholic, Norbu was popular with everyone, staff and customers alike. He was brought from Tibet to India as a child in order to receive an education. He grew up essentially an orphan at a Tibetan Children's Village school. A sensitive artistic soul lacking the support of family, he lost his way. When I first met him in 2010, he ran a very small business, but spent most evenings at the bar drinking beer and sniffing glue. Over the months that followed, he managed to free himself of his glue dependency, but he remained an alcoholic.

This was not the first time that the police had beaten Norbu. One evening in the winter of 2010, he appeared at the bar with his face bruised and his forehead swollen. "The police beat me for no reason," he told me. I didn't know him very well at that point, and I knew he had a drinking problem, but his story was confirmed by a staff member that I had known for years, "When we closed, I walked to the main square with him. He was being quiet and good, but the police took him and beat him. You know how it is here; I wanted to help him, but I could do nothing."

The second beating occurred some months later. The witnesses saw Norbu walking alone in the street. A police jeep pulled up. A group of policemen alighted from the vehicle, searched Norbu's pockets, found nothing, but proceeded to beat him with their belts as he writhed on the ground crying in pain and begging for mercy. According to the witnesses that I spoke to, who were Indian, Tibetan,

Kashmiri, and Western, watchmen employed by the Tibetan community stood by and did nothing. When the police were finished with their fun, they left Norbu lying in the square, got into their vehicle, and took off. As they drove away, the onlookers observed a Tibetan man, who had also witnessed the beating but from the street, strike the window of the police vehicle, but it didn't stop. Perhaps the police had realized the size of their audience in what had appeared to be a deserted part of town.

The next day, I asked a Tibetan friend to see if Norbu was willing to be photographed. That afternoon the friend dropped by my house and gave me photographs that he had taken with his mobile phone. Norbu had agreed to be photographed as long as his face wasn't shown, and I made sure that the police didn't know that they were of him. (To achieve that aim, I knew that I had to wait a very long time before sharing them with anyone.) Norbu's legs were covered with huge black and purple bruises, and his hand was badly swollen. There were concerns that it might be broken. "What kind of hate does it take to beat someone like that?" the photographer asked as we looked at the photographs "Norbu never harms anyone."

Another Tibetan friend, Nyima, had shown up as the photographs were being taken. According to the photographer, he broke down in tears when he saw the extent of Norbu's injuries. Although he was already an alcoholic, that day Nyima began more seriously abusing drugs and alcohol—I saw him at the bar that night and he was a complete mess. In the days that followed, he lost his mind. As I write many months later, he has still not regained his sanity.

As always, friends discussed what could be done, but nothing seemed to hold promise. Norbu was understandably afraid, and worse events had occurred over the years with no comment or action from human rights organizations. The Tibetan government in exile is always silent when refugees are beaten by the police, and, unfortunately, there seems to be a perception in the community that those who are drunk or on the street late at night deserve to be beaten. Although the Dalai Lama has thrown his support behind Kunphen, a Western-style awareness and treatment organization, when Tibetans become alcoholics or drug addicts, little sympathy or understanding is shown in the general community. It is apparent from talking to the addicts that many of them suffer from PTSD and other mental health issues such as depression. Often, the beatings further their substance abuse problems.

Those who are beaten are seldom arrested for any offence. Sometimes the police simply crack a Tibetan across the head when they pass him on the street at night. One friend complained that he still had trouble hearing weeks after such an assault. Another friend told me that the police dragged him around by the hair while calling him an "animal." I have never seen similar attacks occur against middle-class and wealthy Indians no matter how drunk or badly behaved they are. Victims appear to be intentionally chosen because they are known to be poor and marginalized.

Aside from occasionally being violent, the police also have a reputation for extorting money and demanding bribes. I had my own experience with baksheesh, as it is known. If you get married, you need to have a document signed by the police. Everyone we knew who married in 2003 had to pay bribes. We were told that it was important not to meet the police in your home or they might help themselves to your possessions, so we arranged to meet in a restaurant. A scrawny, seedy looking officer arrived several hours late for the appointment. He didn't even bother to appear official and immediately and furtively suggested that we palm him 150 rupees before he signed the document. A couple that we knew visited the police station to have their documents signed. They were told to bring a chicken and a bottle of whiskey as payment. They were a quiet couple who didn't drink, which made their story even funnier.

Sometimes the police would pretend there was a curfew. Several times over the years, I was stopped at night, before midnight during the off-season, and told that it was illegal to be on the street at night. Tibetans told me that the same thing happened to them all of the time. In the case of Tibetans, the police usually demanded a "fine." The late-night shakedowns for cash seem to be happening less frequently, although one friend reported that he had all of his money taken because he couldn't produce an R.C. in the spring of 2012. He had stopped being a monk—presumably he was classified as a "student"— so he could no longer renew it. He was expected to return to Ngawa[2] in Tibet where most of the self-immolations were occurring.

In January of 2012 one afternoon, I watched a group of policemen fine a street vendor 500 rupees for having large heavy-duty plastic bags that the shawls that she was selling were stored in. (In order to combat the tremendous waste disposal problems, it is illegal for shop-keepers to put purchases in flimsy plastic bags in Himachal Pradesh, although heavy-duty plastic shopping bags seemed to be legal.) A production was made of producing a receipt book, but I watched carefully and no receipt was actually written up. They simply placed the money in the receipt book and moved on to their next victim.

What is particularly worrisome about policing that seems to be focused on beating poor people and collecting fines and baksheesh is that Dharamsala is a major tourist destination and therefore an ideal target for terrorist attacks. Indians who appear wealthy can act with impunity. This utter lack of professionalism does not bode well for public safety in that the truly dangerous would recognize security weaknesses and capitalize on them. The few serious crimes that do occur are seldom solved; rather than undertaking careful detective work, suspects tend to be those who are easiest to nab. Assaults and robberies, including those involving tourists, are often laughed off. Most locals are afraid to call the police. Although policing has improved in the past nine years, it has a long way to go.

In absence of law and order, traditional Tibetan methods of resolving serious situations are sometimes employed. I went out for drinks one night with friends whom I will call Eric, Dr Banoffee, and Khonthar. We drank a few beers and unlike on most nights, which were usually mostly devoted to gossiping about ourselves, spent the evening engaged in a long-winded discussion of the Tibetan language. My son was the D.J. in the bar that night. As always, the music was shut off at midnight so that the neighbors wouldn't complain. A Tibetan at a nearby table began loudly cursing my son in Tibetan for turning off the music. Khonthar, who was a bit drunk and protective of my son, told the guy to shut up and get over it. After words were exchanged for a few minutes, we continued our conversation, finished our beers, and left for home.

We hadn't noticed that the heckler had followed us outside. In the street, he approached Khonthar in a rage, and they exchanged several punches. Eric, who was very well versed in martial arts but was loathe to take down a local without extreme provocation, stepped in. Things seemed to calm down for a moment, but suddenly the angry young man hit Khonthar hard in the face. Blood began to gush from a large cut on his forehead. In a split second, he was drenched in it, and it was pouring onto the road. The culprit and his friends ran away. I put my first aid skills to use stopping the bleeding and took Khonthar to the hospital in a taxi where the gash was cleaned and stitched shut.

The story didn't end there. Several days later a monk appeared at Khonthar's home, an emissary from the attacker. The monk explained that the attacker wished to apologize for stabbing Khonthar and, to compensate, would pay his medical bills and replace his glasses, which had been broken. Khonthar, who has exceptional English and is a socially involved intellectual, knows that such problems are handled very differently elsewhere. He took an unusual stance for a Tibetan in India, telling the monk that he was considering going to the police. The monk implored him to change his mind. Khonthar said that he needed to think it over. The next day, new emissaries came begging Khonthar to accept the proposal. Khonthar agreed, but explained that if the attacker bothered him again, he would go to the police. The money was handed over, and Khonthar then met the attacker for tea. They agreed to end further hostilities.

Although such methods of conflict resolution work to a certain extent— only with those with some sense of social responsibility— it is certain that fights, especially violent ones, would occur less frequently if the police were fair and trustworthy. Tibetans I know who were quick to fight in India were far less likely to do so once they arrived in the West (even those who were still suffering from anger management problems) because they understood that people, including bar staff, were not afraid to call the police. Despite its spiritual aspects, McLeod Ganj in many ways resembles the "Wild West."

Chapter 19

When I first went to India, I was intrigued by Buddhism. When I arrived in McLeod Ganj, many Tibetans asked me if I were a Buddhist, but something about their body language when they posed the question made me hesitant, so I always answered, "No," although I qualified the statement by explaining my deep respect for and interest in their religion. I soon learned that Western Buddhists have mixed reputations: some were admired for their kindness and the genuineness of their faith, while others were seen as mentally troubled and unstable. Some Tibetans referred to red-robed Western nuns as "gas bottles." In India, the gas cylinders used for cook stoves are big, round, red, and considered prone to explode.

In their defense, I did meet many foreign practitioners of Tibetan Buddhism who were well-adjusted. Some of the nicest foreigners that I met were Buddhists. Most admirable to me were those who defied the odds by also being socially and/or politically involved. However, in part because so many converts are self-centered, intolerant, mentally unhinged, and whiny, my focus stayed more on social issues. In Dharamsala, when they weren't practicing their faith, foreign Buddhists could usually be found sitting in McLeod Ganj restaurants—where they always seemed to congregate and where lazy me ate most of my dinners—complaining about the food or the service oblivious to the poor trudging past or Tibetan demonstrators filing by carrying photos of political prisoners or Tibetans who had self-immolated. If they weren't obsessing over their spiritual development, they were usually moaning about something: the traffic, the noise, and other deficiencies—their way of life involved too much nit-picking for me. My friend Dolkar, a newcomer who was trapped in India, had a fitting comment for the whiners and complainers, "If they don't like it here, they can go home."

Western Buddhist converts, born-again Christians, and converts to other faiths share a lot of similarities. Gusto for religion seemed to prohibit many Western Buddhists from behaving like normal human beings, and they displayed little tolerance for those who did. They tended to be fanatical about their newfound religion to the point that they looked down on most Tibetans for not being pious enough. "I have to keep away from Tibetans if I want to practice Buddhism," an American man in my Buddhism class told me darkly.

Tibetans are not known for proselytizing. They virtually closed off their country to the outside world until the Chinese invasion. In most places, foreigners wishing to study their religion were not welcomed; indeed, they were most often deported. The current Dalai Lama teaches tolerance and respect for all religions, a view which was true of Tibetans in the past as well; in old Tibet, the holy city of Lhasa and other regions were home to Muslims who were free to openly practice their religion.[1] Tibetans usually willingly discussed aspects of their religion and were often pleased if foreigners were Buddhist, but they usually refrained from pushing their faith on others. There are also apparently rules, which I don't pretend to understand, against the teaching or professing of expert knowledge of texts without having passed certain exams.

None of this stopped the more obnoxious variety of Western Buddhists from grilling people on their religious practices and preaching to anyone who would listen. I tried to avoid conversations with these sorts of people. If I did speak to them, they were usually incapable of normal small talk. Their conversation-opener was usually something like, "Are you familiar with the teachings of Rama Lama Ding Dong?" One of my settler Tibetan friends uncharitably referred to the plethora of rinpoches, there are hundreds of them, as "Lama Bow Wow and Lama Woof Woof." If I didn't express great interest in or knowledge of their acclaimed teacher, I received a look of barely veiled disgust. My explanation that I was more involved in social and human rights issues usually caused their eyes to glaze over.

Their reaction was not entirely surprising: Tibetans teaching Buddhism in the West almost never bring up the sometimes horrific situation in their homeland, although the Tibetan religious community, particularly young monks and nuns, have been at the forefront of protest both in Tibet and in India. But traditionally, most spiritual advisors have kept out of politics. Some of those teaching in the West are still involved with their monasteries in Tibet; discussion of politics on their part could be disastrous because the Chinese might put an end to their work and cause tremendous trouble for their monasteries in Tibet. Tibetans understand these realities, so they do not look to Rinpoches and other teachers for direction regarding protest.

Western Buddhists were, for the most part, conspicuously absent from demonstrations or even tranquil candle-light vigils. Rather than becoming a part of the Tibetan community through their conversion, most showed little interest in anything Tibetan other than teachings, rituals, and religious paraphernalia and books, although they might eat vegetarian momos from time to time. Typically, they sucked everything that they could out of the religion–usually in the name of their own personal development—but had no interest in the suffering of the society that created and embodies their newfound faith. This may seem a harsh assessment, but having attended many Tibet-related events and discussed the situation with numerous activists, it is, unfortunately, an accurate one.

Demonstrations rocked Tibet in March of 2008, making front-page headlines and becoming the leading story in news coverage around the world. Thousands of Tibetans, including many monks and nuns, were imprisoned and many are believed to have been killed. I found no mention of what transpired in the Western Buddhist magazines. Following the demonstrations *Tricycle* magazine encouraged readers to "Make Peace with Your Demons" while Tibetans were being tortured in Chinese prisons.[2]

Tibetans were usually polite and tolerant when it came to the indifference to their plight and the mind numbingly boring and superior-minded babblings about Buddhism by foreign visitors. No matter how off-base the foreigners were in their religious interpretations, Tibetans seldom contradicted them and usually tried to be encouraging. I grew to cherish rare words of dissent. One of the funniest conversations that I ever overheard took place at the Library Canteen as I was having tea one morning. A Western man in his 50's sat down and was soon joined by a Tibetan in his early twenties who did his best to listen attentively as the Westerner discussed his simplistic and odd theories of Buddhism. It was fortunate that I didn't tune out the conversation as I so often did.

"Have you read my teachings on emptiness?" The Westerner asked the Tibetan. "No," the young man replied. "I'll have to give you a copy," said the Western man. With a deadpan expression and in a monotone voice, the Tibetan responded, "No, I don't want it." I almost spit up my tea. The Westerner didn't even blink and started going on about his book. The Tibetan listened for a time then politely said good bye and left.

Most converts' ideas of intensive Buddhist practice weren't the same as those of my Tibetan neighbors in their meditation cells: they didn't find a tiny dark room to eat, sleep, and pray in, tuning out the world while the dogs barked all night and the neighbors shouted drunkenly. They wanted the serenity experienced by an aesthetic meditating on a mountain in a cave, but they needed their comfortable rooms, their e-mails, and beverages and foods that met their standards.

It was very strange. I'd read the Dalai Lama's books and taken classes at the Library. The message that I had received was that nothing is permanent, and given the right attitude, any suffering can be endured. Tibetans on the whole tended to be more stoic about inconveniences such as an indifferent omelet or a badly made cappuccino. Their Buddhist heroes were those who somehow managed to keep up their Buddhist practice under adverse conditions, for example, in Chinese prisons.

After six months of classes at the Library, I realized that many of these people just didn't get it—any of it. The classroom was gorgeously painted and decorated with Tibetan motifs and religious art. The teacher, referred to as Geshe la, an honorific term for a graduate of the highest level of Buddhist study, was a shy and dignified monk. When he arrived at the classroom, we would all remove our shoes and pad in silently. I was lucky in that I had a lot of friends who had been or still were monks or nuns. I tried as best as I could to follow their descriptions of suitable behavior in class. My friends had told me that novice monks were given a whack whenever they squirmed around until they learned to sit still. My knees would seize up, forcing me to change position at least once, but some of the students managed to sit cross-legged and perfectly still for the entire hour.

Others were not so disciplined. They would enter the classroom and perform elaborate prostrations (bows that resemble push-ups) before Geshe la and then disrupt the class by rummaging in their bags for water bottles which crackled and crinkled as they frequently rehydrated themselves. One young man placed himself dead centre in the room for all to see. He struck a torturous cross-legged posture, his back ram-rod straight, and his hands clasped at his chest as if in prayer. He remained thus for about fifteen minutes. Then he seemed to forget where he was, for, much to my amusement, he began intently picking his nose and carefully examining its contents. Geshe la somehow maintained his usual inscrutable expression.

A few days later, a new student arrived and seated himself directly in front of Geshe la. He whipped out a laptop and typed away furiously for the duration of the class. Geshe la didn't say anything and appeared to completely ignore the spectacle. The next day the same thing happened. This time, Geshe la interrupted his usual teachings to give a subtle lesson on classroom etiquette and electronic devices in particular. Unfortunately, the typist didn't seem to understand, although he transcribed the lecture with all of the concentration of a court reporter.

A few days later, Geshe la gently chastised the students for putting their prayer books on the floor; among other things, religious books are not supposed to be placed where you put your potentially dirty feet. The American man who needed to stay away from Tibetans to practice Buddhism had been a repeat offender in this regard; funny enough, he dropped the class several days later because it was "not advanced enough." The student with the best attendance and consistently appropriate behavior was a Korean man who often arrived hung-over after staying up late drinking with his Indian neighbors.

After class one day, I joked to Geshe la's translator that besides sending Geshe la to teach, the Nechung Monastery should also provide a disciplinarian to beat students monastic style so that we would all learn to behave properly in class. The translator laughed and from then on chatted with me when we ran into one another. I kept hoping that a sign with simple instructions would be posted or we would receive a hand-out on etiquette, but from the way that Tibetans in the vicinity of the classroom almost always avoided eye contact and conversation with foreign students, I suspect that we were all seen as potentially volatile and mentally unstable—not to be antagonized.

Geshe la was a very reserved man who spoke very little English, so I never knew what he thought. A "Geshe" is somewhat equivalent to a Western PhD in Tibetan Buddhist philosophy, although the candidates appear to study longer and harder than Western PhD students. I felt embarrassed that such a learned man was teaching our group of nit-wits, but perhaps he found us entertaining after the solemnity of classes in the monastery. It was impossible to know from his Sphinx-like expression.

I respected our teacher for his standoffish behavior, for there is seemingly no greater threat to a monk's vows than female western Buddhists. I don't know what it is about celibate Tibetan men in robes that brings out the worst in some Western women. Asian women of various ethnicities also seem to be drawn to them in a way that is, frankly, rather creepy. Someone should conduct research on the phenomenon. Maybe it is the excitement of chasing the seemingly unobtainable or some twisted desire to have something they consider innocent and pure. Maybe monks seem safer than other men. It was clear from their talk and the excitement in their voices that, even if they would never admit it, some women were not just after platonic friendships or teachings.

I had a monk friend, Rabten, who made friends on Facebook with a number of strangers. He was a very intelligent and moral young man with excellent English. I tutored him every couple of weeks, and one of the things that he wanted to learn was Facebook security and etiquette. One day he told me that he had inadvertently made friends with two women whose behavior was suspect. "Is it normal to send a friend a heart symbol?" he asked me. "Not usually, unless she is a wife or girlfriend," I replied. "That's what I was thinking," Rabten said in dismay.

He went on to tell me that the women one from the U.S.A. and the other from Taiwan, had been hitting on him. He had innocently given the Taiwanese woman his phone number, and she wouldn't stop calling. "I am a monk," he then told the women, "I can't have a girlfriend." The American backed off, but the Taiwanese was more difficult to get rid of without rudely blocking her. "She tried changing her Facebook relationship status to 'In a Relationship' with me," he told me in horror about a week later.

I told my son. He laughed: "Mother, you know what women are like. (My son always calls me "Mother" when he thinks that I am being stupid.) Haven't you noticed how good looking Rabten is?" I had to admit that I hadn't noticed; I tried not to look at monks in that way. My son mentioned a very handsome, young, long-haired Tibetan man who was chased after by an endless parade of foreign women. "Imagine Rabten with long hair," my son said in exasperation, "He looks almost exactly like him." I thought about it and laughed. He was right. Poor Rabten was a chick magnet.

Not all monks took their vows as seriously as Rabten and most others did. During my first week in McLeod Ganj in 2003, I was staying in a cheap room at a friendly little guest house called Himalaya. I shared a toilet with a pretty young Western girl who was staying in the room next door. It was a tiny guest house, with a couple of rooms only, so I ran into her often. She made friends with a handsome young monk. On several occasions, I saw her answer her door to him clad in little more than underpants. He came and went several times a day, and from the guilty expression on his face whenever I ran into him in the corridor, it appeared that he wasn't just going to her room for English lessons.

The guesthouse staff were really angry and quick to set me straight on what was considered appropriate behavior. They didn't blame the girl because she was just a tourist who didn't know better. Most of the staff were ex-monks from Tibet who had left their monasteries. Quitting was fine. They felt that it was important that only those who were truly committed remain monks. What they did not tolerate was monks breaking their vows or chasing girls while still wearing robes. They explained to me that a proper monk should not be hanging around with girls and women, certainly not touching or hugging them. (Over the years, I have hugged three monk friends when I left to go back to Canada but only after they had become almost like family.) Even handshakes should be avoided. If a monk did need to shake hands with a woman – in order to avoid appearing rude to someone who did not understand their culture—he should keep contact to a minimum. He should preferably not visit women's rooms alone, certainly not the room of a girl who was usually scantily clad. Apparently, the guest house staff had been listening at the door and were convinced that the pair was up to no good. Luckily, the girl left town because the staff were so angry that I feared that they might give the monk a beating.

This was my first experience with monks on the prowl. There were hundreds of monks in McLeod Ganj, and at any given time, several seemed to be devoted to chasing girls; there was always a lot of gossip but few actual offenders. I spoke to Western girls and women who had innocently begun friendships with such monks, only to discover that they were after more. Sometimes the women were English teachers and the monks were hoping for a different kind of instruction. Other times monks would offer to teach them about Buddhism and then begin hitting on them. One woman had given a monk her phone number because he told her that he wanted English lessons. He began sending her romantic text messages and then started stalking her. He figured out her routine and would always be loitering in places that she visited. She tried to be polite and keep her distance, but he continued. This went on for weeks until she finally lost her temper.

The problem for such monks is that they often don't know what they will do if they leave their monasteries. Realistically, most don't have a lot of skills and unemployment levels are high. Even worse for those who have recently fled Tibet is that their R.C.'s are extremely difficult to renew if they stop studying. Still, the social stigma in the Tibetan community is huge, so very few purposely chase women.

It can all be a bit confusing, for plenty of monks are in the company of foreign women for perfectly good reasons. Foreigners volunteer as tutors and computer teachers and on projects for monasteries. Many monasteries have meditation centres and conduct fund raising abroad, and their foreign practitioners often visit India. Monks act as hosts and show them around. Some monks run charities. Visitors are often very curious about monks and Buddhism and enjoy talking to them. Some monks are very interested in learning about other cultures and traditions. I met plenty of dedicated monks who had foreign friends, both male and female. Still, after all that I have seen and the terrible reputation of foreign women, I couldn't help but sometimes feel awkward being seen with monk friends or students in public places.

Some of the tourist women were just hot after monks and tried to seduce them. On a number of occasions, monks left their monasteries for such women. They believed that their love was true, but usually, once the women left town, they dumped the now ex-monks on flimsy pretexts. The affairs were obviously just holiday games for the women. The former monks were left with nothing but broken hearts. No home, no job, and no skills. Some of them became Salai gyals.

Some foreigners had what could be referred to as "pet monks." These foreigners were usually religious. They would have likely preferred a high status pet monk with a title: a rinpoche, tulku, geshe or lama. But if they couldn't get enough attention from one of those, they sought out regular monks. From observing them in action, listening in on conversations, and occasionally speaking to them, I noticed that the pet monks made them feel like important practitioners and in some cases fulfilled the roles of mental-health services providers.

Foreigners with pet monks could often spotted in coffee shops. When they made eye contact with me, they often had a proud and superior expression as if to say, "Look at me. I have a monk and you don't." They were usually droning on and on about Buddhism, not lively discussions of complex topics, but rather monologues or discussions of things the monks would have learned as small children.

Sometimes, they were discussing their personal problems such as their divorces or their relationships with their mothers or children. Often, I wondered whether the monks could even understand what they were talking about given that they babbled on about their problems at a high speed and used vocabulary not generally learned by monastics. The monks listened patiently and offered simple advice based on Buddhist teachings or expressed empathy with the baffling problems.

Many of the foreigners went on and on about the emptiness of Western culture and how everyone in the West is obsessed with money. They were usually well dressed, staying in expensive guest houses, and frequenting the nicest restaurants in town. I tended to assume, from their patience with the incredibly boring conversations, that the pet monks were hoping that some of the despised money would benefit them in the form of a new pair of shoes, a gift of cash, or, if they were really lucky, a laptop. I couldn't help but feel that they truly deserved such rewards.

Chapter 20

Because people knew that I was looking at the Salai gyal issue, they encouraged me to write about the high-profile Tibetans who have had relationships with or married foreigners. Over the years, gossip suggested that numerous scandals had occurred. But on investigation, evidence was hard to come by, and it seemed unfair to discuss successful Tibetan men, both settlement Tibetans and newcomers, who could be termed Salai gyals but who had quite ordinary relationships. I researched the "scandals," many related to religious teachers, but most such figures were dubious foreigners who had adopted Tibetan names. Still, there were a few involving reincarnate lamas, often referred to as rinpoches or tulkus, and they were interesting in relation to how the cultures misunderstood each other and how some Tibetan Buddhist practices are marketed by outsiders. Not surprisingly, the perversion of certain traditions met with little objection from the average Tibetan and indeed was encouraged by some, for who would not want to be acclaimed for their mastery of the bedroom arts? But before delving into the strange world of "tantra," perhaps first it is best to explore the few newsworthy scandals and what seems to be a lack of cultural awareness.

It is a complex matter, but rinpoches or "tulkus" as they are sometimes referred to are recognized as the reincarnations of their predecessors, generally at a very young age. Some lineages traditionally marry, while most typically remain celibate. Disrobing, dating, marrying, and even shocking behavior have no effect on their titles. Once recognized as such, they remain rinpoches until they die even if they were to, for example, give up their duties, marry bar maids, and spend their lives working in supermarkets somewhere in Texas. This occasionally leads to confusion in the minds of followers who are not Tibetan, for they erroneously imagine that rinpoches are bound by a strict code of conduct and that all are highly educated and considered distinguished teachers.

That said, some rinpoches are well educated, respected teachers, dedicated to ethical behavior. Some are responsible for monasteries with numerous monks dependent upon them, whereas others, especially some in exile who have lost their traditional monastery in Tibet, are independent with a limited number of followers. Rinpoches have disrobed and married yet continued to be excellent teachers and/or philanthropists. It seems that Tibetans are relatively open to almost any sort of behavior as long as rinpoches are not intentionally deceiving anyone or abusing the prestige of their titles, although if their behavior is non-traditional, they often are not thought of very highly.

In 2011, the young Gomo Tulku advertised the release of his hip-hop C.D. on Phayul. A debate ensued in the Phayul forum. Many of the Tibetans who commented felt that he should not use his title of tulku in his stage name and criticized the accompanying, rather tame, music video for showing him in the company of "half naked Western sluts." Others had no problem whatsoever with what the young tulku was doing. Some praised him for his honesty and openness, and one even went so far as to say that his music could be considered religious practice.[1] Later, in an article in *Details* magazine, Gomo Tulku was presented as a young man pursuing his musical career with monk-like devotion. The video that created such a fuss was apparently the brain-child of its director; Gomo Tulku was seemingly more concerned with his music than girls.[2]

It will seem strange to many that within Tibetan Buddhism, there is room for behavior that is not pious, but over the centuries, some acclaimed teachers have been considered practitioners of something known as "crazy wisdom." "Crazy wisdom" is a term best used to describe a small number of hugely influential teachers over the centuries who in many ways behaved like madmen, but, as one scholarly Tibetan friend put it, "their level of craziness was far beyond normal people's reach, energized by wisdom above wisdom." Crazy wisdom is an important concept because within Tibetan Buddhism, exceptional teachers can deviate radically from traditional and often rather conservative confines of acceptable behavior. Several of the ancient Buddhist masters practiced crazy wisdom at some points in their lives, including Marpa and Padmasambhava. Crazy wisdom is considered to be quite different from ordinary bad behavior, although the line sometimes seems to blur, especially when foreign converts are involved.

Perhaps the most controversial figure in 20th century Tibetan Buddhism is Chogyam Trungpa. Many consider him the most influential figure in the introduction of Buddhism to the West; others view him as a fraudulent creep with a substance-abuse problem. Chogyam Trungpa was a rinpoche born in Kham, Tibet. In 1959, he was one of the tens of thousands of Tibetans who escaped to exile in India. In 1963 at the age of twenty four, he obtained a scholarship to Oxford University. Several years after arriving in the U.K., Trungpa disrobed, took up drinking, doing drugs, and smoking. He also began sleeping with numerous female students. His explanation was that his monk's robes and traditional lifestyle had created a cultural barrier between him and his Western students. This was during the 1970's when "free love" and the use of drugs to expand one's consciousness were becoming a somewhat socially acceptable and important part of youth culture. Trungka married a sixteen-year-old British student; by all accounts their unconventional marriage was a success and ended only with his death. Trungpa was an unperturbed and devoted parent even though he was not the biological father of their youngest son, Ashoka.[3] Trungpa would show up at his teachings late and sometimes drunk and hosted debauched parties. By chance, I learned that one of my son's high-school teachers had attended one of Trungpa's drunken teachings. He was vilified by some and deified by others for his unconventional teaching methods and lifestyle. I began reading *Dragon Thunder*, Trungpa's wife Diana's autobiography, with a great deal of skepticism, but by the end, I came to the conclusion that Trungpa was a remarkable genius.

Trungpa translated many important Tibetan texts into English and authored numerous books that eloquently presented Tibetan Buddhism in a manner easily understood by Western students. He established over one hundred centres that endure under the Shambala name. He founded the Naropa University and a multitude of other smaller yet influential institutions and organizations.

Trungpa suffered a head injury as the result of a fall, and his behavior became increasingly erratic.[4] He died at the age of forty eight following a stroke that was likely brought on by alcoholism and diabetes. According to reports from his followers, his body did not begin to decay for five days, and other traditional signals of Buddhist enlightenment were observed. In an introduction to a biography of Chogyam Trungpa, the Dalai Lama praised his work, especially his writing: "Exceptional as one of the first Tibetan lamas to become fully assimilated into Western culture, he made a powerful contribution to revealing the Tibetan approach to inner peace in the West."[5]

Other rinpoches have been accused of seedy and surreptitious behavior with their Western disciples. The previous Kalu Rinpoche, not to be confused with the current Kalu Rinpoche, was accused of sexual misconduct by a former student, June Campbell. She alleges that he coerced her into having a secret relationship—in the name of tantric practice—that she considered abusive and that lasted for several years when she was in her twenties and he was nearly seventy. By the time she made the accusations, he was unable to defend himself, having died some years previously at the age of eighty four. Campbell wrote a ranting yet academic book, *Traveller in Space: Gender, Identity and Tibetan Buddhism,* in which she discusses the role of women in Tibetan Buddhism and exposes the ancient custom—no secret whatsoever to Tibetans— of small numbers of highly trained monastics having secretive sexual relationships with women as a part of their practice. An anonymous yet somehow compelling review of the book on the Amazon website claims personal knowledge that Campbell's accusations against Kalu Rinpoche are unbelievable.[6]

Sogyal Rinpoche, author of the best-seller *The Tibetan Book of Living and Dying,* settled a lawsuit out of court. "The suit accused him of fraud, assault and battery, infliction of emotional distress and breach of fiduciary duty. It also charged that he 'seduced many other female students for his own sexual gratification.'"[7] Little is known of the validity of the claims; Sogyal Rinpoche has, so far, remained silent on the matter.

In 2011, in Australia, Lama Choedak Rinpoche was also involved in a scandal. According to the Sunday *Canberra Times*, his marriage had dissolved, and he then engaged in a series of relationships with students. When his dating practices were exposed, he released a statement apologizing if "changes that his personal life has gone through have caused any confusion." It appears that there was a lot of confusion, as "the women said they were shocked to discover that their 'spiritual leader' was engaged in multiple affairs within the group because Lama Choedak was considered a 'respected teacher and family man'"[8] Wisely, the Rinpoche headed to Nepal for a retreat.

I couldn't find any other examples. Considering the number of rinpoches who have taught in the West over the past five decades, the list is short, and many of the allegations aren't terribly shocking, given that some Western converts behave much differently with Asian gurus than they would with Christian priests or ministers. Churches actively discourage activities that can lead to inappropriate behavior on the part of either clergy or practitioners. Tibetans have the same traditions and a myriad of often unspoken rules governing appropriate behavior that are largely ignored by or unknown to practitioners in the West. Informal private audiences and social interactions that could lead to trouble are rare in the Tibetan world.

It's hard for me to decide if those rinpoches are unfortunate or lucky. Most female members of Christian congregations wouldn't be lining up when their middle-aged minister divorced. (Or maybe they would be?) I imagine typical priests would have a much harder time getting lucky than their Tibetan counterparts in the West. Then again, the rinpoches are subject to allegations that wouldn't hold much weight in Christian circles. What goes on behind closed doors between consenting adults is generally a private matter in the West, and people are expected to use their common sense. But it seems that when a foreign religion is involved, some people lose theirs.

One Western friend who is a long-term Buddhism practitioner and academic was cynical, "I've seen how women throw themselves at these guys. Then they act all surprised and shocked when something happens." He was right. I've seen enough such behavior to share his cynicism. Some of the women I observed seem to have unhealthy obsessions with their teachers. I don't doubt that deep-down many would feel very special if they could bed and would gladly marry their rinpoche or lama. Nor do I doubt that some of the disgruntled women weren't so much opposed to the sex as to the lack of long-term commitment and the rinpoches' refusals to publically acknowledge the relationships.

The most ridiculously inappropriate behavior that I witnessed was reserved for the Karmapa, who is one of the most important lamas in Tibetan Buddhism. Unfortunately for him, he was blessed with rather striking good looks that have only been somewhat compromised by a recent gain in weight. Even when he was a teenager—as I write he is only 26—I overheard Western women, some old enough to be his mother or even grandmother, gushing and even shrieking over his appearance, "Oh my god, he is so gorgeous." or worse, "He is so hot." It seemed as though practically every woman who came to town was headed down the hill for one of his public audiences. His official title in English is "His Holiness the Karmapa," but many Westerners and even some Tibetans jokingly referred to him as "His Hotness."

There seemed to be a lot more women than men almost permanently camped out at the Gyuto Monastery, where the poor Karmapa is confined to a small building. (As mentioned earlier, since his escape from Tibet in 2000, the Karmapa has not yet been able to establish his own suitable residence. He lacks even a small compound in which to roam freely.) No doubt some of these women are genuine practitioners entirely unmotivated by the Karmapa's appearance, but the Tibetans for their part are embarrassed, amused, or disgusted by the behavior of the "crazy Injis." (Inji means foreigner.) The Karmapa seems a quiet and serious young man. I often wonder what he thinks.

My friend Alex was part of the Karmapa's security team when he went to America for the first time. He told me that while inspecting the then twenty-three-year-old Karmapa's hotel room prior to his arrival, security discovered that American women who were high-up in the organization had hidden notes and other gifts for the Karmapa to find while they were ostensibly preparing and decorating the room for his arrival. According to Alex, security constantly has to be on guard to protect the Karmapa from some of his female followers.

I experienced Tibetan Buddhism only as it is practiced by Tibetans, so I was often perturbed and bemused by some of the Western converts who, if you didn't know better, would appear to be practicing an entirely different religion. I needed to learn more about their world, but I didn't really want to. I was fortunate to have met the informative Alex and a PhD candidate who we nicknamed "Dr. Banoffee." Between the two of them, they filled me in on some of the more bizarre aspects of Tibetan Buddhism as it is practiced and interpreted by some Westerners.

"Do you have any books on tantra?" an Australian woman loudly asked the clerk in a book shop where Dr Banoffee was loitering. Dr Banoffee loves books and can seemingly memorize entire documents in one reading. He'll quote virtually an entire esoteric text on almost any topic at the dinner table or even during drunken conversation at a dance party—if you don't stop him. Besides trying to find books that he hadn't already memorized while listening to Lady Gaga at full volume, Dr Banoffee also enjoyed hanging around McLeod Ganj book shops just to listen to the customers.

The woman chose a title and was thumbing through it when Dr Banoffee felt it was his duty as a budding scholar to inform her: "That is a very serious book meant for practitioners with many years of training. You need to have received numerous empowerments to study it." She was not put off. "I know all about taaiintra," she drawled back at him.

Tantra, an ancient form of Hindu spiritualism that pre-dates the Buddha, forms a major component of Tibetan Buddhism. Despite what a visit to a local book shop might tell you, most tantric practices are entirely devoid of a sexual element. Even at the highest levels of those few practices that do include a sexual component, the sexual act is usually visualized. Only a very tiny number of practitioners are considered advanced or specialized enough to practice with partners.

The secrets of high-level tantra are passed on by a guru. What is well-known and undisputed is that sexual pleasure is not the goal of genuine tantric practice. Rather, sexual energy is channeled in such a way that practitioners endeavor to achieve enlightenment.

I was too embarrassed to visit McLeod Ganj bookshops to see what was available on the topic. I was too well known in the community. The owner of one book store— a man renowned for his chronically morose expression—would develop a mischievous grin whenever I appeared in his tiny shop or when he saw me on the street. As his was the only shop in town that carried it, I had already purchased from him several copies of Jeffrey Hopkin's translation of the *Arts of Love* by Gendun Choephel. Worse yet, whenever someone was looking for the book, I took them to his store. I had bought serious works on other topics, but I feared gaining a reputation—or even more of a reputation—as some kind of Inji Buddhist sex maniac.

Instead, I went on-line. Amazon.com offered hundreds of titles on tantra, ranging from scholarly works to light-weight pop philosophy. For religious practices that are usually devoid of sexual acts and whose purposes are to achieve genuine spiritual enlightenment, an awful lot of books on sex were available—dozens of them in fact. Most of the genuine religious and academic books looked like heavy going and, to put it mildly, didn't make tantra seem like much fun. They didn't even mention sex, which is not surprising because, as I understand it, the highest level tantric texts are secret and not available for translation. That hasn't prevented Western writers from being very creative. I found books on massage tantra, tantra sex games, gay tantra, and masturbation tantra. There was even a *Complete Idiot's Guide to Tantric Sex*. Some were guised as spiritual teachings while others were essentially pornography. No wonder so many people had baffling ideas about the relationship between Tibetan Buddhism and sex.

Chapter 21

Visits during the mid to late 2000's were, in many ways, my favorite times in McLeod Ganj. I was earning good money at the time, so I was able to visit almost every winter. Most of my Tibetan friends were at least marginally better off, so they were happier and more hopeful. Each time I arrived, I discovered that a few acquaintances had gone abroad and others back to Tibet. But I made new friends and despite on-going development—mostly in the form of restaurants, coffee shops, and guest houses that all represented jobs for locals—with each arrival, I felt as if I had come home.

Because of the winter cold, very few foreigners visited, and McLeod Ganj had not yet become a major destination for domestic tourists from the plains with hopes of experiencing snow. What has since become a passion for large numbers of Indian tourists is difficult to understand, for when it did snow, the charm quickly evaporated for most. Negotiating the sodden streets while being pelted with chunks of snow by fellow tourists and bombed with more of the same by gleeful restaurant workers perched on roof-tops—their small revenge for the indignities they suffer—was followed by a return to a frigid concrete hotel; the arrival of snowflakes inevitably led to a town-wide electricity failure lasting days. Under the amused gaze of locals, the tourists made doomed attempts to leave town, mostly ending after less than a few metres of hopeless tire spinning. Snow plows and sand trucks are understandably not in the budget of Indian towns that experience only a few days a year of snowfall.

I didn't mind the snow and the frigid temperatures; the weather gave me a chance to show off my stoicism—buildings did not have heating so it was a bit like winter camping without a campfire—and usually repelled prima donna tourists. In any event, I usually spent cold nights drinking with friends; after a Kingfisher or two, the cold disappeared, hence the "stoicism." Because of the temperatures and subsequent dearth of tourists, including, to my amusement, foreigners who pretended that they lived there year round, but actually usually left for the winter and sometimes even the monsoon, many service industry businesses closed during January and February. My McLeod Ganj became a place of quiet streets, shuttered shops, and almost empty guesthouses.

Tashi Sonam had begun running a popular local restaurant—so he had moved up in the world. It was on the third floor of a building that stood alone, with no neighbors, on a little-developed stretch of Temple Road. Every winter it closed for two months and every night in the restaurant, gregarious Tashi Sonam held court; along with his old friends he had acquired a number of new ones and despite seldom ever seeming to leave the building, even when the restaurant was closed, he somehow also amassed a number of interesting foreign friends, most of whom were intellectual booze hounds. Despite being closed for business, the kitchen produced endless thermoses of tea and hot water and an occasional spectacular dinner party. Truth be told, the whisky manufacturers were also kept very busy. "Let's do the Dew!" became a popular expression, and somehow the mixture of half cheap whiskey and half Mountain Dew—Tibetans tend to mix killer drinks—was unexpectedly enjoyable.

Aside from running the restaurant, Sonam Tashi worked for a human rights organization and administered a small volunteer placement organization. His pet project was finding English teachers for Tibetan nuns, whom he saw as largely neglected. His feminist tendencies did not stop him from regaling visitors with outlandish Tibetan folk tales concerning Aku Tonpa—a roguish character who, in one of the more famous stories, sold penises to nuns.

Tashi Sonam was a great friend and also a wonderful source of information because he had his finger on the pulse of news and gossip in the community. He presented information for what it was: substantiated fact, gossip, or malicious rumor. He also seemed to know everything that there was to be known about the situation in Tibet on any given day. Although he had always spoken of remaining in India, eventually he married and went abroad. In many ways, I was happy for him, for although he had been a monk in Tibet and studied only at Tibetan Transit School in India, once in the West he was able to fulfill his dream of attending university. Still, I felt sad that I would never again enjoy the lively gatherings that he had hosted. His Tibetan friends who remained in India were sadder still. McLeod Ganj was never quite the same without him.

During that time, changes among the Salai gyals were already becoming apparent. As some of the young newcomers became financially independent and even successful, more were dating foreign women on their own terms and some even ended up supporting them. One story was very romantic. A foreign woman had visited India and married a Tibetan that she had known only for a short time. On returning home, the marriage seemed insane. She returned to India in order to divorce, but on reuniting with her husband, she fell in love with him again. I knew him; he was a really nice guy with a successful business. When I ran into them in Delhi, she had long since run out of money. He was supporting her. He emigrated, and their marriage has, not surprisingly, endured.

Chapter 22

Despite almost annual visits of up to six weeks, it wasn't until 2010 that I returned to Dharamsala for an extended period of time. Canada was in the depths of a recession, the job market was terrible, and my savings were dwindling rapidly thanks to the high cost of living. My son didn't want to move to a new town for his last two years of high-school, but he had liked living in Dharamsala when he was nine, so he was willing to go back and study by correspondence. At least he already had friends there, and I promised a more exciting lifestyle than we were having, broke, in Canada. The trip was a bit of a gamble, but I felt that my time would be better served by living cheaply while studying and volunteering in India than continuing to apply for almost every job opening within a twenty kilometer radius of where I lived with no response. It seemed that I was overqualified for many jobs, while other potential employers assumed that I was an unreliable hippy (I'd last worked in theatre management), a view that was ironic, considering my workaholic tendencies and disdain for most hippies. "To hell with them," I thought. For the second time, we packed up our lives and flew off to India. We arrived just in time to witness the end of an era.

As mentioned earlier, a series of brutally suppressed demonstrations had broken out across Tibet in March of 2008. Such widespread expression of discontent had not occurred since the Chinese invasion in the 1950's. Although several Chinese were killed in Lhasa— some presumably unintentionally when buildings were set on fire— most demonstrations were remarkably peaceful. The Chinese, however, responded with extreme force and mass arrests. Reports of torture and deaths in detention made their way to the outside world. Around the same time, the Chinese increased security on the border with Nepal to further prevent Tibetans from escaping.

According to International Campaign for Tibet, who use data collected by the United Nations High Commission for Refugees, 2007 had been a fairly typical year with 2163 escapes. In 2008, only 652 managed to get out, and there were fewer than 900 in each of the three following years. Increased border security was doubtless a major contributor to the decrease, but a number of Tibetans told me that many people back home no longer wanted to flee to India. It was becoming known that they were neither welcome nor allowed to stay in India. As well, economic prospects were improving in Tibet, so the desire to escape in order to help support impoverished families was becoming less common, and as we shall see, within Tibet, a cultural and linguistic renaissance had also begun. But for those who did want or need to escape, the situation on the border was more than troubling.

I arrived to a strange new McLeod Ganj. On every previous visit, new arrivals from Tibet were plentiful, but a new reception centre had just opened down in the Kangra Valley, and according to all reports, it was run like a prison. New arrivals were not allowed to leave, although they could receive visitors. Foreigners were not allowed to visit without official permission. In a year and a half, neither I nor my son, who travelled in different circles, met anyone who had recently escaped from Tibet, and we never saw them in the street. They are hard to miss; recent arrivals have distinctive dress and mannerisms, many also sporting rosy cheeks from exposure to the sun and wind.

Apparently, those young enough to attend school were held at the Reception Centre until they were transferred to boarding schools, while monks and nuns were sent to monasteries and nunneries. Lay people, seemingly over the age of twenty-five—I could not find the exact age but that had been the age limit for admittance to Transit School— were kept for a month or so, during that time they met the Dalai Lama and then were sent back to Tibet. I had hoped to obtain detailed information concerning new arrivals from exile government officials, but I was told by the Department of Information that they wouldn't give me any, so I gave up. In any event, their information was not required, for anyone could see that there were no new arrivals present. People, even newcomers, told me that almost no one had escaped from Tibet since 2008, but in 2010 when I was there, according to the U.N.H.C.R., 874 refugees fled,[1] but in Dharamsala, it was as if they had never existed, they were locked away.

An exception was being made for several hundred "pilgrims"[2] who had fled in past years. How they were selected has not been publically revealed. But ex-monks and former students that I met whom had been in India for a number of years and did not want to return, were living as fugitives. Many couldn't handle the stress and went back to Tibet.

The lack of new arrivals wasn't the only dramatic change. There were almost no Salai gyals. There were still plenty of young single men from Tibet who had arrived some years earlier, but very few were pursuing the stereotypical Salai gyal lifestyle. It was strange not to see Salai gyals everywhere. No one hung out at the bus stand or the chai shop on Bhagsu Road. No hopeful faces peered from roof-top restaurants and street-front patios. Most Tibetan men in restaurants and bars were engrossed in conversations with their Tibetan friends and paid little if any attention to foreigners at tables surrounding them. A few were dating foreigners, but almost all of them were in committed relationships. Some were pursuing foreign women for casual sex and affection— there was still an extreme shortage of Tibetan women— but the intensity and desperation had all but disappeared. I immediately discussed this development with my friend Clive, who had spent much of the past ten years in McLeod Ganj. He was as perplexed as I was and wondered if they had gone "underground," but neither of us could see how that could happen in a small town.

My friend Tinley was back in McLeod Ganj after a five-year absence. He had never been a typical Salai gyal. He was too serious for that, but, like many of my friends, he had met and married a young foreign woman, which made him a Salai gyal in the broadest definition of the term. Both he and his wife, who was a teenager when they met, had since studied at university in the U.K. and both had very good jobs. (As she laughingly told me when she later arrived in McLeod Ganj, the volunteer program that she had originally come to work for had revamped its rules on consorting with locals as a result of her relationship with Tinley.) We met up in Mountview for a reunion. "Pauline, what happened to all of the Salai gyals?" was one of his first questions. "Olivia was so worried about me coming here alone and hanging around with Salai gyals. She thought their bad behavior would rub off on me. When I got here, I called her and told her, 'Don't worry. There aren't any Salai gyals anymore.' She couldn't believe me."

Discussions with my young, single, male Tibetan friends were illuminating. Gonpo Tsering, a former Salai gyal, was sent money by his family in Tibet and no longer needed to rely on foreign sources for funds. He told me that many families in Tibet were now financially better off and able to send money to relatives in India who couldn't find employment or needed help. He also told me that some Tibetans were purposely choosing to return to Tibet rather than trying to go abroad if they couldn't make lives for themselves in India. "People have other options now. Most don't want to get married to foreigners unless they really love them and have confidence that the relationships will last. It needs to be the right person or there can be a lot of problems. And the wives need to be comfortable with us always sending money home to our families in Tibet."

I couldn't help but notice that there were also far more entry-level jobs in McLeod Ganj. While the economy in the West was depressed, new businesses, particularly restaurants, had sprung up all over McLeod Ganj in the past several years. Many were staffed by young Tibetans, usually newcomers. Others with skills and experience had found work with the now numerous N.G.O.'s around town. A lot more jobs were available, with less competition for them. I met very few newcomers who didn't have work.

Remittances from Tibet frequently supplemented wages that were, especially in the service industry, often below the legal minimum. A Tibetan friend who ran an N.G.O. committed to stamping out child labor and ensuring that employment laws were followed by the Tibetan community told me that as a result of his efforts, he was threatened by wealthy Tibetan business people and even played me a recording in which he was verbally abused by staff in the Tibetan Settlement office in Delhi when he confronted them over the issue. Tibetan restaurant workers were fortunate if they earned $50 a month; many received less, and Indians from poor regions such as Bihar often earned the very least. Still, with occasional donations from family and friends, most newcomers enjoyed a better lifestyle and much improved nutrition. They also usually helped their friends who were not so fortunate.

Many of those who wanted to go abroad had found ways that didn't involve getting married. I purposely didn't ask many questions, but a lot of newcomers that I knew had made their way to Europe. I spoke to Rinchen, who lived in Europe, shortly after he had vacationed in Belgium. "So many of our friends are there now," he told me. "And it's not just Amdo people. There are people from Kham and U-Tsang and lots of settlement Tibetans."

Many settlement Tibetans had long been successfully engaging in efforts to get to the West. Although their legal status was safer than that of the newcomers, they, too, felt insecure. A friend who travelled to various settlements on his vacations told me that almost everyone that he spoke to was hoping to go abroad, and he hoped that someone would explore their reasons for so urgently wanting to get out— perhaps secrets lay buried there, too. I'd heard rumors of problems with relations with Indians, and it seemed that lack of documentation that would enable them to fulfill their potentials career-wise and the precarious nature of R.C. renewal were both issues, but doubtless there were many other factors. They, like the newcomers, wanted to be secure and independent.

A friend returned from Europe to arrange the paperwork for her children, who had been unable to accompany her initially. I admired her guts. She was a resourceful single mother who had left for Europe little more than a year earlier alone and virtually illiterate. Now she was back: cosmopolitan and boldly dressed in European fashions. She was all business. She laughed when she told me that someone in the exile government's Tibetan Settlement Office—formerly the Tibetan Welfare Office (the name change was essential in my opinion, as in my years in India, I had never heard of them showing interest the welfare of anyone that I knew)— told her that the exile government didn't want Tibetans going abroad. If she had followed their rules, she would have abandoned her children in India and returned to Tibet more than a decade earlier. Instead, she had scraped out a life in India and despite her illiteracy done well for herself, but the time had come for her and her children to join the free world. She spent most of her visit with her lawyer drawing up paperwork. "I'm so proud of my mom," her teenage daughter told me.

Besides increased opportunities for some, other factors benefitted the lives of newcomers. Access to communications technology had had a tremendous impact. In 2003, not one of my friends had a phone, and calls from a phone booth—in India, amusingly referred to as an "STD," but meaning "Sexually Transmitted Disease" in my country—to countries abroad cost thirty three cents a minute, a fortune in India. By 2010, all of my Tibetan friends had cell phones, for they had become incredibly cheap, and calls abroad, including to Tibet, had dropped to around four cents a minute. During that time, mobile phone service also became almost universal across Tibet. The impact on newcomers was dramatic. Many had not spoken to their families since they had left. Suddenly, most could talk to them as often as they wanted. With tears and laughter families reunited over the phone and parents began parenting again, albeit long distance. For some, though, reunification was not so sweet. Families of a few of those who had stopped being monks refused to speak to them. But for most, reunification brought joy or at least peace of mind—parents often begged their children to come home, and that could be tough, particularly for those who were politically active or never wanted to return to the oppression.

Internet service had improved to the point that voice chat became reliable. Previously, voices were often garbled or the connection was too slow to work at all. Skype, Yahoo Messenger, QQ and other services began to allow friends and family to have voice conversations and use web-cams, and Tibetan fonts became compatible with Skype, Facebook, and other software. Tibetan-language news websites and blogging proliferated. Although most Tibetans didn't own their own computers, some used them at work, and Internet cafes were plentiful. Internet access on mobile phones became available and affordable for as little as two dollars a month.

The impact of Facebook on Tibetans' lives cannot be understated. The site is blocked by the Chinese government, but Tibetans elsewhere have become enthusiastic users. Links to news articles, photos, and blogs are shared, along with personal photos, observations, gossip and rumors, and conversations both serious and frivolous. Arguably, its most important function is the sharing of information on the political situation in Tibet, but the importance and influence of personal communications cannot be understated.

The effect of Facebook on Salai gyals was sometimes amusing. In 2003, I knew a number of young men who had multiple e-mail addresses for their multiple girlfriends. They would often give their girlfriend the passwords to e-mail accounts in order to "prove" that they were faithful. Unbeknownst to the women, other girlfriends had passwords to other e-mail accounts held by the same guy. The arrival of Facebook mostly put an end to such deceptions. Jamyang related an amusing story of a Salai gyal who had two girlfriends, both of whom he added as "friends" on Facebook. The Salai gyal had little understanding of how the then new medium of communication worked, but one aspect became very clear when the new girlfriend posted a romantic message on his wall, and his other girlfriend read it.

Tibetans abroad began having long discussions with their friends in India about the difficulties that they faced, although many, especially those who had lived in abject poverty in India, had done remarkably well for themselves. Some of the friendships that I made in 2003 have endured almost a decade. I saw many, who had little more than a change of clothes when I met them, slowly create comfortable lives in the West. Undernourished, directionless, and seemingly unmotivated and helpless young men transformed themselves into strapping, confident, and productive people. Many are now able to help support their parents and families in Tibet. Some still struggle with lack of language skills and education, as well as loss of community and culture; demons and darkness sometimes linger beneath the surface, but almost everyone I know has been transformed. A few, though, it must be said seem doomed to a life of struggle.

Tibetans who went abroad often became deeply involved in Tibetan activism and cultural preservation. Even those without the time or skills to contribute directly turn out to support Tibet and raise awareness at events in their new countries. Almost all of those whom I know are under thirty five. A number of Exile Tibet's prominent and respected elite married foreigners and went abroad in the 70's and 80's. Who knows what some of the Salai gyals of the 2000's will achieve in the coming decades?

Most interesting of all, despite the cynical view that Tibetans marry foreigners only for visas, around half of the marriages that I am aware of succeeded, a success rate that is about the same as that of the general population of Canada where four out of ten first marriages fail.[3] Many are raising families while juggling mortgages and car payments and supporting families in Tibet, often paying for their relatives' children in Tibet to go to school and even university. Their lives are not always easy, and they are quick to tell people in India not to marry foreigners unless they are in very strong relationships.

Marriages failed for reasons that are not always what cynics would expect. Certainly, a number of the Tibetans were entirely insincere. But often the marriages broke down during the difficult period of culture shock and adaptation experienced by most Tibetans following their arrival in the West. A surprising number of the separations were initiated by the Western wives because their husbands, who had been outgoing and even successful in India, did not make friends or adapt with the ease that both had expected. Instead, many spent months or years struggling to come to terms with their new lives, often suffering from depression and occasionally anger, substance abuse, and gambling problems. Many of them appeared to suffer from PTSD and other mental health issues that they were almost always in denial of. I spoke to some of the men whose marriages had failed, and all of them felt ashamed even though separation sometimes seemed essential. A few of my friends married women who turned out to be mentally unstable. One left, partially on my advice, after his wife, who previously unbeknownst to him had a drug problem, assaulted him and threw a lamp at his head.

Some spent hours outlining what had led to the breakdown of their marriages. A young man explained how hard things had been when he first arrived in the U.K. In India, he and his wife had had so much fun together, but when he got to the U.K., she was immersed in university studies: "She was always doing work on her computer even on my days off. For example, once on my day off, the weather was beautiful and I asked if we could go to the beach even just for an hour or two. She said, 'No, I have to study all day today.' I was so angry and thought she was just being mean. It was always like that. She never had time for anything, and if we did make plans, she often forgot or changed them at the last minute. Of course, now I understand that it can be like that when people are in school, but at the time, I felt that she didn't care about me at all. It was very hard for me. After she forgot about a special day together that we had planned, I was so fed up that I left. To tell you the truth, I still love her. She did so much for me, and she is a beautiful person."

The Tibetans that I have seen adapt the least well to life in the West are Tibetan-language scholars and writers. Aside from a few who went abroad when they were young, most are unemployed or underemployed in their fields. Tibetan Studies is dominated by Westerners. Unfortunately, no educational upgrading is available to provide the intensive study required for Tibetan adults, no matter how accomplished or talented, to obtain the academic skills required to work effectively in their field in English and other languages.

Many Tibetan intellectuals languish in obscurity, working at menial jobs and suffering from depression. They usually have families to support, so they cannot afford to attend university; many would, realistically, need to complete high school first in order to achieve their potential. Some had no idea how hard it would be, but many understood the fate that awaited them and had taken opportunities to emigrate for the sake of their families. One Tibetan I met who had gone to North America on a rare scholarship had, within weeks of arriving, been coerced by his wife into dropping out of school and declaring refugee status. Just before he did so, against the advice of all of his friends, he told me that she was calling him every day begging:

"You must do it for our children." The last that I heard, he was working the night shift stocking shelves at a big box store. The pressure wasn't imaginary; another friend in India, who wanted to stay there because he knew that he had terrible prospects abroad, was broken hearted after being dumped by his Tibetan wife because he had failed to get her to the West.

The situation of Tibetan academics is frustrating, for although much of the work produced by foreigners in Tibetan studies is impressive, some extremely so, in numerous cases, the situation I saw was befuddling. Outsiders were almost always deciding what was important to study, and due to the nature of academia, they usually arrived in Dharamsala with preconceived notions based on the work of other outsiders. In certain fields, some were led around by the nose, either by Tibetans or by their own preconceptions and misinterpretations. Much of the research that I read and even used as sources was riddled with mistakes that were apparent even to me and would never pass muster if knowledgeable Tibetans critiqued them.

I knew a number of Tibetans who had the abilities to provide the insight that I so badly needed for my own writing, but due to the nature of my findings, I didn't want to share my writing with them until it was published, for fear that they would be blamed by association. (Or that they would freak out at the possible implications of some of what I have written and try to force me to change my book. It must be said that even some newcomers think that most other newcomers should be sent back to Tibet, just not them and their friends.) But at the end, I sent my manuscript to a carefully chosen Tibetan for assessment. He explained and corrected a number of small but important mistakes that no one without his particular scope of knowledge of Tibetan society would have caught. I don't pretend that my book is academic, but its need for evaluation by a qualified Tibetan was no less critical. Until numerous Tibetans, those born in exile, newcomers, and those within Tibet, become a part of academia, the record will continue to fall short in many areas.

Chapter 23

While the Internet opened up communications among Tibetans, other technological developments were enabling sinister forces to help themselves to what was said. In the 2000's, spying moved from the ground into the cyber world as was dramatically brought to light when, in 2009, researchers from the somewhat aptly named Munk Centre in Toronto unveiled the results of a nine-month investigation. "Their sleuthing opened a window into a broader operation that, in less than two years, has infiltrated at least 1,295 computers in 103 countries, including many belonging to embassies, foreign ministries and other government offices, as well as the Dalai Lama's Tibetan exile centers in India, Brussels, London and New York."[1] Conclusive proof that the Chinese government was directly behind the spying could not be established; however, the intelligence gathering was traced to computers based in mainland China:

> The Canadian researchers were also presented with concrete examples where the virtual snooping had real-world implications. In one case, a young woman who works for a Tibetan outreach group was detained by Chinese intelligence agents at the Nepalese-Tibetan border and interrogated. During the interrogation, she was presented with transcripts of her on-line chats dating back years.[2]

In the Dalai Lama's offices, hackers were able to take complete control of infected computers, open and copy files, and even gather information by turning on webcams and microphones. Greg Walton, who has worked on computer security issues for the Tibetan exile community for many years and had been the man on the ground collecting data and monitoring the spying on the Dalai Lama's private office, told me that similar forms of spying are endemic and on-going and include many soft targets—individuals with limited connection to high profile organizations.

Greg said that he suspected that many Tibetan organizations and individuals continue not to take Internet security seriously. My own observations led me to agree with him. Very few Tibetans that I spoke to seemed concerned about or fully understood the importance of Internet security. The strangest conversation that I had about Internet spying was with a university-educated staff member of exile Tibet's highest profile English-language media outlet. He told me that it had been discovered that his e-mail account had been hacked. "I was really shocked," he told me. "Why would the Chinese want to read my e-mail?"

As people in Tibet increasingly began protesting against Chinese policies by lighting themselves on fire, among my friends, discussions began regarding how information from Tibet was being gathered and how exile activists should respond. Activists were neither discouraging such extreme protest nor encouraging potential protesters to escape into exile to protest safely without sacrificing their lives. As usual, none of them campaigned for newcomers to be allowed to remain in India.

There seemed to be an ongoing race for the latest news out of Tibet because releasing photographs or videos of self-immolations and protests virtually guaranteed human rights organizations at least a mention of their names in the *New York Times* or other high-profile media. A friend who knew well both how the Chinese and many activists operate was disgusted: "They don't seem to care what happens to the people in Tibet who give them information. It's not safe to call or send e-mails right now. The most important thing should be the safety of people in Tibet, not getting news, pictures, and videos out as fast as possible." People in Tibet were willing to risk their lives to get information out. Unfortunately, no matter how many photographs and accounts were published, the reality was that there was next to nothing that other countries were willing or able to do to help those in Tibet.

A friend from Amdo was extremely angry, accusing exile activists of being bigoted against people from Tibet while making a living off them. He felt that they were endangering the lives of people in Tibet by publicizing personal details of dissidents and celebrating activism within Tibet without concern for the participants' welfare: "Bigotry from ordinary settlement Tibetans is a problem, but most of them are just ignorant. The activists are despicable. Most of them hate us [newcomers] and just use people in Tibet to make money. They don't care about people in Tibet at all. If they did, they wouldn't be doing what they are doing." I didn't believe that the carelessness and hypocrisy were intentional, but it seemed that there was a huge gap between what settler and even foreign activists fought for and how they regarded and treated those who had grown up in Tibet.

Instead of whispering in the dark about hidden meaning in Tibetan songs and poems like people in Tibet did, activists and Tibetans in exile openly discussed the artists work in articles and on blogs and Youtube. If the artists weren't already being tortured in prisons, I suspected they would be soon because it is well known that the Chinese monitor Tibet related internet content. Sometimes it was hard to figure out whose side the activists were on.

Although newcomers do the majority of leg-work for activists because they can read their language well and speak the dialects, I seldom saw newcomers among the numerous groups of exile and foreign activists that I observed having dinner in restaurants and partying together. Behind the public face of activism, I sensed a great deal of paranoia and exclusion. In the absence of genuine friendships and understanding, there was a lack of trust. One of my foreign friends was spending an evening with a prominent settlement Tibetan activist when he received an e-mail written in Tibetan regarding a protest that had just occurred in Tibet. She texted me that he was translating it and would let us know what had transpired. Half an hour later, she texted that he was still trying to translate it. It became apparent that like many settlers, he not only could not read his own language effectively but didn't have a newcomer friend to forward it to for swift translation. If he had friends who were newcomers, it seemed that he didn't trust them enough to do the translation.

I couldn't help but notice that many human rights groups run by foreigners were just as guilty of not protecting people inside Tibet. Disturbingly, I heard that some pressured their Tibetan staff in India to report absolutely everything they learned from their sources and encourage people inside Tibet to provide information when it was unsafe to do so. To make matters worse, the photographs and videos that are such coveted prizes endanger the lives of demonstrators and even bystanders who can then be identified and arrested by the Chinese. There were some rare exceptions. Organizations such as Canada Tibet Committee and Human Rights Watch did not join the media frenzy and carefully chose the information that they released, I suspect for the very reasons that my friends and I were so concerned. Shortly after conversations with my Tibetan friends about dubious ethical practices, hackers, who were likely Chinese, hacked one of the organizations in question and apparently stole all of their e-mails and files. Whether or not individuals in Tibet were arrested as a result and what happened to them if they were will likely never be known.

I had always been concerned about Internet security, but living in Dharamsala took my paranoia to a new level. Greg Walton's comments about soft targets made me look more carefully at how average people in the Tibetan world protected themselves. Greg had told me that not only were unimportant people being hacked as a way of gaining information about their more important friends, but that social media including Facebook, Tibet-related news forums, the Chinese version of Skype, and QQ were all used by the Chinese government to gather information. Websites can be hacked and e-mail addresses and other personal information can be gathered about those who believe themselves to be anonymously posting on forums and blogs.

Using Facebook alone, one can mine massive amounts of data and gather photos of people and their families. I've received dozens of "friend" requests from individuals with Tibetan names who provide no personal information in their profiles. I've noticed that many of my Tibetan friends and Western Tibet supporters have accepted friend requests from these unknown persons, allowing them access to everything that appears on their Facebook pages, which of course includes the comments of their friends. In any event, most Tibetans do not have privacy settings engaged. Many didn't understand what could happen and were unconcerned.

Many Tibetans also erroneously presume that communicating in the Tibetan language is somehow like using secret code, seemingly blissfully unaware that anyone on the planet can learn their language. In 2010, the website lhakar.org, set up by high-profile activists, urged exile Tibetans to "send an occasional e-mail in Tibetan – it will surprise your parents, delight your friends, and confound the hackers!"[3] How many Chinese hackers are fluent in Tibetan is impossible to know, but one would assume that a small army of them exists, so this advice seems naive at best.

Will told me that while at his university in the United States, he had received a friend request from a very beautiful Tibetan girl. He examined her profile and immediately became suspicious when he saw that it contained only a photo. She provided no personal information, and she posted nothing even remotely personal on her wall. He ignored the request because he was suspicious that she was a spy. He said that others in his department had accepted the friend request.

Several days after signing up for an innocuous Buddhism course in Dharamsala in 2010, I received the following e-mail with an attachment. It was from someone calling himself Gyatso, a common Tibetan name shared by the Dalai Lama and a former director of the institution where I had registered:

"My beloved,

I am So glad you are back. You just have no idea how much I missed you!! My arms missed holding you. My eyes missed your smile. My ears missed the sound of your laugh. I missed the smell of your hair and the taste of your lips. I missed your head resting on my chest. I missed snuggling close to you in front of the fireplace. I missed looking at you across the couch as I rub your leg. I missed brushing back your hair, exposing your neck to loving and tender kisses. I missed holding your face in my hand and staring into your beautiful blue eyes. I missed being held by you. I missed being near you. I missed you.

With love from a longing heart,— G"

Tempting though it was, I did not open the attachment. The e-mail originated from a .cn e-mail address, I don't have blue eyes, and, sadly, I had never experienced the encounter described. Cyber spying appeared to have intruded even on my dull little world, although I never knew for certain.

Chapter 24

Although spying on the ground appeared to have become redundant, the exile government still seemed reticent to hire newcomers; I had just one acquaintance who worked for it in 2011. "Newcomers aren't qualified," people often squawked, but their assertions rang false because among other things, newcomers were working with and running many of the most successful and innovative N.G.O.'s in town. One friend, although mostly self-taught, had a myriad of office skills and university-level English along with excellent Tibetan. He had approached the exile government several times but was always rejected. Fortunately, a foreign university recognized his talent. Working part-time for it, he was earning three times what he would have in a full-time, entry-level position with the exile government.

The exile Tibetans have lost out by marginalizing the newcomers, their greatest source of potential talent, for there are only a very small number of Tibetans in exile. The 2009 Demographic Survey of Tibetans in Exile recorded only 127,935 outside of Tibet.[1] This is little more than the population of a large town, not an enormous brain pool to draw from considering the diverse needs of the exile community. So far, no system is in place to identify particularly bright and talented adult newcomers and give them the tools or education that they need in order to benefit society. Among the tens of thousands that escaped, many must have had great potential. But as we know, mature adult newcomers are mostly unceremoniously shipped back to Tibet.

Dropping by the offices of the Central Tibetan Administration—the official name of the exile government—could be disheartening. Over the years, I visited various offices on numerous occasions. Some of the staff were bright, efficient, and helpful. Many others, including young people who had obviously been hired fairly recently, were so lethargic that they appeared to be in the depths of a good heroin buzz. When I entered an office, sometimes no one would greet me or even look up, although they were obviously not all busy. Finally, someone would shuffle towards me and ask what I wanted with an expression and tone that clearly showed that they were not the least interested in helping me. Usually, they claimed to be unaware of whatever information I was looking for, even when it was something that I had read about in a report they produced. They often told me to seek what I needed at the Library, pointing vaguely in its general direction. Other times, I was told that they were no longer releasing the information that I requested, the sort of data that is freely available in most democracies. I became increasingly paranoid that there was something wrong with how I presented myself.

Fortunately, I spoke to other foreigners who had had similar experiences. I expressed my fears to a PhD candidate and she laughed. "They did the same thing to me. They wouldn't help me with anything." I suggested that she go back and tell them that she was a scholar and produce a card from her university. "That seems so tacky. I'm just a student," she replied, making a face. "Just do it and see what happens," I suggested. When I saw her several days later, she smiled, "I did what you said and it worked. They were more helpful." We joked that I should make a business card from my alma mater, the University of Hardknocks, that I could whip out when the need arose.

I never told any officials what I was doing or asked for their assistance. Even researchers from universities were often stonewalled when seeking information related to newcomers, and I didn't think that my project would prove popular with exile-government officials. There was potential for retribution against those who had even unknowingly assisted me, and I might have been fed false or misleading information. Instead, I hunted on-line and in books for what I needed.

I heard rumblings and grumblings from other academics and skilled volunteers. In 2003, foreigners had been mostly positive when discussing the exile government. The prevailing attitude was that it was doing its best under challenging circumstances with a limited budget. By 2010, the mood was quite different. Even die-hard, long-term supporters were becoming critical. "It's a mess. All of the best people have left or are leaving to go abroad," a volunteer who had spent the past few years doing various work in various departments of the exile government told me.

The volunteer in question gave the impression of being a keener, but as I got to know him a little better, I discovered that he was also very cynical. "They need to figure out a way to stop the brain drain. It's such an uninspiring place to work that the best people mostly leave. Once they have gone abroad, it is impossible to get them back. Even if they want to come back and contribute, they can't afford to. Most of them help support their families in India with their Western wages."

Some Tibetans were actually happy about the deterioration in the treatment of foreigners in the exile government offices. In the eight years that I had been visiting Dharamsala, I had heard hundreds of complaints from Tibetans, mostly newcomers, about how they were treated when they visited the offices. "They are nice when foreigners go in there, but they treat us like shit," was a typical comment from a newcomer friend. There were also accusations of endless "tea breaks" and other inefficiencies. When I told newcomers about the bad service that I usually received and that I had heard similar complaints from settlers, some were pleased. "That's good! Maybe they are finally starting to treat everyone equally," Lhamo Sham told me with her slyest smile.

Chapter 25

Over the years, some Tibetans have managed to get permission from the Chinese embassy in Delhi to return to Tibet. In the 1980's, for a period of several years, travel between India and Tibet was fairly open, although the Tibetan Government in Exile granted only those who were considered upstanding citizens the permission required to return home to Tibet for a visit. Tibetans who could not be counted upon to project a desirable image of exile life were not provided with the documentation that they needed to leave India.[1] Many who returned never came back, but how they fared in the long-run is largely unknown.

In 2010, seemingly unnoticed by almost everyone except those concerned, newcomers began heading back to Tibet at an alarming rate. These were often established newcomers who had obtained proper R.C.'s. The Chinese were issuing travel documents to virtually everyone who applied. This meant that Tibetans didn't have to try to sneak back on foot or face arrest at the border. At first, people, especially those with R.C.'s, were suspicious and few were interested. But as time passed, more and more went back and reported that they had not experienced problems. By the fall of 2011, almost every newcomer that I spoke to was intending to go back. Some were only planning to visit family, but most had no intention of returning to India.

As I write, the exodus has not been mentioned by English-language media or by human rights groups even though with every week, the number of newcomers declines. It seems impossible that the exile government hasn't noticed. But perhaps it is so out of touch with the newcomer community that it hasn't, or perhaps it doesn't serve its interests to talk about it.

A rare article on the subject that was translated for me from *Tibet Times* provides insight into the disillusionment of newcomers:

> When I meet other newcomers like me, I can't help but frequently discuss the rapid decline in the number of

newcomers living in Dharamsala. Some of them mentioned to me that "the decline in the number of newcomers residing in India means the end of miserable lives as newcomers, and that is good thing." They also added, "There is no use in newcomers settling in Dharamsala. They won't be given land or be protected. [Land for settlements had been given to the settler Tibetans shortly after they arrived in exile decades earlier, but like proper R.C.'s, newcomers were not entitled to the same.] It is better to go [back to Tibet or abroad] if there is a better option so that they at least can be independent. [2]

No one seems to know what the motivation was for the change in the Chinese government's policy. Some feel that it wants to cause a "brain drain" in the exile population or demonstrate that the situation in Tibet is not bad if Tibetans are choosing to return, but the latter seems unlikely given that the Chinese have also remained silent on the matter. Certainly, cyber spying has made torturing random individuals on their return to Tibet obsolete. Whatever the reasons, many newcomers were obtaining the documents and taking their chances.

Many of them had been in India for years and did not have any problems with their R.C.'s. Some were fed up with their situations and told me that they wanted to go back in order to have careers, get married, and live "normal" lives; others wanted to do what they could to preserve their culture back home as they didn't see much serious interest in cultural preservation in exile. Some were planning to teach English or found N.G.O.'s. A few told me that they would continue trying to find a way to the West, but if they couldn't, they would return to Tibet shortly. Some were angry and hated Tibetan society in India: "In Tibet, our own people are not our enemy. People from different regions of Tibet treat each other with respect. These people [settler Tibetans] hate us. I am going back to tell everyone in Tibet what it is really like here. People in Tibet need to know that they should not come here."

I ran into Kelsang, who had just visited Tibet: "A lot of the old Salai gyals from here who went back are working as tour guides. Some are now dating Western tourists who visit there!" We both laughed. "If you have good English it is quite easy to get a job as a tour guide, and the pay can be good." Many of those who had gone back were calling India and telling their friends to join them. They made it sound as though there were lots of jobs and no troubles even when they had been home only a week and had yet to find employment. A rumor was going around that it if things weren't up to expectations in Tibet, it was easy to get to the West from there. To some, Tibet was the new Promised Land.

"People want to go where they can live a good life," Gendun told me. It was his leaving party. As was typical, it was a small, quiet affair at a table in a bar, entirely unlike the more elaborate leaving parties of those who had married and gone abroad. Many told only a few of their closest friends that they were going back to Tibet as if speaking of what they were doing would somehow bring them bad luck or draw the attention of sinister elements. Gendun was leaving in the next couple of days. Despite his great personality, near perfect English,both spoken and written, knowledge of spoken Hindi, and the courses that he had taken in India, he had been unable to find a job that paid enough to cover his basic expenses. At his last job, he had been earning only 1500 rupees (30 dollars) a month.

"I used to want to try to go to the West because there are no opportunities here, but it hasn't happened. I don't just want to live here in some small room and earn a few thousand rupees a month for the rest of my life. I've been talking to a lot of people who have gone back to Tibet, and they tell me there are real opportunities. I want to help my family. What country I go to is not important. I am so tired of wasting my life. Other people are, too. I know at least twenty guys who are planning to go back after the Kalachakra in January."

Tsering, who was drinking with us, looked sad, and his mind seemed far away. Tsering is intelligent and handsome and also has almost perfect English. He had been with the same Western woman, an educated and beautiful girl that I knew slightly, for a number of years. Some of the guys working at the Library nicknamed him and a close friend of his "Killer Number One and Killer Number Two" because of their gorgeous girlfriends. "She has sacrificed so much for me. But I don't want to leave Asia," he told me sadly. It was interesting that Tsering of all people didn't want to go abroad. He, far more than most, had skills that could make him successful there, and he made friends easily

Lodoe wanted to go abroad, but he had just passed up an opportunity. A woman had agreed to marry him to help him out, but when she came to India to do so, she confessed that she wanted more. "I couldn't pretend," he told me. "I want to leave, but not like that. I'm not going back to Tibet. Maybe I'll be stuck here forever. I'll be the last newcomer in Dharamsala!"

For one fortunate friend there was no pretending. He had fallen in love. I had known Dawa for nine years. Although he always acted cheerful, I could see that he harbored an inner sadness. On my last trip, I began seeing him around town with a lovely volunteer of my acquaintance. Over the months that followed, their romance blossomed, and he lost his wistful look. One night Dawa, who seldom went to the bar, appeared in a beautiful chuba, looking radiant. "She is the most wonderful woman that I have ever met. I love her so much," he told me. "She is pregnant and we are having a baby!" His partner had gone back to her country and was starting the sponsorship process.

Other news was not so joyous. If people did go back to Tibet for a visit using the Chinese government travel document, their families put a lot pressure on them to stay. One friend had gone back and he was apparently not really happy in Tibet, but a friend told me that his family had confiscated all of the documents that he needed to return to India. "We are worried about him," she said. "You know how he likes to talk. He is having a hard time keeping his mouth shut." Other Tibetans who had returned were, as expected, not only unimpressed by the Chinese regime but also disappointed because "corruption is worse than in India" and society in Tibet was so status oriented: "If you don't have money there, you are nothing." Another friend later concurred and elaborated, "Tibet is status oriented and competitive. The guys that are going back are so far behind other Tibetans their age there. They are just getting shitty jobs."

My greatest concern was shared by many. Once they had moved back to Tibet, the newcomers were vulnerable to the Chinese regime. Even if they avoided anything political, they would come under suspicion whenever there were incidents. My heart filled with fear whenever someone told me that he or she was returning. I felt that many would live to regret their decisions, but their options were so limited and unappealing that I couldn't help but sympathize with their decisions. I breathed a sigh of relief on the occasions when I heard that a friend had returned to India.

Despite the optimism of many, some had been far less than impressed. I heard that Lhasa and other places were virtually under martial law and that the situation for Tibetans was terrible. There were other troubling experiences: Namgyal had returned to Tibet with the Chinese travel document to visit family but had been arrested as soon as he arrived. He was detained for more than a week. "They had copies of all of the articles that I had written in India. They showed them to me! I was really worried that they were going to put me in prison. When they did release me, they told me not to tell my family that I had been detained. What was I supposed to say? Why wouldn't I have called to tell them where I was? I stayed in Tibet for a while and visited my family, but I was under constant watch by security. I can't live like that. I was afraid that they wouldn't let me come back here, but finally they agreed. I don't ever want to go back there."

I didn't see Namgyal around for a few weeks after that. One day, a mutual friend told me that Namgyal hadn't answered his phone for a week, and he was getting worried. Several days later, he informed me that Namgyal had called with some shocking news: "I'm in Europe. I'm applying for refugee status." Like so many who, thankfully, found ways to go abroad, Namgyal had told no one he was leaving. "I feel so sad," my friend told me. "Namgyal was my closest friend. Almost all of my friends are gone now."

Still, although they were not naïve concerning the dangers, there were people with good plans and some confidence. Over the past few years, an informal movement had begun in Tibet, and many wanted to go back to contribute. Inside Tibet, people were increasingly focusing on preserving and improving their language and culture, an objective that many felt could be achieved within the Chinese system. Some wanted to establish Tibetan-language schools or work in other areas such as improving health awareness or confronting social issues. Many planned to teach English because they felt that it was essential to life in the modern world and would enable Tibetans to participate successfully in the growing tourism industry. Some had come to their decisions through discussions with those who had returned to Tibet in the past and were working successfully in those fields. But it was unclear how easily such dreams could be made a reality.

I learned that in Tibet, new words were being created to describe modern things, from the parts of motorcycle engines to Microsoft Office software. People from all walks of life were learning and using the new vocabulary. Families and friends reported to Tibetans in India that if someone did use Chinese needlessly, fellow Tibetans pretended that they couldn't understand: "What are you trying to say?" Sometimes, they just gave them a blank stare or even demanded a fine. A friend told me that he spoke to his mom, who is illiterate, on the phone. She admonished and corrected him when he used a Chinese word. "I couldn't believe that she knew the new Tibetan word. I knew it, but I couldn't imagine that she would. That is why I used Chinese. Even ordinary people are taking this very seriously." Another Tibetan friend who had recently visited his homeland told me that older people were not always so enthusiastic. Some seemed afraid that speaking pure Tibetan could be perceived as being anti-Chinese.

The movement wasn't just restricted to spoken language. Reading and literacy were also undergoing a renaissance. In Tibet, new technologies were being developed to allow Tibetans to use phones and computers more easily in their own language. Mobile phone applications and hand-held devices, including dictionaries, were being developed or expanded on. People had become much more concerned with social issues. I was told that many young people were giving up formerly very popular unhealthy habits such as smoking and excessive drinking. The movement wasn't about following old ways; it was about creating a modern, dynamic, distinctly Tibetan society that changed and adapted with the times without creating conflict with the Chinese regime. "Of course Tibetans want their own country," a friend told me. "But the Chinese aren't going anywhere for now, so we need to do something sensible to save our culture before it's too late." Despite the self-immolations that at times were occurring every few days, some positive news was coming out of Tibet, and many newcomers in exile wanted to get back home as soon as possible to join in.

In India, many newcomers with no intention of going back were also participating. They were learning the new vocabulary and no longer used Chinese words unless they were speaking to a Chinese person. (Many Chinese visit India, and, surprisingly, most newcomers are not racist towards them. Communicating with the Chinese was also seen as important, and many worked hard to keep-up and improve their language skills.) Newcomers also seldom used English words unless they were speaking English. They were blogging and using social media in Tibetan. It was encouraging to see how much real and enduring effort and progress that newcomers made during my sixteen months in McLeod Ganj.

I was pleased when I read on Phayul that when people from Tibet sent messages congratulating Lobsang Sangay on becoming the new exile prime minister, they also urged exile Tibetans to speak their language properly. "Along with the messages of congratulations to the new Kalon Tripa, the Tibetan youngsters requested Tibetans outside Tibet to respect their mother tongue and speak in pure Tibetan. 'When we appeal for the preservation of our language, we don't mean to undervalue other languages,' one Tibetan youth clarified. Anyone can speak Chinese or English but please preserve our language well."[3] Unfortunately, their plea was largely ignored by settlement Tibetans, at least in Dharamsala. A little over a month later, a singing competition was held in McLeod Ganj at the T.C.V. day school. Dozens competed, and the event went on for hours, the top prize being 10,000 rupees ($200), a sizable sum in India. The only stipulation was that songs must be sung in pure Tibetan although any dialect and any style of music were welcome. I was told that not one settler was among the competitors.

Very few exile-born Tibetans that I observed were interested in participating in preservation and revitalization in a meaningful way. They didn't seem to think that their culture or language was in danger, even when it seemed that half the words that they were using in conversation were English or Hindi. No one seemed interested in learning new words. Signs were put up in McLeod Ganj and articles appeared in English stating that people in Tibet were speaking pure Tibetan, reading Tibetan books and newspapers, and wearing Tibetan dress on Wednesdays. The movement is known as "Lhakar," meaning "white Wednesday," and the exiles seemed under the impression that it needed to be observed only once a week.

It was clear that the movement was intentionally not political, so I was disgusted by the way that some of the activists did their best to make it appear that way. This was erroneous and dangerous for the entire movement in Tibet. Some Tibetans to whom I spoke were very angry. They didn't like Lhakar being manipulated, and they saw exile Tibetans as needing to embrace it more than anyone. I entirely got their point when I looked at the lhakar.org website. It was disturbing; everything people were doing in Tibet was presented as a protest or a boycott; it was almost as though the activists wanted innocent people to be arrested.

Some of the website's advice for exile Tibetans was good, but much was feeble. The website made no mention of speaking pure Tibetan or learning new words. Exile Tibetans were encouraged to read a Tibetan newspaper and post in Tibetan on Facebook once a week. Later, the website announced that children at T.C.V. would wear Tibetan dress once a month, calling this move a "landmark event in the development of Lhakar as a powerful movement not only in Tibet but also in the diaspora."[4] The website seemed oblivious to the fact that Tibetans in Tibet, and some in exile, were working to save their language and culture every single day, not just with token gestures on Wednesdays.

I know how lacking in effect small gestures can be. I grew up in a country mostly populated by immigrants. For a number of years, I lived in Edmonton, which has a large number of residents of Ukrainian and Polish ancestry, me included. They were often skilled at traditional dancing and owned beautiful ethnic costumes. Homes were decorated with traditional arts. Many people attended their traditional churches, which were decorated like those "back in the old country." The strongest connection was to food with recipes for cabbage rolls and pyrogies—dumplings that resemble Tibetan momos—often being passed down from generation to generation. But none of my friends could speak their languages; they were virtually indistinguishable from other Canadians.

To be fair to the settlement Tibetans, many had received little education in their own language, so reading and writing are tasks rather than a joy for many. Despite many recent improvements to the educational system, the exiles still only teach a form of handwriting called "Ume" to children in the primary grades. Apparently, this is a tradition that comes from the Lhasa region. In Amdo, beginning in elementary school, children are taught "Uchen," the script used in books and newspapers and on signs and menus.[5] Not surprisingly, Amdo people are renowned among Tibetans for their writing skills, for they obviously enjoy a tremendous advantage. Some of my settlement Tibetan friends told me that they were very good at reading and writing Ume, but they had never quite mastered Uchen, so they never read books or newspapers. It was a very odd system. As a child, at the age of seven, I had begun reading novels meant for teens and adults.

The settlement Tibetans' situation depressed me; they had so many problems of their own with human rights in India, and I despaired that they would never fit in when or if they got their country back. But my friend Antonio had spent a great deal of time in Tibet and knew both cultures well: "Some of the people here would never want to go back to Tibet because India really is their home. They would miss their ice creams and the food. They wouldn't understand the culture. I think a lot of them would settle in Lhasa where they would create their own "Little India" neighborhood. They imagine that they will be in charge, but most of them won't be. There are far more diversely skilled Tibetans in Tibet that know the country, and they would be running everything. But these people will be very valuable to the society, especially because of their English and should do well for themselves. A lot of them would stay in Lhasa pining for India, but I think that many of them would hit the ground running and never look back."

Chapter 26

The Dharamsala that I inhabited was not that of yoga studios and meditation classes nor the rarified world of the successful refugee elite. During the day, I attended class, volunteered, and worked at home. It was mostly at night, when I roamed the darkened streets and haunted the bars and coffee shops, that my exile world really came alive. It was a sometimes brutal regime: I rose early and worked long hours, my desk a sea of Post-It Notes, cigarette ash, and discarded coffee cups. As darkness fell, I often made my way to a restaurant in search of dinner and conversation and later still to the bar where the lives of newcomers unfolded before me, usually in thought-provoking or lively conversations but sometimes in violence and bloodshed.

Cooks were sometimes also historians. Waiters read literature and the reluctant bouncer, hired for his size but of the gentlest nature, blogged and wrote poetry—"No fighting. No fighting," he would always sing at the crowd whenever "Hips Don't Lie" played on the sound system. Stylish young guys chatting up girls sometimes turned out to be highly educated ex-political prisoners. The young man who, in a drunken brawl, smashed plates and bottles over the heads of his adversaries, with the speed and grace of a kung fu master, was observant and analytical. Ex-monks with long hair dressed in traditional Tibetan chubas drank tea or chugged beer and rocked out on the dance floor. Bright young men struggled in broken English to explain to me their feelings of frustration and hopelessness and their dreams for the future. A grown man, an artistic soul, was essentially an orphan, having been sent from Tibet as a child to study in India. He would furtively inhale deeply into a bag of glue and pass out at the table. Tibetan men debated, talked politics, and joked in a myriad of Tibetan dialects, some trying to get up the nerve to talk to the foreign girls sitting at the next table. There were never more than a couple of Tibetan girls in attendance.

Some guys, little more than teenagers, posed and did their best to look cool, in their hip-hop clothes and trendy sunglasses, as they sucked back Kingfisher Strong, only to end their night early, vomiting gracelessly into the toilet. Others acted tough, their shirt sleeves rolled up to show off not usually very impressive muscles. A vicious fight would sometimes break out for no apparent reason. Shards of glass would fly as the adversaries would briefly attack each other with beer bottles and glasses before the perpetrator was dragged from the bar by staff and friends, leaving streaks and droplets of blood in his wake. Foreign tourists would dash to the counter, pay their bill and leave, spooked by the extremity and unexpectedness of the violence. Waiters would quickly sweep up the evidence and mop the stains off the floor. Everyone would grumble about the stupidity of such behavior and try to relax and go back to their drinking as if nothing had happened, but the mood was strained. A fresh group would arrive, cheerfully unaware of what had just transpired. The D.J. would seize the moment to play "Waving Flag" by K'naan, and the room would be rejuvenated with the new arrivals' carefree dancing.

As the situation in Tibet deteriorated and increasing numbers of newcomers vowed that they were going back anyway, dance party nights became more and more popular. In many ways, their world was disintegrating and it seemed no one wanted to miss "the party at the end of the world," as I began to mentally refer to the increasingly animated nightlife.

In 2003, I hadn't known more than a few Tibetans who could afford to pay for their own drinks, but now they had more disposable income than ever before. Aside from the few long-term Tibetan/foreign couples and some Tibetan guys who were courting foreign girls, most Tibetans stuck to themselves. Many were going back to Tibet, so friends were enjoying their last few weeks or months together. On occasional nights, though, it was hard to imagine that it wasn't 2003.

On one evening in particular, I arrived before 9 pm, and the dance floor was already packed. This in itself wasn't unusual, for the bar had to turn off the music by 11 pm in order to appease the neighbors. What was unusual was the number of Tibetan men on the dance floor with foreign women; usually, it was mostly men dancing—my son noted that the fewer women there were on the dance floor, the more complaints he heard about the quality of the music. The place was so packed that there were no spare chairs, so as I often did, I bought a beer and stood at the bar, where I always knew someone, and watched the antics.

Although it was common to see foreign girls dancing, to my surprise I noticed something that I hadn't seen in a very long time. A number of unfamiliar girls were dancing lasciviously with Tibetan guys. The girls looked overly pleased with themselves, and one, who was grinding up against a Tibetan who looked literally entranced by his good fortune, immediately shot me a look that said, "Look what I've got and you don't." Later, as I was chatting to a Tibetan friend, yet another gave me the same look as she made-out with her new friend in the middle of the bar. They must have felt very superior to poor old me because although I was talking to a lot of different Tibetans, I was obviously failing to find myself an exotic lover as they had.

Over the months, I began making new friends because so many of those that I knew left for Tibet. Over time, I got to know many hitherto strangers, from the town drunks to young intellectuals. Although I was terrified of the long-term foreigners because many of them were insane, I hesitantly met a number who weren't and were usually ready to tip back a few drinks by the weekend. Previously, Tibetans had seldom socialized with the many Kashmiris who migrate to Dharamsala for work and are also stereotyped because some have disastrous relationships with foreign women—one friend referred to them as "the new Sali gyals"—but my son made friends with a witty young Kashmiri tour guide. Once the Tibetans got to know him, they wondered how they could ever have been so prejudiced, and he overcame his prejudices as well.

Another barrier was slowly coming down: Tibetan women were beginning to go out to the bars as well. Although the 6th Dalai Lama had apparently hung around in bars with Tibetan women in the 18th century, Ekai Kawaguchi had commented on their "love of liquor and unclean habits" at the dawn of the 20th century, and women I knew who had grown up in Lhasa spoke of drinking parties, public drinking had been off limits to Tibetan women for most of my years in Dharamsala. This was changing, and seemingly every month a few more women were brave enough to face the sour looks of some. Settler Tibetan girls had been the first to step forward, no doubt inspired by the many educated young Indian women in places like Mumbai and Delhi who were increasingly rejecting the notion that they should remain at home.

But I was still shocked when on Valentine's Day, I went to a lavish new bar with a group of settler Tibetan girl friends and discovered that the place was packed with women, both Tibetan and Indian. They were sipping cocktails and drinking beer. Some were smoking cigarettes. (Long before, I had discovered that many Tibetan women smoke in secret. In 2003, I was frequently annoyed that my middle-aged neighbor was always in the toilet when I needed it, until one day I came across her carelessly exiting in a haze of cigarette smoke.) As I moved around the crowded dance floor, I came across a friend's teenage daughter dancing with her trans-gendered dance instructor from Taiwan. That night I realized that real, unstoppable change was occurring. Still, on a typical night, only a handful of Tibetan women ventured out.

"She is not good." I had mentioned the name of an Amdo woman friend who occasionally went out for beer to a by-all-appearances modern young male Tibetan friend. A number of other Tibetan men, especially those who knew her well, spoke of her with awe and respect as she balanced a modern lifestyle with great parenting abilities. She was famous for her kindness and generosity and her homemaking and cooking skills. But my friend made an ugly face. "She is not a proper Tibetan woman. She goes to the bar and has boyfriends. No good." It was a funny comment coming from him because he was obsessed with chasing Western girls, to the point of appearing sleazy, and he didn't mind if they drank. He had little luck with the girls, no doubt due to his warped values. Double standards and attitudes like his were slowly dying out, but for many, the sight of a woman – other than a foreigner—with a glass of beer or a cigarette was still a shocking and unacceptable sight.

Domestic tourism had also changed the late-night social landscape of Dharamsala. In 2010, Indian Premier League cricket matches began being hosted at the new stadium in Dharamsala. During the events, for several days, traffic in McLeod Ganj backed up for kilometers, but the publicity that the televised matches garnered also led to a massive influx of domestic tourists, particularly during the summer and monsoon months. The natural beauty and climate were a major draw, as was the cosmopolitan nature of the small town.

Unfortunately, not all of the domestic tourists had the best manners. Those with the worst reputation were the "Punjabi" tourists, specifically young Indian men not always actually from Punjab, who seemed to go to McLeod Ganj with the express purpose of looking at foreign women, getting drunk, and misbehaving. Despite stereotypes, most Indian men were gentlemen. Even the tourists from areas that seldom saw foreign visitors didn't usually pay much attention at all to Western women, but during busy seasons, there were dozens in town who stared at Western women as though they were watching television for the first time in their lives. My lethal looking umbrella kept them at bay; they had a deserved reputation for groping and otherwise sexually harassing women.

Many of the tourists from Punjab loved to dance. This wouldn't have been problematic except that they tended to be huge and danced with exceptional vigor on the tiny dance floors. Some sashayed a little too close for comfort. An American friend referred to them as "the jocks of India," a rather apt comparison because they often resembled frat boys out on a tear. The ordinary "Punjabi" tourists hated their antics, and local Indians hated them even more. "These guys are ruining the night," a pleasant group of young Punjabi tourists told my son one evening at Mountview as close to a dozen of their enormous countrymen were bounding and gyrating together on the dance floor, carelessly whacking the star-shaped ceiling lights with their arms as they leapt about. They bumped into chairs and continuously tried to get disgruntled strangers, both men and women, to dance with them. It was only 9 pm, and no one else was even remotely drunk yet.

The staff at McLlo was expert at dealing with problems and shuffling customers around to prevent trouble, so despite the crowds of overly friendly young Punjabi tourists who frequented the bar, it was a surprisingly pleasant place to hang out. "Pauline you sit over there," the head waiter would say, pointing to the end of a table of young Indian men that were obviously tourists. "Those guys are good. They won't bother you." And he was, as usual, right. The waiters never ceased to amaze me with their powers of observation and immediate reactions to even the slightest signs of trouble. When he wasn't serving, another waiter friend always stood near the counter watching the tables. His eyes widened into giant globes when he spotted anything even remotely unacceptable. I learned to sit facing the counter. You didn't need to watch the tables around you if he was within sight; you only needed to glance at his facial expressions.

You never know what you will come across in McLeod Ganj. One night I went out for dinner at McLlo with a friend. A large delegation of British Members of Parliament was dining with the Dalai Lama's nephew. At another table, the waiter informed us, were members of a Mumbai cricket team. The latter spent the evening with their eyes glued to a match on the big screen T.V. Locals knocked back beers and chatted, ignoring the VIP's. In walked "Floor Man," a local guy whom I had thus nicknamed following a night when he passed out in the middle of the floor in a bar. Luckily, he didn't do so that night. It was a somewhat surreal and unlikely scene to witness in a small town in a remote corner of India, but that is McLeod Ganj.

Other nights were even more bizarre. During Losar in 2011, I had a number of Tibetan friends over to my place one afternoon for food and drinks. By 6 pm, my supply of beer and whiskey was exhausted and most friends had headed on to other soirées or gone home. The night being young and being only somewhat drunk, Kunchok and I decided to head for McLlo. The place was already hopping, and the entire staff of a local restaurant was celebrating enthusiastically at a big table in the back. A neatly groomed, professional looking, middle-aged

Western man in a black suit was at the table closest to us with a group of young Tibetans. I was surprised when he rudely shouted at the Indian staff to hurry up with his order. I could only see part of his profile, but his face wore an ugly sneer.

A celebrant from the big table stood up. "Free Tibet," he hollered raising his glass to the room. The crowd fell silent when the well-groomed foreigner scornfully shouted at the top of his voice, "Tibet belongs to China. You FUCKING IDIOT!" The Tibetans at the man's table looked frightened, and Kunchok eyed the beer bottles on our table. I knew what he was thinking; the same idea was crossing my mind. But I wasn't frightened: if a fight started, the staff was always on my side. I'd been friends with many of them for years, and they were doubtlessly already displeased, for the man had been abusing them as well. "I think you'd better shut up," I informed the well-dressed man. He turned his head towards me with a menacing expression, "You don't know who I am," he growled. "Oh yes I do," I retorted. "You are one of the crazy foreigners who comes here, and I think it's a good idea if you shut up." The Tibetan sitting next to him whispered frantically for a few minutes, and although the man continued muttering and sneering, he never raised his voice again. Oddly, the Tibetans seated with him did not leave; they placated and remained with him until we left hours later, as the bar was closing.

The next day I was walking down Temple Road when I saw an unusual sight: a priest in a black suit was walking up the road towards me. As he got closer, I realized that it was the mad man from the night before. At McLlo, his seat had been angled away from mine so I had not noticed his clerical collar. Intrigued, I followed him, but he was walking fast and there was a lot of traffic in the streets. Although I got my camera out of my bag to photograph him, he ducked into Hotel Tibet, and I never saw him again.

With Tibetans and local Indians, it was relatively easy to find out almost anything about their backgrounds, although it sometimes took time to eliminate gossip, but outsiders could become almost anyone they wanted to be. Anyone could create a Tibet support group with a blog or Facebook. People who had never been published and had no credentials whatsoever showed up and pretended to be journalists. The frauds were often taken seriously. Certainly, many of the delusional creatures believed that they were doing very important work and even fund raised in that regard. In some respects it was hilarious, but in the end, they were wasting people's time and money and often disseminating inaccurate information.

Sometimes it was difficult to tell who was for real and who wasn't. My son was at Mountview one night with one of his friends whom I will call Jim. Jim had worked in media and IT for a number of years and was in Dharamsala studying Buddhism. One of my friends whom I will call Max showed up, and my son introduced them to each other. Max is a legitimate expert in a number of areas, and his work has been the subject of articles in newspapers such as the *New York Times*. But on the night in question, Max was extremely drunk, so much so that he made no sense whatsoever; in fact, as he attempted to explain what it was that he did, he only succeeded in convincing Jim that he was a complete fraud. Even worse, Max then began flirting with one of my son's teenaged friends. To be fair to Max, he had no idea of her age, and she could pass for a woman in her twenties, although she was actually fifteen. It was all too much for Jim. He, too, was drunk, and he completely lost his temper. The next day I looked up some articles about Max for my son to give to Jim. Jim headed back to the meditation centre, and Max was so horrified by his own behavior that he quit drinking for at least a week and never got quite so drunk again.

Sometimes I saw people around town who looked as though they might be interesting. One afternoon, a bearded man in a stylish overcoat carrying an odd looking musical instrument passed through the bus stand. He was interesting as it turned out, but for all the wrong reasons. That night I arrived at McLlo, and he was sitting with some of my friends, "Tashi Delek!" he exclaimed loudly when I sat down. Groaning inside at his horrible pronunciation and ridiculous use of Tibetan when speaking to a fellow North American, I said "Hello" and introduced myself. "My name is Yak," the stranger proclaimed. He also proclaimed that he was a great Tibet supporter, implying that he did important work.

Yak was a fixture in the town for a week or two and invaded my watering holes nightly. "Tashi Delek!" he would shout whenever he saw me, at least whenever he was drunk, which was every evening. I nicknamed him "Captain Creech" after a lecherous character in Gerald Durrell's hilarious autobiographies, for he somewhat resembled an old fashioned sea captain. Yak's attempts at winning my heart were rebuffed, a point which he would loudly lament to whoever was at the table. He didn't seem too heartbroken, however. When he wasn't pouring liquor down his throat and practicing using his three words of Tibetan, he would rise to his feet, command the entire bar to be silent, and bellow out tuneless songs that he seemed to be making up on the spot. Despite his behavior, it was dreadfully cold, I wasn't about to give up drinking at the bars every night and stay home in my freezing apartment in order to avoid him. Instead I drank more, as, it seemed, did everyone else that he inflicted himself upon. Once everyone was drunk, the bellowing of nonsense and horrific singing were more amusing. Like many of the odd, extroverted, yet secretive characters who showed up, there was something not quite right about him, and he also had a habit of sticking locals with his bar bills, by accident or design it was hard to know. Thankfully, he finally left town.

Time marched on. Every time that I left my house, I saw fewer people that I recognized. For those who remained, the exodus sometimes created an unexpected bonanza. One very poor but popular friend had over time been given a refrigerator, T.V., and D.V.D. player. Another friend's room was crammed with possessions left by those who had suggested that they might come back but never did. Many of my friends and acquaintances told me that they, too, would be going back to Tibet shortly after I returned to Canada. It seemed as though the time of the newcomers had come to an end, although there were many who were planning to stay. Aside from a few scathing mentions in print, it seemed that the Salai gyals would soon be a small, forgotten part of Tibetan history. But one could not be entirely certain.

One day, I was walking down Jogibara road to my Tibetan language class at the library. A recent landside had caused the road to be closed to traffic. As I meandered along listening to the birds and the sound of the creek rushing far below, I noticed a young monk coming up the hill towards me. As he walked, he was intently studying a notebook and reading aloud. As he came closer, I heard him reciting: "I want to be Salai gyal. I want to be Salai gyal." My eyes almost bugged out of my head. Luckily, the monk was so engrossed in his study that he didn't notice. I stopped and listened carefully while pretending to send a text message on my phone. He corrected himself. "I want to be A Salai gyal," he said loudly and clearly as he passed me. He continued his strange recitation as he disappeared up the hill.

Chapter 27

As my time to return to Canada approached, I wasn't leaving the Tibetan community; it was leaving me. In Bodh Gaya, the Dalai Lama was holding a Kalachakra initiation (an important twelve-day-long series of teachings) in January of 2012. Many newcomers told me that they were planning to attend and then return to Tibet in the spring. Throughout December, Tibetans began leaving for Bodh Gaya. Some were preparing to set up businesses to serve the thousands of pilgrims that would converge on the town. Others were headed to Delhi and even Nepal to collect relatives arriving from Tibet for the teachings. The Chinese government had allowed a few thousand people from Tibet to go to India. (Many were subsequently arrested on their return and sent to detention centres for reeducation.)

For a few weeks, McLeod Ganj was inundated by around 1000 people from Tibet who had come to catch short teachings that the Dalai Lama was giving before heading off to Bodh Gaya. The pilgrims were easily recognizable from their clothing: often regional dress with jaunty cowboy hats and fedoras. They were not disheveled, sunburned, and exhausted like escapees. They had money and were dependent on no one. As they had arrived on Chinese passports and had not escaped through the Himalayas, they were not locked up at the reception centre but were free to do as they pleased. They were civilized and polite. They reminded me of the adult refugees who had stayed at the old reception centre in McLeod Ganj waiting to meet the Dalai Lama before they were sent back to Tibet.

Just before the teachings began, I stepped out into the street one morning to see that all of the street vendors' stalls had been carted away. Instead of being lined with their colorful wares, there was a new view of ugly concrete walls and the open sewers, which quickly filled with garbage. As I stood on Jogibara Road looking at the sorry sight, I was joined by the fat manager of Black Magic, the most opulent new restaurant in town. "Those people are not poor either," he told me, implying that the street vendors were wealthy like him, so the vendors' loss of their livelihoods should be of little concern. That the fat manager was wealthy was undoubtable: he had displayed tens of thousands of rupees and offered hard drugs to my teenage son if my son would produce a Western woman for him to have sex with. My opinion of the place worsened in later that year when the management and staff of Black Magic severely beat two Tibetan customers before stripping them naked, urinating on them, and dumping them in the jungle outside town. The fat manager did not seem the most trustworthy source of information or, for that matter, very smart when it came to marketing his business or the town. He didn't seem to realize that the street stalls added much needed tourist appeal to what is essentially a concrete jungle.

The visitors from Tibet couldn't have helped but notice the removal of the street stalls. I was glad that they got to see this example of Tibetan life in India. Apparently, the street stalls were illegal, although they shouldn't have been because they added charm and character to the otherwise dull streets. Vendors told me that they had to pay a bribe of 3,000 rupees in order to lay out their wares again. On this occasion, most chose not to because they were headed off to the Kalachakra. A handful couldn't go, so they paid up, but they were few in number. For the month that I remained, the streets assumed a seedy look, with an ongoing garbage strike only adding to the aura of dereliction.

Once the teachings ended, organized chaos reigned at the bus station, for it seemed that everyone was going to the Kalachakra. Each night in the gloom of the massive structure, dozens of busses jockeyed for position while hundreds of Tibetans gathered with their baggage. In the days and nights that followed, the town emptied. Even most of the drunks and drug addicts headed off to the Kalachakra. Many secular friends were not planning to attend the Kalachakra initiation but were going to man booths educating people on various issues or were taking advantage of an opportunity to sell books and other materials. Some went for the chance to connect with friends. Many of the poor who could afford to get there went to find work selling things or preparing meals for the thousands of pilgrims that would be attending.

Within days, most of the Tibetan shops and restaurants closed. I couldn't tell how many Tibetans were gone, but a conservative guess is 80%. There were almost no customers in the many Indian and Kashmiri shops, and the taxi drivers loitered forlornly; walking in the streets became a delight thanks to the absence of their vehicles, but I knew that a lot of families were going hungry. The street dogs became quiet as their rations of scraps disappeared. Barely a Tibetan face could be seen on the streets. The few open restaurants were deserted save for a few local Indians and domestic tourists. "This is a disaster," a nut seller from Kashmir told me. "My business is 5% of what it usually is." He didn't seem worried, but I saw a lot of long faces. I had wondered what McLeod Ganj would be like without Tibetans. Without them, much of the economy was on the verge of collapse. I imagined the apartment buildings abandoned and the jungle taking over.

Many of the Indian tourists appeared bored and confused. A few Indian street vendors had paid their bribes to reopen their stalls, but on Temple Road, there wasn't a single Tibetan merchant. There were no monks. There was almost no Tibetan food. The Tibetan temples and monasteries were practically deserted. The Library was shuttered. They had come to see "Little Lhasa," but Little Lhasa was gone.

Just before midnight our group ventured next door to Mountview, where an all male Punjabi dance party was in its death throes. Most of the patrons were so drunk that they could barely walk. The scouts that we sent upstairs reported that some were passed out on tables and the floor. One unconscious drunk was seen being dragged shoeless back into the fray. We hung out downstairs until the music was shut off. The last drunks staggered out at 12:30 am, and the staff locked the security gate.

Upstairs, it looked as though the Mongol Hordes had invaded. The furniture was topsy turvy and the celebrants had smashed the paper light shades like piñatas. Broken glass and spilled beer were everywhere. There was vomit. "Pirates!" the bartender exclaimed pointing at the room with a big grin when I walked in. "Do you want us to leave?" I asked "No!" he shouted with glee. "We want to celebrate that they are GONE!"

One of the Tibetans in our group swept up the worst of the glass and puke. Leaving the staff to relax, we slid the big long table back to its rightful place and found chairs that weren't wet with beer, creating a patch of relative civility in the midst of the mess. Then we danced in the sticky mucky spilled beer. By the time that we left at 2 am, the streets were deserted, the main square a sea of broken liquor bottles.

The following day, almost all of the Indian tourists left, and an unimaginable silence descended over the town. Even my tortured mind seemed to calm itself as I abandoned my writing to wander the streets to witness the impact of the absence of Tibetans and chat with Indian merchant friends who had much time on their hands. My peace of mind lasted one day.

On January 2, Phayul reported that the exile government had concerns: "In information that we have received, we suspect there might be 1000 to 1500 spies attending the Kalachakra teachings sent by China to study and report on the Tibetan leaders and their activities in the exile community." The ludicrous inference was that up to 21% of the visitors from Tibet, who were mostly old people, were spies. The next day there was more fear mongering in the Times of India. Apparently, many of the pilgrims from Tibet had not reported to the Refugee Reception Centre when they passed through Kathmandu. This was not surprising in that most of them had come for the Kalachakra, not to attempt to seek asylum that they would not be granted. Apparently, Tibetan officials were concerned that some of them were headed to McLeod Ganj and had increased security at the Temple: "Tibetans dressed in camouflage would keep an eye over offices. We fear that the Chinese spies might want to destroy our records. Tibetan volunteers from Dehradoon are here for the purpose."

I began to frequent the Temple and roamed the town in search of suspicious characters. On my first visit to the Temple, I saw a couple of security guards, but otherwise the complex was almost abandoned. The only sign of life was an Indian family who held up their children to spin the prayer wheels. My next visit showed more promise, for I spotted a lone Tibetan girl, but, as is customary, she only circumambulated the complex three times and then left. I went at night and I went in the afternoon, but other than a handful of security guards, no one was there. As I sat in coffee shops watching, the streets were almost deserted. The only Asian visitors in town were a pair of Korean nuns. Perhaps they were spies? Needless to say, nothing happened.

At the same time that the Kalachakra ended, it was our time to leave. On the bus ride to Delhi, I reflected on what I had learned through my research and the promises that I had made to the newcomers. "Write the truth," people had told me as they shared even unsavory aspects of their lives. They knew some of the truth, but it seemed that the truth was more complicated than they realized. I wondered how many settlement Tibetans knew that new arrivals were forced to go back to Tibet. It was possible that even many of the activists had no idea. There was so little communication between the parties involved that it was possible. No journalists or academics had reported on what transpired. The only human rights organization to have documented some of the problems was the Tibet Justice Institute in a report released in September of 2011. Perhaps the researchers, like me, had been tormented by their findings and troubled that the truth could be detrimental to the Tibetan cause. But the damning information contained in the report was never mentioned on-line or in the press. It was tucked away on page 49, separate from the section on R.C.'s, which was several pages earlier. In legal language that may have been too complex for some, it explained how new arrivals were now dealt with by being given Special Entry Permits for their pilgrimage or study. I knew that an exception was going to be made for about 300 newcomers. But there was no other whisper of change.

None of the numbers reporting how many people had escaped from Tibet matched, but somewhere between 57,178 and 87,096 had gotten out since 1979. I knew that tens of thousands were missing. I'd seen so much bizarre math that I didn't trust much of it, but exile government officials had stated that 46,620 "pilgrims" had returned to Tibet; no mention had been made of "students." Had children sent from Tibet for education been sent back unwillingly once their studies were complete? How many newcomers who wanted to had managed to remain in exile was a big question. Samdhong Rinpoche had mentioned that 30% of Dharamsala Tibetans were newcomers. If the figure was accurate, that accounted for only 4,113 of them. There were no other settlements in India with sizable newcomer populations except in the monasteries; the current numbers of monks were illusive, but I heard mention of 20,000 monks, including those born in India. I couldn't see that more than a few thousand newcomers had made it abroad. "What have you done with them?" I wanted to scream at exile government officials. "Show me the raw data from the 2009 survey."

I wanted to know the details concerning how so many had been sent back unnoticed and with little complaint. Had they been shipped back to Nepal for the journey home to re-enter Tibet on foot or to surrender to border officials? Most new arrivals were unable to speak Hindi, Nepali, or English effectively. They couldn't have made the arrangements on their own. Were they now being taken to Delhi to apply for Chinese travel documents? Were they convinced to go only because they were told that they would get no help in India or were they convinced to do so for the good of their country? Or did they leave without question because they understood that that was what the Dalai Lama wanted them to do? It seemed that there was no better way to convince Tibetans to go along with proposals than pulling what is referred to as "the Dalai Lama card." I was left with more questions than answers.

There had been hope, but it appeared to have been dashed. It had seemed that the new Tibetan exile prime minister, Lobsang Sangay, was concerned about the problems of newcomers, at least that is what he had said during his campaign. Certainly, most of my friends had voted for him, for he had promised to make the problems of newcomers a top priority. Shortly after his election, my hopes had been dampened when I spoke to a volunteer who worked with the exile government: "I think it is a disaster that he was elected. He [Lobsang Sangay] doesn't have experience dealing with people who work for the exile government. They don't want anything to change. The way things are serves their interests. I don't think he has the personality or the experience needed to deal with them. Intelligent discussion and debate at Harvard are no preparation for this snake pit. I hope I'm wrong."

Back in Canada, as I wrote, I kept hoping for change that would give my book a positive ending, but in the many months that followed, none was forthcoming. The number of self-immolations increased, and there was no word on anything more being done to help refugees who did not want to return to Tibet. Then the ongoing horror inside Tibet was joined by horror in exile.

In the middle of February 2012, I read an article in Phayul in which a member of Tibetan Youth Congress claimed that it was planning something "big and effective." The only thing that I could think of that would actually be effective would be something that influenced Chinese policies. Such seemed unlikely to be achieved by an organization devoted to protest and dedicated to Tibet regaining independence. "I hope it's not a fucking self-immolation," I swore to myself out loud.

Weeks later on March 26th, a Tibetan man self-immolated at a demonstration in Delhi in front of world media. Horrific images of his act brought enormous international media coverage which included some disturbing information. "They [activists] were telling me that there's going to be something different from the regular stuff, and that you are going to see something happening today that you have never seen before. A lot of media people were guessing that it might just be someone self-immolating," Neha Sethi reported to Voice of America. In the Huffington Post, I learned more: "While activists had been whispering Monday morning that something dramatic was expected at the protest, organizers insisted they were not behind the self-immolation." Who knew and who didn't will likely never be known, but apparently some did, and seemingly no one tried to stop the man. I felt sick to my stomach. "Who could let their friend do this?" I thought, imagining that he was an exile activist. But he was not one of their own.

It was soon revealed that the self-immolator was an unemployed member of the lowest "caste" in exile society. His name was Jamphel Yeshi. He was a newcomer who had grown up in Kham and escaped from Tibet in 2006. But now he was no longer the object of scorn. It had taken an unimaginable act, but a newcomer had achieved a status that I had never witnessed in the exile community—that of hero. An elaborate funeral was held for him in Dharamsala. It appeared that almost the entire town turned out to mourn his passing and show respect as his flag-draped coffin was carried through the streets on its way to the crematorium.

The End

Endnotes

Introduction

[1] *Demographics Survey of Tibetans in Exile—2009*, p. 41, Planning Commission, Central Tibetan Administration, Dharamsala, 2009, CD-ROM

[2] United Nations, UNESCO Institute for Statistics, "Regional Literacy Rates for Youth (15-24) and Adults (15+), 2005 - 2010," *unesco.org,* Web, July 9, 2012

Chapter 1

[1] "The New Arrivals Are Intolerant," *Outlook*, June 7, 2010, Web, July 20, 2011

[2] "Tibet's Stateless Nationals II: Tibetan Refugees in India," p. 49, Tibet Justice Center, September 2011, Web, September 20, 2011

[3] India, Bureau of Immigration, Ministry of Home Affairs, "Information Pertaining [sic] Tibetan Nationals, " Government of India, Web, July 12, 2011

[4] Walker, Vanessa, *Mantras & Misdemeanors*, p. 122, Crows Nest (Sydney), Allen & Unwin, 2006, Print

[5] Mohan, Vibhor, "Tibetans Going in for Foreign Spouses," *Tribune*, June 14, 2005

[6] I was told that the two most common spellings are "Salai Gyal (གསལ་ལེ་རྒྱལ)" and "Zalai Gyal (ཟ་ལེ་རྒྱལ)."

[7] Tenzin, Kyabje Kirti Rinpoche Lobsang, *Supplementary Chapters on Gedun Choephel*, p. 33, Dharamsala, T.C.K.M., 2008, Print

[8] Chopel, Gedun, *Tibetan Arts of Love,* Trans. Jeffrey Hopkins, Dorje Yudon Yuthok, pp. 14-16, Ithica, Snow Lion Publications, 1992, Print (A variety of spellings are sometimes employed to convert Tibetan names and words into English. The spelling that I am most familiar with and employed is "Gendun Choephel," which varies from that used by Hopkirk.)

[9] Ibid., p. 275

[10] A friend provided further information that he considered of note: "The name of the village in Menla Kyab's comic cassette is 'Same Chong Dewa' (སེམས་ཆུང་བདེ་བ), literally meaning 'Village With Careful Mind.' The name symbolizes that the village is somehow remote and backward, so the villagers always go against new things such as having marriages with western women, etc. The villagers are very careful about maintaining their culture and customs.

In the series, there are some comic pieces related to this village, including "Same Chong Dewa's Thief" (the village's problem with a thief.), "Same Chong Dewa's War for Region," "Same Chong Dewa's Lama" (actually a fake lama), "Same Chong Dewa's Wedding Ceremony," and "Same Chong Dewa's Marriage" (the Salai Gyal episode).

[11] *Demographics Survey of Tibetans in Exile—2009*, p. 29, Planning Commission, Central Tibetan Administration, Dharamsala, 2009, CD-ROM

[12] "Sex Ratio," *The World Factbook*, Central Intelligence Agency, 2011, Web, March 7, 2012

[13] *Demographics Survey of Tibetans in Exile—2009*, p. 28, Planning Commission, Central Tibetan Administration, Dharamsala, 2009, CD-ROM

[14] Ibid., p. 29

[15] *Tibetan Demographic Survey: 1998, Volume II*, p. 739, Planning Council, Central Tibetan Administration, Dharamsala, 2000, Print

[16] *Tibetan Demographic Survey: 1998, Volume I*, pp. 59 and 216, Planning Council, Central Tibetan Administration, Dharamsala, 2000, Print

[17] In 2011, my request to the Department of Information for statistical data on newcomers was denied.

[18] Gupta, Naveen, Surender Nikhil Gupta, "Outbreak of Gastroenteritis in Tibetan Transit School, Dharamshala, Himachal Pradesh, India," p. 99 (Table 1), *Indian Journal of Community Medicine*, 2006, Web, August 3, 2011 ("Dharamshala" is a common alternate spelling of "Dharamsala.")

[19] Mills, Edward J., et al., "Prevalence of Mental Disorders and Torture among Tibetan Refugees: A Systematic Review," p. 3, *BMC International Health and Human Rights*, 2005, PDF
Terheggen, Maaike A., Margaret S. Stroebe, Rolf J. Kleber, "Western Conceptualizations and Eastern Experience: A Cross-Cultural Study of Traumatic Stress Reactions among Tibetan Refugees in India," p. 394, *Journal of Traumatic Stress*, Vol. 14, No. 2, 2001, PDF

[20] Mercer, Stewart W., Alastair Ager, Eshani Ruwanpura, "Psychosocial Distress of Tibetans in Exile: Integrating Western Interventions with Traditional Beliefs and Practice," pp. 179 and 185, *Social Science and Medicine*, Vol. 60, 2005, PDF

[21] "Tibet's Stateless Nationals II: Tibetan Refugees in India," pp. 132-133, *Tibet Justice Center*, September 2011, Web, September 20, 2011

[22] U.S. Embassy Cable, "10NewDelhi290, Tibet Growing Frustration after Latest Round," *Wikileaks*, February 11, 2010, Web, July 6, 2010

[23] "Dangerous Crossings: Conditions Impacting the Flight of Tibetan Refugees in 2001," *International Campaign for Tibet*, 2002

[24] *Tibetan Demographic Survey: 1998, Volume I,* p. 365, Planning Council, Dharamsala, Central Tibetan Administration, 2000

Chapter 2
[1] "A Culture at Risk: An Initial Assessment of Seismic Vulnerabilities in Upper Dharamsala, India," pp. 2-3, *GeoHazards International*, 2006, Web, July 11, 2011

Chapter 3
[1] Associated Press, "Tibetan Monk Sets Himself on Fire," *The Guardian*, February 18, 2012, Web, February 18, 2012

[2] Ponnudurai, Parameswaran, "Popular Tibetan Writer Detained," *Radio Free Asia*, February 18, 2012, Web, February 18 2012

[3] Watts, Jonathan, Ken Macfarlane, "Inside Tibet's Heart of Protest," *The Guardian*, February 10, 2012, Web, February 10, 2012

[4] *Tibetan Demographic Survey:1998, Volume I*, pp. 180-183, Planning Council, Central Tibetan Administration, Dharamsala, 2000, Print

[5] Angry Tibetan Guy, "Tibetan Language," *Angry Tibetan Guy*, September 2011, Web, September 30, 2011

[6] Iyer, Pico, *The Open Road, The Global Journey of the Fourteenth Dalai Lama*, p. 167, New Delhi, Penguin Group, 2008, Print

[7] Ibid., p. 169

[8] Ibid., p. 167

[9] Ibid., p. 35

[10] Post, Audrey, *Precious Pills: Medicine and Social Change among Tibetan Refugees in India*, p. 70, Oxford, New York, Berghahn Books, 2008, Print

[11] Schrempf, Mona, *Soundings in Tibetan Medicine*, p. 56, Leiden, Brill, 2008, Print

[12] Yeh, Emily "Will the Real Tibetan Please Stand Up! Identity Politics in the Tibetan Diaspora," p. 243, *Tibet, Self and the Tibetan Diaspora: Voices of Difference*, IATS, 2000, Print

[13] Hess, Julia Meredith, *Immigrant Ambassadors: Citizenship and Belonging in the Tibetan Diaspora*, p. 147, Stanford, Stanford University Press, 2009, Print

[14] Ibid., p. 66

[15] Diehl, Keila, *Echoes from Dharamsala*, p. 64, Berkley and Los Angeles, University of California Press, 2002

[16] Bernabei, Matilde, "A Case Study of Tibetan Educators in India and Nepal: Constructing Community in the Diaspora," p. 118, Diss., Simon Fraser University, 2011, Print

[17] For readers not familiar with residential schools, until only a few decades ago indigenous children in Canada were removed from their homes and placed in boarding schools. The goal was to strip them of their language and culture and assimilate them into white society. The results were disastrous. The Canadian prime minister issued an official apology in 2008. Investigations and lawsuits are ongoing.

[18] Ibid., p. 113

Chapter 4

[1] Sharlho, Tseten Wangchuk, "China's Reforms in Tibet: Issues and Dilemmas," p. 47, *The Journal of Contemporary China*, Volume 1, Number 1, Fall 1992, Web, August 4, 2011

[2] Klieger, Paul Christiaan, "Accomplishing Tibetan Identity: The Constitution of a National Consciousness," Diss., University of Hawaii, 1989, Web, July 13, 2011

[3] Shakya, Tsering, *The Dragon in the Land of the Snows: A History of Modern Tibet Since 1947*, pp. 348 to 448, London, Pimlico, 1999, Print

Chapter 5

[1] Dogra, Chander Suta, "Tocsin on Mount Exile," *Outlook*, June 7, 2010, Web, July 22, 2011

[2] Post, Audrey, *Precious Pills: Medicine and Social Change among Tibetan Refugees in India*, p. 67, Oxford, New York, Berghahn Books, 2008, Print

[3] Christie, Lotte, "Mindful Adult Education: Theory and Practical Suggestions," p. 14, *Danish Centre for Conflict Resolution*, 2004, Web, July 17, 2011

[4] "Sherab Gatsal Lobling, History," *Sambhota Tibetan Schools Society*, Web, July 24, 2011 (Sherab Gatsel Lobling is now the official name of Tibetan Transit School; however, the new name is almost never used by anyone including students, past or present.)

[5] "Six Months without a Bath," Tibet Society United Kingdom, Autumn 1998, *World Tibet News Network*, Canada Tibet Committee, Web, Aug 1, 2012

[6] Tribune News Service, "Twenty-Nine More Suspected of Food-Poisoning," *The Tribune*, September 17, 2004, Web, August 1, 2011

[7] Holtz, Timothy, *A Doctor in Little Lhasa*, Indianapolis, Dog Ear Publishing, 2009, Print

[8] Gupta, Surender Nikhil, Naveen Gupta, "Outbreak of Gastroenteritis in Tibetan Transit School, Dharamshala, Himachal Pradesh, India," p. 97, *Indian Journal of Community Medicine*, 2006, Web, August 3, 2011

[9] Ibid., p. 98

[10] "LAFOT Brings Clean, Safe Water to Tibetan Students in Dharamsala," Los Angeles Friends of Tibet, *Facebook*, December 22, 2009, Web, August 10, 2011

Chapter 6

[1] Jigme, Hortsang, *Under a Blue Sky*, Trans. Lobsang Dawa, Guusje de Schot, p. 84, Dharamsala, Self-Published, 1998, Print

[2] Corry, Tara, et. al. "Tibetans in Exile," *Oxford University*, July 1994, Web, July 10, 2011

[3] Knorbu30, "Shapaley-Shapale Song (Tibetan rap)," *Youtube*, March 24, 2011, Web, July 26, 2011

[4] Saunders, Kate, "Tibetan Rap on Chinese Knuckles Flusters Beijing," *The Guardian*, November 25, 2011, Web, November 26, 2011

Chapter 7

[1] Meo, Nick, "The Pick-Up Paradise," *The Times*, July 22, 2004, Web, August 10, 2011 (The article is only available on *The Times* website to those with a subscription; however, it is currently also available via *Google News*.)

[2] Regg Cohn, Martin, "Little Lhasa Belies Tibet Ideal," *Toronto Star*, December 8, 2003, Web, July 10, 2011

Chapter 8

[1] Klieger, Paul Christiaan, "Accomplishing Tibetan Identity: The Constitution of a National Consciousness," p. 235, Diss., University of Hawaii," 1989, Web, July 13, 2011

[2] Ibid., p. 242

[3] Ruwanpura, Eshani, et al., "Cultural and Spiritual Constructions of Mental Distress and Associated Coping Mechanisms of Tibetans in Exile: Implications for Western Interventions," p. 194, *Journal of Refugee Studies, Vol. 19, No.2*, Oxford University Press, 2006, PDF

[4] Ibid., p. 194

Chapter 9
[1] "Dangerous Crossings," Reports 2001 to 2010, *International Campaign for Tibet*, 2002 to 2011, PDF
[2] *Tibetan Demographic Survey, Volume II*, p. 739, Planning Council, Central Tibetan Administration, Dharamsala, 2000, Print
[3] "Dangerous Crossings: Conditions Impacting the Flight of Tibetan Refugees, 2006 Report," p. 30, *International Campaign for Tibet*, 2007, PDF
[4] Terheggen, Maaike A., Margaret S. Stroebe, Rolf J. Kleber, "Western Conceptualizations and Eastern Experience: A Cross-Cultural Study of Traumatic Stress Reactions among Tibetan Refugees in India," p. 394, *Journal of Traumatic Stress*, Vol. 14, No. 2, 2001, PDF
[5] Gupta, Surender Nikhil, Naveen Gupta, "Outbreak of Gastroenteritis in Tibetan Transit School, Dharamshala, Himachal Pradesh," India, p. 99, *Indian Journal of Community Medicine*, 2006, Web, August 3, 2011
[6] Sachs, Emily, et al., "Entering Exile: Trauma, Mental Health, and Coping among Tibetan Refugees Arriving in Dharamsala, India," p. 202, *Journal of Traumatic Stress*, Vol. 21, No. 2, April 2008, PDF
[7] Bhatia, Shushum, Tsegyal Dranyia, Derrick Rowley, "A Social and Demographic Study of Tibetan Refugees in India," p. 414, *Social Science and Medicine*, Vol. 54, 2002, PDF
  Wangmo, Rinzin, "Status of Tibetan Refugees in India: A Case Study of Bylakuppe," p. 70, Stella Maris College, 2008, PDF
  "In India: Situation of Tibetan Refugees and Those Not Recognized as Refugees; Including Legal Rights and Living Conditions," Refworld, UNHCR, December 23, 1999, Web, August 12, 2011
[8] Kawaguchi, Ekai, *Three Years in Tibet*, p. 476, Delhi, Book Faith India, 1995, Print
[9] Rockhill, William Woodville, The *Land of the Lamas: Notes on a Journey Through China, Mongolia, and Tibet*, p. 212, Varanasi, Pilgrims Publishing, 2000, Print
[10] Ibid., p. 213
[11] Ibid., p. 213
[12] "Tibet's Stateless Nationals II: Tibetan Refugees in India," p. 15, Tibet Justice Center, September 2011, Web, September 20, 2011

Chapter 10
[1] "4 in 10 First Marriages End in Divorce: Report," *cbc.ca*, October 4, 2010, Web, February 11, 2012
[2] India, Office of the Registrar General and Census Commissioner, Ministry of Home Affairs, "Abstract of Speakers' Strength of Languages and Mother Tongues—2001," Ministry of Home Affairs, Web, February 11, 2012

Chapter 11
[1] United Nations, UNHCR, "States Parties [sic] to the 1951 Convention Relating to the Status of Refugees and the 1967 Protocol," *unhcr.org*, Web, August 18, 2011
[2] "Tibet's Stateless Nationals II: Tibetan Refugees in India," p. 46, Tibet Justice Center, September 2011, Web, September 20, 2011

[3] "Six Months without a Bath," Tibet Society United Kingdom, Autumn 1998, *World Tibet News Network*, Canada Tibet Committee, Web, August 1, 2012

[4] "Tibet's Stateless Nationals II: Tibetan Refugees in India," p. 49, Tibet Justice Center, September 2011, Web, September 20, 2011

[5] Dogra, Chander Suta, "Tocsin on Mount Exile," *Outlook*, June 7, 2010, Web, July 22, 2011

[6] McDonald, Angus, "Love Across the Divide," *South China Morning Post*, August 30, 2003
Web, July 17, 2011

[7] "Tibet's Stateless Nationals II: Tibetan Refugees in India," p. 132, Tibet Justice Center, September 2011, Web, September 20, 2011

[8] "Tibet's Stateless Nationals II: Tibetan Refugees in India," p. 47, Tibet Justice Center, September 2011, Web, September 20, 2011

[9] Thinley, Phurbu, "Tibetans to Boycott Local Taxi and Auto Rickshaw Service in McLeod Gunj [sic]," *Phayul,* May 4, 2007, Web, May 4, 2007 (Article deleted but available elsewhere on-line.)

[10] "Tibet's Stateless Nationals II: Tibetan Refugees in India," p. 47, Tibet Justice Center, September 2011, Web, September 20, 2011

Chapter 12
[1] "The New Arrivals Are Intolerant," *Outlook*, June 7, 2010, Web, July 20, 2011

[2] Sonam, Tenzin, "A Tibet of the Mind" *Phayul*, December 2, 2010, Web, December 20, 2010

[3] "Violence against a Tibetan Woman in Tenzinghang: TWA's Report," pp. 1-11, Tibetan Women's Association, September 2011, Web, October 3, 2011

[4] Ibid., p. 4

[5] Ibid., p. 11

[6] Tsering, Tendar, "Israel Farming Programme Now Open to Non-Farming Settlements," *Phayul*, May 18, 2012, Web, May 19, 2012 (The article also mentions that most newcomers were prevented from joining the program because completion of grade ten was required of participants from Dharamsala. The rule did not apply to residents of other settlements.)

Chapter 13
[1] "Emotional and Psychological Trauma: Causes and Effects, Symptoms and Treatment," *healingresources.info*, Santa Barbara Graduate Institute Center for Clinical Studies and Research and L.A. County Early Identification Group, Web, September 3, 2011

[2] Walker, Joyce, "Teens in Distress Series: Adolescent Stress and Depression," University of Minnesota, 2005, Web, September 3, 2011

[3] Brock, Dylan, "Taming the Mind: Current Mental Health Treatments and Obstacles to Expanding a Western Model in a Tibetan Exile Community, p. 9, " SIT Study Abroad, Digital Collections, World Learning, 2008, PDF

[4] Ibid., p. 30

[5] Terheggen, Maaike A., Margaret S. Stroebe, Rolf J. Kleber, "Western Conceptualizations and Eastern Experience: A Cross-Cultural Study of Traumatic Stress Reactions among Tibetan Refugees in India," pp. 400-401, *Journal of Traumatic Stress,* Vol. 14, No 2, 2001, PDF

[6] Keller, Allen S., "Striking Hard: Torture in Tibet," p. 3, *Physicians For Human Rights*, 1997, PDF

[7] Sevan-Schreiber, David, Brigitte Le Lin, Boris Birmaher, "Prevalence of Posttraumatic Stress Disorder and Major Depressive Disorder in Tibetan Refugee Children," *Journal of the American Academy of Child and Adolescent Psychiatry*, Abstract, August 1, 1998, Web, October 1, 2011

[8] Evans, Dabney, et al., "Shattered Shangri-La: Differences in Depressive and Anxiety Symptoms in Students Born in Tibet Compared to Tibetan Students Born in Exile," p. 4, *Social Psychiatry and Psychiatric Epidemiology*, 2008, PDF

[9] "Mission," Tibetan Children's Village, *Tibetan Children's Education Welfare Fund*, Central Tibetan Administration, Web, October 1, 2011

[10] "Another Death Due to Drug Overdose," *kunphen.org*, Web, December 15, 2011

[11] Evans, Dabney, et al., "Shattered Shangri-La: Differences in Depressive and Anxiety Symptoms in Students Born in Tibet Compared to Tibetan Students Born in Exile," p. 3, *Social Psychiatry and Psychiatric Epidemiology*, 2008, PDF

[12] "Tibetan Torture Survivors [sic] Program," Department of Health, *Central Tibetan Administration*, Web, October 1, 2011

[13] "Tibetan Medicare System (TMS)," Department of Health, *Central Tibetan Administration,* Web, July 1, 2012

[14] Puri, S. Gopal, "Tibetan Administration Plans Moral Offensive to Counter Chinese Infiltration," *The Times of India*, May 1, 2012, Web, May 2, 2012,

[15] Katayama, Lisa, "Brothers First," *Buddhadharma*, Fall 2008, Web, May 12, 2012

Chapter 14
[1] Murphy, Dervla, *Tibetan Foothold*, London, Harper Collins, 2000, Print

[2] Klieger, Paul Christiaan, "Accomplishing Tibetan Identity: The Constitution of a National Consciousness, pp. 228-233, Diss., University of Hawaii," 1989, Web, July 13, 2011

[3] Dogra, Chander Suta, "Tocsin on Mount Exile," *Outlook*, June 7, 2010, Web, July 22, 2011

[4] Desai, Sonalde B., et al., *Human Development Survey: Challenges for a Society in Transition*, p. 161, New Delhi, Oxford University Press, 2005, PDF

[5] Desai, Sonalde B., et al., *Human Development Survey: Challenges for a Society in Transition* p. 13, New Delhi, Oxford University Press, 2005, PDF

[6] "Himachal Pradesh HC Issues Notice to Centre, State of Himachal Pradesh, Dalai Lama and Others Seeking Removal of all Flags of Tibetan Government-in-Exile from the Indian Soil," *indlawnews.com*, November 17, 2010, Web, August 12, 2011

[7] Mohan, Lalit, "Tibetans Warned Against Defacing Rocks, Trees," *The Tribune*, August 31, 2012

[8] "High Court Issues Notice to Tibetans [sic] Administration over Encroachments," *The Himachal*," April 15, 2012, Web, September 1, 2012

[9] Tribune News Service, "State Cabinet Okays Amendments to Rules," *The Tribune*, July 27, 2011, Web, July 28, 2011

[10] India, Census of India, "Figures at a Glance: Provisional Population Totals, Himachal Pradesh," Ministry of Home Affairs, 2011, Web, July 18, 2012

[11] Raote, Rrishi, "Unease in Dharamsala," *Business Standard*, March 19, 2011, Web, September 3, 2011

[12] Canada, Statistics Canada, "Population By Selected Ethnic Origins, by Province and Territory (2006 Census)," Statistics Canada, Web, July 18, 2012

[13] Desai, Sonalde B., et al., *Human Development Survey: Challenges for a Society in Transition*, pp. 49 and 50, New Delhi, Oxford University Press, 2005, PDF

[14] *Demographics Survey of Tibetans in Exile—2009*, p. 54, Planning Commission, Central Tibetan Administration, Dharamsala, 2009, CD-ROM

[15] Desai, Sonalde B., et al., *Human Development Survey: Challenges for a Society in Transition*, p. 49 and 50, New Delhi, Oxford University Press, 2005, PDF

[16] *Demographics Survey of Tibetans in Exile—2009*, p. 38-40, Planning Commission, Central Tibetan Administration, Dharamsala, 2009, CD-ROM

[17] India, Office of the Registrar General, "Maternal and Child Mortality and Total Fertility Rates," p. 20, Ministry of Home Affairs, 2011, PDF,

[18] *Demographics Survey of Tibetans in Exile—2009*, p. 13, Planning Commission, Central Tibetan Administration, Dharamsala, 2009, CD-ROM

[19] Ibid.

[20] Ibid.

[21] Yee, Amy, "Young Lawyer Aids Exile Tibetans with His Language and Legal Skills," *The Christian Science Monitor*, September 6, 2011, Web, September 8, 2011

Chapter 15

[1] McGirk, Tim, "Hate Campaign Shatters Calm of Dalai Lama," *The Independent*, May 11, 1994, Web, July 14, 2011

[2] Dhondup, K., "Dharamsala Revisited: Shangrila [sic] or Sarajevo," *Tibetan Review*, July 1994, Web, August 7, 2011 (Available on several websites.)

[3] Ibid.

[4] Ibid.

[5] Thinley, Phurbu, "Tibetans to Boycott Local Taxi and Auto Rickshaw Service in McLeod Gunj [sic]," *Phayul*, May 4, 2007, Web, May 5, 2007 (Original link removed, but the article is available from other on-line sources.)

[6] Nazreen, Wasfia, "McLeod Ganj Clash: A Non-Tibetan's Reflection," *Phayul*, May 4, 2007, Web, May 5, 2007 (Original link removed, archived by Canada Tibet Committee's *World Tibet Network News*.)

[7] Tsering, Topden, "Making Sense of the Senseless: Violence in Dharamsala," *Phayul*, May 4, 2007, Web, May 5, 2007 (Original link removed, archived by Canada Tibet Committee's *World Tibet Network News*.)

[8] "Press Statement – Phayul Regrets Article," *Phayul*, May 7, 2007, Web, May 8, 2007

[9] "Joint Press Statement Resolving McLeod Ganj Clash," *Phayul*, May 11, 2007, Web, May 12, 2007

[10] Tsering, Topden, "Making Sense of the Senseless: Violence in Dharamsala," *Phayul*, May 4, 2007, Web, May 5, 2007 (Original link removed, archived by Canada Tibet Committee's *World Tibet Network News*)

[11] Main Page (On-Line, Himachal Pradesh Section), *The Tribune*, August 14, 2007, Web, August 15, 2007

[12] Tribune News Service, "Taxi Operators on Strike Again," *The Tribune*, August 12, 2007, Web, August 13, 2007

Main Page (On-Line, Himachal Pradesh Section), *The Tribune*, August 17, 2007, Web, August 18, 2007

[13] Tribune News Service, "3 Tibetan Security Officials Held," *The Tribune*, April 2, 2010, Web, April 4, 2010

[14] Wangyal, Lobsang, "Three Tibetans Arrested for Attacking Local Indians," *Tibet Sun*, April 5, 2010, Web April 7, 2010, (Article and photo since removed from website.) http://www.tibetsun.com/news/2010/04/05/three-tibetans-arrested-for-attacking-local-indians/

Chapter 16
[1] Mohan, Lalit, "China Link Surfaces; Karmapa Likely to be Questioned," *The Tribune*, January 28, 2011, Web, January 30, 2011

[2] Jain, Meetu, "Himachal Police Grills [sic] Karmapa over Raids," *IBN Live*, January 29, 2011, Web, January 29, 2011

[3] NDTV Correspondent, "Karmapa Money Trail: Recovered Cash Came From Nepal," *NDTV*, January 31, 2011, Web, January 31, 2011

[4] Mohan, Lalit, "Virbhadra Bats for Karmapa," *The Tribune*, February 4, 2011, Web, February 4, 2011

"Tibetans Protest, Say Karmapa Not a Spy," *IBN Live*, February 8, 2011, Web, February 8, 2011

Chapter 17
[1] "Press Freedom Index 2011/2012," *Reporters without Borders*, Web, January 13, 2013

[2] Tribune News Service, "Shops Gutted in McLeodganj [sic]," *The Tribune*, December 1, 2010, Web, December 2, 2010

[3] Mohan, Lalit, "Rains Take a Toll on Dharamsala Roads," *The Tribune*, August 19, 2011, Web, August 20, 2011

[4] Mohan, Lalit, "Tibetans Deported from Kinnaur Being Released," *Tribune*, September 27, 2012, Web, September 28, 2012

Chapter 18
[1] Younghusband Francis E., *India and Tibet,* p. 196, New Delhi, Asian Educational Services, 2005, Print

[2] Ngawa is also known as Ngaba (Lhasa dialect) and Aba (Chinese)

Chapter 19
[1] Amir-uddin Nadwi, Abu Bakr, *Tibet and Tibetan Muslims*, p. 50-59, LTWA, 2004, Print
[2] *Tricycle*, Summer, 2008, Web, September 5, 2011

Chapter 20
[1] Link is currently unavailable because the forum is not operational. If the forum is reinstated, the thread can be located using the following information: Phayul Forum, thread name: "Gomo-tulku [sic] Photograph," Thread started: August 29, 2011
[2] Hooper, Joseph, "Leaving Om: Buddhism's Lost Lamas," *Details*, August, 2012, Web, September 3, 2012
[3] Ibid.
[4] Mukpo, Diana, *My Life with Chogyam Trungpa*, pp. 338-382, Boston & London, Shambhala, 2006
[5] Midal, Fabrice, *Recalling Chogyam Trungpa*, pp. ix-x, Boston, Shambhala Publication, 2005, Print
[6] River Sky, "To Be Avoided As Delusional and Counterproductive," Customer Review, *amazon.com*, December 31, 2004, Web, March 21, 2012
[7] Oakley, Richard, "Shock at Lama Sogyal Rinpoche's Past," *The Sunday Times*, July 4, 2009, Web, October 4, 2011
[8] Stewart, Francis, "Lama Choedak Rinpoche Apologizes," *The Canberra Times*, May 1, 2011, Web, October 1, 2011

Chapter 22
[1] "Dangerous Crossing: Conditions Impacting the Flight of Tibetan Refugees, 2010 Update," *International Campaign for Tibet*, Washington DC, 2011, PDF
[2] Tsering, Tendar, "382 Tibetans will not be deported: Additional SP," *Phayul*, July 5, 2012, Web, July 5, 2012
[3] "4 in 10 First Marriages End in Divorce: Report," cbc.ca, October 4, 2010, Web, February 16, 2012

Chapter 23
[1] Markoff, John, "Vast Spy System Loots Computers in 103 Countries," *The New York Times*, March 28, 2009, Web, March 29, 2009
[2] El Akkad, Omar, "Meet the Canadians Who Busted Ghostnet," *The Globe and Mail*, March 30, 2009, Web, March 31, 2009
[3] "Ten Ways to Promote Tibetan Language," lhakar.org, Web, May 1, 2011

Chapter 24
[1] *Demographics Survey of Tibetans in Exile—2009*, p. 13, Planning Commission, Central Tibetan Administration, Dharamsala, 2009, CD-ROM

Chapter 25

[1] Klieger, Paul Christiaan, "Accomplishing Tibetan Identity: The Constitution of a National Consciousness," pp. 276, 300, and 309, Diss., University of Hawaii," 1989, Web, July 13, 2011

[2] Germay, Arig, "The Home on Foreign Soil," Trans. Anonymous, *Tibet Times*, May 1, 2012
Original Tibetan language link:
http://tibettimes.net/blogs.php?id=6&post_id=20419

[3] Tsering, Tendar, "Tibetans Inside Tibet Give Two Thumbs Up to New Kalon Tripa," *Phayul*, August 10, 2011, Web, August 11, 2011

[4] Tendor, "A Lhakar Milestone," lhakar.org, April 4, 2012, Web May 13, 2012

[5] Rgyal, Lha Byams, Kuo-ming Sung, *Colloquial Amdo Tibetan: A Complete Course for Adult English Speakers*, pp. 4 and 5, Beijing, National Press For Tibetan Studies, 2005

Bibliography

Achin, Kurt, "Tibetan Protestor Self-Immolates in Indian Capital Ahead of China Summit," *Voice of America*, March 25, 2012

AFP, "Indian Tibetans Fight for Symbolic Homeland," *Agence France-Press*, April 16, 2008

Amir-uddin Nadwi, Abu Bakr, *Tibet and Tibetan Muslims*, Dharamsala, LTWA, 2004

Andre, Annette, "Education in Exile: Present and Future Situation," *Tibetan Bulletin*, Vol. 13, No. 3, May–June, 2009

Angry Tibetan Guy, "Tibetan Language," *Angry Tibetan Guy*, September, 2011

"Another Death Due to Drug Overdose," *kunphen.org*, December 15, 2011

Arnold, Rebecca, "Unemployment in the Tibetan Community in Exile," Independent Study Paper, Emory Study Abroad Program, Emory University, 2009

Artiles, Claudia, "Tibetan Refugees' Rights and Services in India," Minority Rights, *Human Rights and Human Welfare Journal,* 2011

Associated Press, "Jampa Yeshi, Tibetan Exile, Sets Self on Fire in Self-Immolation Anti-China Protest," *The Huffington Post*, March 26, 2012

Associated Press, "Tibetan Monk Sets Himself on Fire," *The Guardian*, February 18, 2012

Avedon, John F., *In Exile from the Land of Snows*, New Delhi, Viking, 1997

Basu, Sundeep, "Organizing for Exile! 'Self-help' among Tibetan Refugees in an Indian Town," *Refugee Watch*, No. 35, June, 2010

Bell, Charles, *The People of Tibet*, Delhi, Book Faith India, 1998

Bernabei, Matilde, "A Case Study of Tibetan Educators in India and Nepal: Constructing Community in the Diaspora," Diss., Simon Fraser University, 2011

Bhatia, Shushum, Tsegyal Dranyi, Derrick Rowley, "A Social and Demographic Study of Tibetan Refugees in India," *Social Science & Medicine*, Vol. 54, 2002

Brock, Dylan, "Taming the Mind: Current Mental Health Treatments and Obstacles to Expanding a Western Model in a Tibetan Exile

Community," Digital Collections, SIT Study Abroad, World Learning, 2008

"Burning and Lootings of Shops and Houses of Tibetan Minority in Manali," *World Tibet Network News*, Canada Tibet Committee, July 8, 1999

Canada, Statistics Canada, "Population by Selected Ethnic Origins, by Province and Territory (2006 Census)," Government of Canada, 2009

Carlson, Catherine, "Substance Abuse among Second-Generation Tibetan Refugees Living in India," Emory Tibetan Studies Program, Emory University, 2003

Chopel, Gedun, *Tibetan Arts of Love*, Trans. Jeffrey Hopkins, Dorje Yudon Yuthok, Ithica, Snow Lion Publications, 1992

Christie, Lotte, et al. "Mindful Adult Education: Theory and Practical Suggestions," Danish Centre for Conflict Resolution, 2004

Cohen, Amy, "Borders without Doctors: The Community Health Workers Program for Tibetan Refugees," Emory-IBD Tibetan Studies Program, Emory University, 2004

Corrigan, Sean, "Beyond Provision: A Comparative Analysis of Two Long-Term Refugee Education Systems," M.A. Thesis, University of Toronto, 2005

Corry, Tara, et al. "Tibetans in Exile," Oxford University, 1994

Craig, Mary, *Kundun*, London, Harper Collins, 1998

Craig, Mary, *Tears of Blood*, New Delhi, Indus, 1993

Crescenzi, Antonella, et al. "Effect of Political Imprisonment and Trauma History on Recent Tibetan Refugees in India," *Journal of Traumatic Stress*, Vol. 15, No. 5, October, 2002

"A Culture at Risk: An Initial Assessment of Seismic Vulnerabilities in Upper Dharamsala," India, *GeoHazards International*, 2006

Dalai Lama, *Awakening the Mind, Lightening the Heart,* New York, Harper Collins, 1995

Dalai Lama, *Essential Teachings*, Berkeley, North Atlantic Books, 1994

Dalai Lama, *How to Practice,* New York, Simon and Schuster Inc., 2002

Dalai Lama, *A Simple Path*, London, Harper Collins, 2000

Dalai Lama, *The Wisdom of Forgiveness,* New York, Penguin, 2004

"Dangerous Crossings: Conditions Impacting the Flight of Tibetan Refugees," *International Campaign for Tibet*, 2002 to 2012

Das, Sarat Chandra *Journey to Lhasa and Central Tibet,* Delhi, Paljor Publications, 2001

Das, Sarat Chandra, *Lhasa and Central Tibet*, Delhi, Book Faith India, 1998

David-Neel, Alexandra, *My Journey to Lhasa*, Boston, Beacon Press, 1993

David-Neel, Alexandra, *Tibetan Journey,* Delhi, Book Faith India, 1992

Davis, Brittany, "Embodying Cultures: Rethreading Meanings of Tibetanness in Dharamsala, India," *Electronic Journal of the ACA-UNCA*, 2010

Demographics Survey of Tibetans in Exile—2009, Planning Commission, Central Tibetan Administration, Dharamsala, 2009

Desai, Sonalde B., et al. *Human Development Survey: Challenges for a Society in Transition*, New Delhi, Oxford University Press, 2005

Dhondup, K., "Dharamsala Revisited: Shangrila [sic] or Sarajevo," *Tibetan Review*, July, 1994

Dhondup, K., *Songs of the Sixth Dalai Lama*, Dharamsala, Library of Tibetan Works and Archives, 1996

Diehl, Keila, *Echoes from Dharamsala*, Berkley and Los Angeles, University of California Press, 2002

"Divorce Rate in Lhasa Remains High," *People's Daily,* April 1, 2001

Dogra, Chander Suta, "Tocsin on Mount Exile," *Outlook*, June 7, 2010

Dolma, Sonam, et al. "Dangerous Journey: Documenting the Experience of Tibetan Refugees," *American Journal of Public Health*, Vol. 96, No.11, 2006

Dowman, Keith, *The Divine Madman*, Varanasi, Pilgrims Publishing, 2000

Duska, Susanne Aranka, "Harmony Ideology and Dispute Resolution: A Legal Ethnography of the Tibetan Diaspora in India," Diss., University of British Columbia, 2008

Editorial Board, "Always Beggars?: A Comment on Gyari Dolma's Interview," *Tibetan Political Review*, June 11, 2010

"Education Policy in Exile," *Office of Tibet, New York*, 2001

"Emotional and Psychological Trauma: Causes and Effects, Symptoms and Treatment," *Healing Resources.info*, Santa Barbara Graduate Institute Center for Clinical Studies and Research and L.A. County Early Identification and Intervention Group, 2012

El Akkad, Omar, "Meet the Canadians Who Busted Ghostnet," *The Globe and Mail*, March 30, 2009

Evans, Dabney, et al. "Shattered Shangri-la: Differences in Depressive and Anxiety Symptoms in Students Born in Tibet Compared to Tibetan Students Born in Exile," *Social Psychiatry and Psychiatric Epidemiology*, 2008

Field, Catherine, Michael Wilson, "Tibetan Children Sent on a Dangerous Journey to Save Lives, Culture," *Ottawa Citizen*, July 17, 1994

Finnigan, Mary, "Lama Sex Abuse Claims Call Buddhist Taboos into Question," *The Guardian*, July 1, 2011

Ford, Julian D., et al. "Trauma among Youth in the Juvenile Justice System: Critical Issues and New Directions," *National Center for Mental Health and Juvenile Justice*, June, 2007

"Forked Tongue: Tibetan Language under Attack," *Free Tibet*, February 21, 2008

"4 in 10 First Marriages End in Divorce: Report," *CBC.ca*, October 4, 2010

Germay, Arig, "The Home on Foreign Soil," Trans. Anonymous, *Tibet Times*, May 1, 2012

Gupta, Surender Nikhil, Naveen Gupta, "Outbreak of Gastroenteritis in Tibetan Transit School, Dharamshala, Himachal Pradesh, India, 2006," *Indian Journal of Community Medicine,* Vol. 34, 2009

Gyatso, Palden, *Fire under the Snow*, London, Harvill Press, 1998

Hamilton, J., "Tibetan Education in Exile: Past, Present, and Future," *Tibet Post International*, April 13, 2009

Harrer, Heinrich, *Seven Years in Tibet*, London, Pan, 1956

Hart, S., "'Yak café, Yak Coffee, Goat Tea Shop,' None of These Names Were Appealing," *Tibet Post International*, May 8, 2009

Henfry, Lee-Anne, Ben Hillman, "Macho Minority: Masculinity and Ethnicity on the Edge of Tibet," *Modern China*, Vol. 32, No. 2, Sage Publications Inc., 2006

Herge, *Tintin in Tibet*, London, Methuen, 1974

Hess, Julia Meredith, *Immigrant Ambassadors: Citizenship and Belonging in the Tibetan Diaspora*, Stanford, Stanford University Press, 2009

Higginson, Richard, "Intercultural Workshop on Conflict Transformation: Exploring Non-Violence with Members of Indian and Tibetan Communities in North and South India," Center for Justice and Peacebuilding, Eastern Mennonite University, 2008

"High Court Issues Notice to Tibetans Administration over Encroachments," *The Himachal*," April 15, 2012

Hillman, Sean, "Health Care in the Tibetan Refugee Community of Dharamsala" *Buddhist Ethics*, April 11, 2011

Hilton, Isabel, *The Search for the Panchen Lama*, London, Penguin Books, 2000

"Himachal Pradesh HC Issues Notice to Centre, State of Himachal Pradesh, Dalai Lama and Others Seeking Removal of all Flags of Tibetan Government-in-Exile from the Indian Soil," *indlawnews.com*, November 17, 2010, Web, August 12, 2011

Holtz, Timothy, *A Doctor in Little Lhasa*, Indianapolis, Dog Ear Publishing, 2009

Holtz, Timothy, "Refugee Trauma versus Torture Trauma: A Retrospective Controlled Cohort Study of Tibetan Refugees," *The Journal of Nervous and Mental Disease*, Vol. 186, January, 1998

Hooper, Joseph, "Leaving Om: Buddhism's Lost Lamas," *Details*, August, 2012

Hopkirk, Peter, *Trespassers on the Roof of the World*, Oxford, Oxford University Press, 1986

"Human Rights Situation in Tibet: Annual Report 2006," Tibetan Centre for Human Rights and Democracy, 2007

Hussain, Dilwar, Braj Bhushan, "Cultural Factors Promoting Coping among Tibetan Refugees: A Qualitative Investigation," *Mental Health Religion and Culture*, Vol. 14, No. 6, Routledge, 2011

Hussain, Dilwar, Braj Bhushan, "Development and Validation of the Refugee Trauma Experience Index," *Psychological Trauma: Theory, Research, Practice, and Policy*, Vol.1, No. 2, American Psychological Association, 2009

IANS, "Chinese Spy Held Near Dalai Lama Palace," *Yahoo News India*, March 20, 2012

India, Bureau of Immigration, Ministry of Home Affairs, "Information Pertaining [sic] Tibetan Nationals," Government of India, 2011

India, Census of India, Ministry of Home Affairs, "Figures at a Glance: Provisional Population Totals, Himachal Pradesh," Government of India, 2011

India, Office of the Registrar General and Census Commissioner, Ministry of Home Affairs, "Abstract of Speakers' Strength of Languages and Mother Tongues – 2001," Government of India, 2012

India, Office of Registrar General, Ministry of Home Affairs, "Maternal & Child Mortality and Total Fertility Rates," Government of India, 2011

"Indian Police Warns of Chinese Agents Sent to "Harm" the Dalai Lama," *Phayul*, January 9, 2012

"Interview with Tsering Dolkar: The Tibetan Mother Theresa," *Dolma*, Summer 2007

Iyer, Pico, *The Open Road, The Global Journey of the Fourteenth Dalai Lama*, New Delhi, Penguin Group, 2008

Iyer, Pico, *Video Night in Kathmandu*, Toronto, Vintage, 1989

Jain, Meetu, "Himachal Police Grills [sic] Karmapa over Raids," *IBN Live*, January 29, 2011

Jigme, Hortsang, *Under a Blue Sky*, Trans. Lobsang Dawa, Guusje de Schot, Dharamsala, Self-Published, 1998

"Joint Press Statement Resolving McLeod Ganj Clash," *Phayul*, May 11, 2007

Jorden, Ngawang, "Education of Tibetan Refugee Children in Exile," Symposium on Contemporary Tibetan Studies, Collected Papers, Mongolian and Tibetan Affairs Commission, 2003

Katayama, Lisa, Brothers First, *Buddhadharma*, Fall 2008

Kaufman, Eileen, "Shelter from the Storm: An Analysis of U.S. Refugee Law as Applied to Tibetans," Touro Law Center, 2009

Kawaguchi, Ekai, *Three Years in Tibet*, Delhi, Book Faith India, 1995

Keller, Allen S., et al. "Striking Hard: Torture in Tibet," *Physicians for Human Rights*, 1997

Klieger, Paul Christiaan, "Accomplishing Tibetan Identity: The Constitution of a National Consciousness," Diss., University of Hawaii, 1989

Kliger, Paul Christiaan, "Will the Real Tibetan Please Stand Up!" *Tibet, Self and the Tibetan Diaspora: Voices of Difference*, IATS, 2000

Knorbu30, "Shapaley - Shapale Song (Tibetan Rap)," March 24, 2011, *Youtube*, July 26, 2011

"LAFOT Brings Clean, Safe Water to Tibetan Students in Dharamsala," Los Angeles Friends of Tibet, *Facebook*, December 22, 2009

MacPherson, Seonaigh, Anne-Sophie Bentz, Dawa Bhuti Ghoso, "The Tibetan Diaspora: Adapting to Life Outside India (Part II)," *Migration Policy Institute*, 2008

Magnier, Mark, "Tibetan Exiles in Dharamsala, India, Settle in with Disillusionment," *Los Angeles Times*, October 4, 2010

Mahajan-Sinh, Nupur, "Little Lhasa of Dehradun," *Uppercrust*, November/December 2011

Main Page (On-Line, Himachal Pradesh Section), *The Tribune,* August 14, 2007

Main Page (On-Line, Himachal Pradesh Section), *The Tribune,* August 17, 2007

Markoff, John, "Vast Spy System Loots Computers in 103 Countries," *The New York Times*, March 28, 2009

McDonald, Angus, "Love across the Divide," *South China Morning Post*, August 30, 2003

McGirk, Tim, "Hate Campaign Shatters Calm of Dalai Lama," *The Independent*, May 11, 1994

McGranahan, Carole, "Truth, Fear and Lies: Exile Politics and Arrested Histories of the Tibetan Resistance," *Cultural Anthropology*, Vol. 20, Issue 4, 2005

Mee, Arthur, *The Children's Encyclopaedia, Volume 9,* London, The Educational Book Company, No Publication Date

Mengele, Irmgard, *dGe-'dun-chos-'phe: A Biography of the 20th Century Tibetan Scholar*, Dharamsala, Library of Tibetan Works and Archives, 1999

Meo, Nick, "The Pick-Up Paradise," *The Times*, July 22, 2004

Mercer, Stewart W., Alastair Ager, Eshani Ruwanpura, "Psychosocial Distress of Tibetans in Exile: Integrating Western Interventions with Traditional Beliefs and Practice," *Social Science and Medicine*, Vol. 60, 2005

Meyer, Karl E., Shareen Blair Brysac, *Tournament of Shadows*, New York, Basic Books, 1999

Midal, Fabrice, *Recalling Chogyam Trungpa*, Boston, Shambhala Publication, 2005

Mills, Edward J., et al. "Prevalence of Mental Disorders and Torture among Tibetan Refugees: A Systematic Review," *BMC International Health and Human Rights*, 2005

"Mission," Tibetan Children's Village, *Tibetan Children's Education Welfare Fund*, Central Tibetan Administration, October 1, 2011

Mohan, Lalit, "China Link Surfaces; Karmapa Likely To Be Questioned," *The Tribune*, January 28, 2011

Mohan, Lalit, "Encroachers Felling Deodar Trees," *The Tribune*, November 13, 2011

Mohan, Lalit, "Food Poisoning Kills Student," *The Tribune*, September 21, 2010

Mohan, Lalit, "Karmapa Absolved of Criminal Charges," *The Tribune*, May 21, 2012

Mohan, Lalit, "Little Israel Loses Buzz Due to Visa Curbs," *The Tribune*, March 7, 2011

Mohan, Lalit, "MHA Seeks Details of Foreigners in Tibetan Schools," *The Tribune*, October 1, 2011

Mohan, Lalit, "No Action on Benami Properties of Tibetans," *The Tribune*, July 28, 2009

Mohan, Lalit, "Rains Take a Toll on Dharamsala Roads," *The Tribune*, August 19, 2011

Mohan, Lalit, "Post Match Pandemonium at McLeodganj [sic]," *The Tribune*, May 20, 2012

Mohan, Lalit, "300 Tibetans to Be Deported," *The Tribune*, April 1, 2011

Mohan, Lalit, "Tibetans Deported from Kinnaur Being Released," *Tribune*, September 27, 2012

Mohan, Lalit, "Tibetans Warned Against Defacing Rocks, Trees," *The Tribune*, August 31, 2012

Mohan, Lalit, "Traffic Stuck for 20 Hours," *The Tribune*, September 7, 2012

Mohan, Lalit, "200 Benami Land Cases against Tibetans Pending in Revenue Courts," *The Tribune*, February 1, 2011

Mohan, Lalit, "Virbhadra Bats For Karmapa," *The Tribune*, February 4, 2011

Mohan, Vibhor, "Crackdown on Drug Peddlers, Addicts Soon," *The Tribune*, July 31, 2005

Mohan, Vibhor, "McLeodganj [sic] Sans Police Basic Facilities," *The Tribune*, May 30, 2005

Mohan, Vibhor, "Scores of Tibetans Staying Illegally," *The Tribune*, August 1, 2006

Mohan, Vibhor, "Tibetans Going in for Foreign Spouses," *The Tribune*, June 14, 2005

Mohan, Vibhor, "Ticket to the West," *The Tribune*, May 10, 2006

Mukpo, Diana, *My Life with Chogyam Trungpa*, Boston & London, Shambhala, 2006

Munis, Marianne, "Mutual and Cooperative Learning at the Foothills of the Himalayas," *SPF International Newsletter*, No. 14, June, 2005

Murphy, Dervla, *Tibetan Foothold*, London, Harper Collins, 2000

Nazreen, Wasfia, "McLeod Ganj Clash: A Non-Tibetan's Reflection," *Phayul*, May 4, 2007

NDTV Correspondent, "Karmapa Money Trail: Recovered Cash Came From Nepal," *NDTV*, January 31, 2011

"The New Arrivals Are Intolerant," *Outlook*, June 7, 2010

"New Exit Permit Regulations to Facilitate Tibetans' Travel Abroad," *Tibet.net*, December 14, 2006

"The New Tibetan Refugees," Office of the Reception Centers, Central Tibetan Administration, 1997

Nietupski, Paul Kocot, *Labrang,* New York, Snow Lion Publications, 1999

Norbu, Jamyang, "Shakabpa and the Awakening of Tibetan History," *jamyangnorbu.com*, December 6, 2011

Oakley, Richard, "Shock at Lama Sogyal Rinpoche's Past," *The Sunday Times*, July 4, 2009

"The Original Buildings," *Tibetan Exile Education Foundation*, February 23, 2011

Oppenheimer, Mark, "Sex Scandal Has U.S. Buddhists Looking Within," *The New York Times*, August 20, 2010

Padma, Vol. 1, Issue 1, Kunphen, June 2010

Palkyi, Tenzin, "Analyzing Educational Attainments and Occupational Outcomes of Tibetan Refugees Living in India," *Uknowledge*, University of Kentucky, 2011

Patial, Shishu, "Police to Check Illegal Foreigners in Kangra," *The Tribune*, November 27, 2002

Pehrson, Charlotte, "Tibetan Migration to India: Why, When, How, and With What Consequences," B.A. Thesis, Lund University, 2003

Ponnudurai, Parameswaran, "Popular Tibetan Writer Detained," *Radio Free Asia*, February 18, 2012

Post, Audrey, *Precious Pills: Medicine and Social Change among Tibetan Refugees in India*, Oxford, New York, Berghahn Books, 2008

"Press Statement – Phayul Regrets Article," *Phayul*, May 7, 2007

PTI, "Foreign Currency Seized from Monastery," *The Hindu*, January 29, 2011

Puri, S. Gopal, "Tibetan Administration Plans Moral Offensive to Counter Chinese Infiltration," *The Times of India*, May 1, 2012

Raote, Rrishi, "Unease In Dharamsala," *Business Standard*, March 19, 2011

"Recent Arrivals and Grassroots," *Tibet Society*, October 9, 2011

Regg Cohn, Martin, "Little Lhasa Belies Tibet Ideal," *Toronto Star*, December 8, 2003

"Report of Refugee Populations in India," Human Rights Law Network, November, 2007

Reuters, "The Wrong Side of the Mountains, *The Economist*, December 24, 2005

Rgyal, Lha Byams, Kuo-ming Sung, *Colloquial Amdo Tibetan: A Complete Course for Adult English Speakers*, Beijing, National Press For Tibetan Studies, 2005

River Sky, "To Be Avoided As Delusional and Counterproductive," Customer Review, *amazon.com*, December 31, 2004

Robertson, Ian, "Like Baboons, Our Elected Leaders are Literally Addicted to Power," *The Telegraph*, April 26, 2012

Rockhill, William Woodville, *The Land of the Lamas: Notes on a Journey Through China Mongolia and Tibet*, Varanasi, Pilgrims Publishing, 2000

Roemischer, Jessica, "Women Who Sleep with Their Gurus and Why They Love It," *What is Enlightenment*, Issue 26, 2004

Ruwanpura, Eshani, et al. "Cultural and Spiritual Constructions of Mental Distress and Associated Coping Mechanisms of Tibetans in Exile: Implications for Western Interventions," *Journal of Refugee Studies*, Vol. 19, No. 2, Oxford University Press, 2006

Sachs, Emily, et al. "Entering Exile: Trauma, Mental Health, and Coping among Tibetan Refugees Arriving in Dharamsala, India," *Journal of Traumatic Stress*, Vol. 21, No. 2, April 2008

Sainath, P., "The High Cost of Some Cheap Weddings," *The Hindu*, May 25, 2010

Samten, Lobsang Choedon, "Tibet House Trust Secretary's Report to Trustees," *Tibet House Trust*, June, 2003

Sandhu, Kulwinder, "Mad about McLeodganj [sic]," *The Tribune*, April 11, 2007

Sandhu, Kulwinder, "16 Tibetan Kids Told to Leave State," *The Tribune*, September 27, 2007

Saunders, Kate, Tibetan Rap on Chinese Knuckles Flusters Beijing, *The Guardian*, November 25, 2011

Schrempf, Mona, *Soundings in Tibetan Medicine,* Leiden, Brill, 2008

Schwartz, Sam, et al. "Investigating the Tibetan Healing System: A Psychosocial Needs Assessment of Tibetan Refugees in Nepal," *Intervention*, Vol. 3, No. 2, 2005

Sevan-Schreiber, David, Brigitte Le Lin, Boris Birmaher, "Prevalence of Posttraumatic Stress Disorder and Major Depressive Disorder in Tibetan Refugee Children," *Journal of the American Academy of Child and Adolescent Psychiatry*, August 1, 1998

Shakya, Tsering, *The Dragon in the Land of the Snows: A History of Modern Tibet Since 1947*, London, Pimlico, 1999

"Sex Ratio," *The World Factbook*, Central Intelligence Agency, 2011

Sharlho, Tseten Wangchuk, "China's Reforms in Tibet: Issues and Dilemmas," *The Journal of Contemporary China*, Volume 1, Number 1, Fall 1992

"Sherab Gatsal Lobling, History," *Sambhota Tibetan Schools Society*, 2012

Shiyong, Wang, "Tibetan Market Participation in China," Diss., University of Helsinki, 2009

"Six Months without a Bath," Tibet Society United Kingdom, Autumn 1998, *World Tibet News Network,* Canada Tibet Committee, October 10, 1998

Sonam, Tenzin, "A Tibet of the Mind" *Phayul*, December 2, 2010

Sood, Ravinder "Tourism Needs a Reality Check," *The Tribune*, June 5, 2011

Sowey, Helen, "Are Refugees at Risk of Substance Misuse? Ed.1," *Drug and Alcohol Multicultural Education Centre*, 2005

"SP and Others (Tibetan – Nepalese Departure – Illegal – Risk) People's Republic of China CG [2007] UKAIT 00021," Asylum and Immigration Tribunal, Issue 45, *Garden Court Chambers*, March 5, 2007

Stewart, Francis, "Lama Choedak Rinpoche Apologizes," *The Canberra Times*, May 1, 2011

"Stitches of Tibet," *Dolma*, Summer 2007

Ta-Young, LoAn, "Assessment of the Community Health Needs of Youth Living in South Parkdale," Parkdale Community Health Centre, 2008

Tarodi, Tunga, "Revisiting Home: Tibetan Refugees, Perceptions of Home (Land) and Politics of Return," Working Paper 266, Bangalore, *The Institute for Social and Economic Change*, 2011

Teichman, Eris, *Travels of a Consular Officer in Eastern Tibet*, Varanasi, Pilgrims Publishing, 2000

"Ten Ways to Promote Tibetan Language," *lhakar.org*, 2012

Tendor, "A Lhakar Milestone," *lhakar.org*, April 4, 2012

Tenzin, Kyabje Kirti Rinpoche Lobsang, *Supplementary Chapters on Gedun Choephel*, Dharamsala, T.C.K.M, 2008

Terheggen, Maaike A., Margaret S. Stroebe, Kleber, Rolf J., "Western Conceptualizations and Eastern Experience: A Cross-Cultural Study of Traumatic Stress Reactions among Tibetan Refugees in India, *Journal of Traumatic Stress*, Vol. 14, No. 2, 2001

"Tibetans Protest, Say Karmapa Not a Spy," *IBN Live*, February 8, 2011

Thinley, Phurbu, "Tibetans to Boycott Local Taxi and Auto Rickshaw Service in McLeod Gunj [sic]," *Phayul* May 4, 2007

"Tibetan Community in Exile, Demographic and Socio-Economic Issues 1998 – 2001," Planning Commission, Central Tibetan Administration, 2004

Tibetan Demographic Survey: 1998, Volume I & II, Planning Council, Dharamsala, Central Tibetan Administration, 2000

"Tibetan Medicare System (TMS)," Department of Health, *Central Tibetan Administration*, July 1, 2012

"Tibetan Torture Survivors [sic] Program," Department of Health, *Central Tibetan Administration*, October 1, 2011

"Tibetans Protest, Say Karmapa Not a Spy," *IBN Live*, February 8, 2011

"Tibet's Stateless Nationals II: Tibetan Refugees in India," Tibet Justice Center, September 2011

TNN, "Chinese Spies in India, Suspects Tibetan Admin," *The Times of India*, Jan 3, 2012

Tribune News Service, "Move to Classify Tibetans," *The Tribune*, September 18, 2005

Tribune News Service, "Shops Gutted in McLeodganj [sic]," *The Tribune*, December 1, 2010

Tribune News Service, "State Cabinet Okays Amendments to Rules," *The Tribune*, July 27, 2011

Tribune News Service, "Taxi Operators on Strike Again," *The Tribune*, August 12, 2007

Tribune News Service, "3 Tibetan Security Officials Held," *The Tribune*, April 2, 2010

Tribune News Service, "Twenty-Nine More Suspected of Food-Poisoning," *The Tribune*, September 17, 2004

Tricycle, Summer 2008

Tsering, Lhasang, *Ocean of Melody*, New Delhi, Rupa, 2009

Tsering, Tendar, "Kalachakra—an Opportunity for Tibet Activism," *Phayul*, January 2, 2012

Tsering, Tendar, "Israel Farming Programme Now Open to Non-Farming Settlements," *Phayul*, May 18, 2012

Tsering, Tendar, "Over a Thousand Chinese Spies Suspected in Bodh Gaya," *Phayul*, January 2, 2012

Tsering, Tendar, "Tibetans in Pain Not Knowing What to Do," *Phayul*, February 12, 2012

Tsering, Tendar, "Tibetans Inside Tibet Give Two Thumbs Up to New Kalon Tripa," *Phayul*, August 10, 2011

Tsering, Tendar, "Troubled RC's to Be Renewed by March 2012," *Phayul*, September 17, 2011

Tsering, Tendar, "382 Tibetans Will Not Be Deported: Additional SP," *Phayul*, July 5, 2012

Tsering, Topden, "Demise of a Place: An Obituary, *tibetwrites.org*, December 27, 2007

Tsering, Topden, "Making Sense of the Senseless: Violence in Dharamsala," *Phayul*, May 4, 2007

United Nations, General Assembly, "Convention and Protocol Relating to the Status of Refugees," *unhcr.org*, 2010

United Nations, General Assembly, "Declaration on the Rights of Indigenous People," *un.org*, 2007

United Nations, UNHCR, "India: Situation of Tibetan Refugees and Those Not Recognized as Refugees; Including Legal Rights and Living Conditions," *Refworld*, unhcr.org, December 23, 1999

United Nations, UNHCR, "Nepal: Situation of Tibetan Refugees and Those Not Recognized As Refugees; Including Legal Rights and Living Conditions (1995-1999)," *Refworld*, December 22, 1999

United Nations, UNESCO Institute for Statistics, "Regional Literacy Rates for Youth (15-24) and Adults (15+), 2005- 2010," unesco.org, 2012

United Nations, UNHCR,"States Parties [sic] to the 1951 Convention Relating to the Status of Refugees and the 1967 Protocol," *unhcr.org*, 2012

U.S. Embassy Cable, "10NewDelhi290, Tibet Growing Frustration after Latest Round," *Wikileaks*, 2010

Van den Dool, Paula, "Diversity and Unity in Exile: Nationalism and Cultural Compromise in the Tibetan Diaspora," M.A. thesis, University of Utrecht, 2009

Vijayendra Rao, "The Economics of Dowries in India," *The Oxford Companion to Economics in India*, Delhi, Oxford University Press, 2007

"Violence against a Tibetan Woman in Tenzinghang: TWA's Report September 2011," Tibetan Women's Association, 2011

Walker, Joyce, "Teens in Distress Series: Adolescent Stress and Depression," University of Minnesota, 2005

Walker, Vanessa, *Mantras & Misdemeanours*, Crows Nest (Sydney), Allen & Unwin, 2006

Wangchuk, Tashi, Sanjor v/s Sarjor, *Migyul,* Issue No. 6, Summer 2005

Wangdu, Kalsang, "Minority Education Policy of China With Reference to Tibet," *Tibetan Review*, June 1, 2011

Wangmo, Rinzin, "Status of Tibetan Refugees in India: A Case Study of Bylakuppe," Stella Maris College, 2008

Wangyal, Lobsang, "Bleeding McLeod Ganj Needs Immediate Tibetan Hands," *lobsangwangyal.com*, May 8, 2007

Wangyal, Lobsang, "Three Tibetans Arrested for Attacking Local Indians," *Tibet Sun*, April 5, 2010

Ward, Shannon, "Performing Diasporic Subjectivities: Gendered Narratives of Cultural Reproduction in a Community of Tibetan Exiles," Honors Thesis, Wellesley College, 2012

Watts, Jonathan, Ken Macfarlane, "Inside Tibet's Heart of Protest," *The Guardian*, February 10, 2012

Welsh, C., *Early Jesuit Travellers in Central Asia,* Delhi, Book Faith India, 1998

Winand, Tammy, "Everyday Exile Project is Evolving," *everydayexile.blogspot.com*, April 25, 2011

Wong, Edward, "Tibetan Exiles Rally around Delhi Self-Immolator," *The New York Times*, March 28, 2012

Yee, Amy, "Indian Monastery Aids Tibetan Monks Facing Crackdown," *The Christian Science Monitor*, July 11, 2011

Yee, Amy, "Young Lawyer Aids Exile Tibetans with His Language and Legal Skills," *The Christian Science Monitor*, September 6, 2011

Younghusband Francis E. Younghusband, *India and Tibet*, New Delhi, Asian Educational Services, 2005

About the Author

Pauline MacDonald is the pseudonym of an independent researcher who inhabits cyberspace. Recently, she completed an employment aptitude analysis that concluded she should work as a crime scene investigator, forensic accountant, or train operator. However, she is not employed in those fields.

CPSIA information can be obtained at www.ICGtesting.com
Printed in the USA
LVOW05s1453110314

376956LV00016B/596/P

9 780992 132002